STECK-VAUGHN THE COMPLETE EDITION

AMERICA'S STORY

BY VIVIAN BERNSTEIN

STECK-VAUGHN
C O M P A N Y
ELEMENTARY • SECONDARY • ADULT • LIBRARY

⚹ ABOUT THE AUTHOR

Vivian Bernstein is the author of *World History and You, World Geography and You, American Government,* and *Decisions for Health.* She received her Master of Arts degree from New York University. Bernstein is active with professional organizations in social studies, education, and reading. She gives presentations to school faculties and professional groups about content area reading. Bernstein was a teacher in the New York City Public School System for a number of years.

⚹ ACKNOWLEDGMENTS

Executive Editor: Diane Sharpe
Senior Editor: Martin S. Saiewitz
Design Manager: Richard Balsam
Designer: Pamela Heaney
Photo Editor: Margie Foster
Electronic Production: Shelly M. Knapp
Cover Production: Claunch Consulting

⚹ CREDITS

Cover Photography: Reagan Bradshaw Photography

Photo Credits: pp. 2–3, 4, 5, 6 The Granger Collection; p. 10 The Bettmann Archive; p. 11a & b The Granger Collection; p. 11c North Wind Picture Archives; p. 15 The Granger Collection; p. 16a The Bettmann Archive; pp. 16b, 17 North Wind Picture Archives; pp. 20, 21, 22, 25, 26, 27a & b The Granger Collection; p. 27c The Bettmann Archive; p. 31 The Granger Collection; p. 32a The Bettmann Archive; pp. 32b & c, 33 The Granger Collection; p. 34 North Wind Picture Archives; pp. 38–39, 40, 41a The Granger Collection; p. 41b © Uniphoto; p. 41c North Wind Picture Archives; p. 42 The Granger Collection; pp. 43, 46 The Bettmann Archive; p. 47a & c The Granger Collection; p. 47b Reagan Bradshaw; p. 48a The Valentine Museum; pp. 48b & c, 49a The Granger Collection; p. 49b The Bettmann Archive; p. 52 The Granger Collection; p. 53a Reagan Bradshaw; p. 53b © Uniphoto; p. 54a Reagan Bradshaw; p. 54b © Henryk T. Kaiser/Photri; p. 54c © Uniphoto; p. 55a © Keith Jewel; p. 55b © Bob Daemmrich/Uniphoto; p. 58 The Bettmann Archive; pp. 59, 60 The Granger Collection; p. 63 The Bettmann Archive; p. 64a The Granger Collection; p. 64b © Uniphoto; pp. 65, 66a The Granger Collection; p. 66b North Wind Picture Archives; pp. 70–71, 72 The Granger Collection; p. 73a The Bettmann Archive; p. 73b North Wind Picture Archives; p. 73c The Granger Collection; p. 74 Courtesy The Missouri Historical Society; pp. 75, 79, 80 The Granger Collection; p. 81a North Wind Picture Archives; pp. 81b, 82, 85, 86, 87a, 88a The Granger Collection; p. 88b North Wind Picture Archives; p. 91 The Granger Collection; p. 92 Mount Holyoke College Art Museum, South Hadley, MA; p. 93a The Granger Collection; p. 93b North Wind Picture Archives; p. 94 The Granger Collection; pp. 98–99 Courtesy The Bucks County Historical Society, Doylestown, PA; pp. 100, 101a North Wind Picture Archives; p. 102a & b Courtesy The Institute for Texan Cultures; p. 102c The Granger Collection; p. 102d © Quinn Stewart; p. 103a Courtesy The Institute for Texan Cultures; p. 103b The Granger Collection; p. 103c Courtesy The Barker Texas History Center, University of Texas, Austin; p. 106 Courtesy Texas State Archives; p. 107a The Bettmann Archive; p. 107b The Granger Collection; pp. 109, 113 North Wind Picture Archives; pp. 115, 116 The Granger Collection; p. 119 The Bettmann Archive; p. 120 The Granger Collection; p. 121a North Wind Picture Archives; p. 121b The Granger Collection; p. 122a The Bettmann Archive; pp. 122b, 125 The Granger Collection; p. 126a © Quinn Stewart; pp. 126b, 127a The Granger Collection; p. 127b Courtesy The Sophia Smith Collection, Smith College; p. 128a The Bettmann Archive; p. 128b The Granger Collection; continued on page 297.

Cartography: Maryland CartoGraphics

Cover artifacts: Courtesy of Richard Balsam, Reagan Bradshaw, Carl Green, John Harrison, Michael and Pamela Heaney, Scott Huber, Michael Kane, Tim Knapp, Sabrina Porch, The Sharper Image®, Betsy Sledge.

CONTENTS

America's Story tells the story of our country, the United States of America. This book tells how our country became a land of freedom. It tells how our nation changed from a small country to a very large one.

Our country's story began with Native Americans. Later, people who came to America from Great Britain started 13 colonies. These colonies were ruled by Great Britain. People in the American colonies fought and won a war against the British. After the war the colonies became a free country called the United States.

The new United States had only 13 states. Slowly the nation grew larger. Americans moved west. More and more states became part of the United States.

As the nation grew, problems between the northern and southern states also grew. People in the North and in the South disagreed about slavery. Some southern states left the United States to start a new nation. This led to a long, terrible war. After the war, the United States became one nation again.

The country continued to change as millions of people from other countries came to live in America. The cities in our country grew larger. More Americans settled in the West.

Later, Americans faced new kinds of problems. They fought in two world wars. The United States became a world leader.

Today the United States continues to change. For more than two hundred years, people have worked to make our country a land of freedom. As you read this book, you will learn about the men and women who were part of America's story.

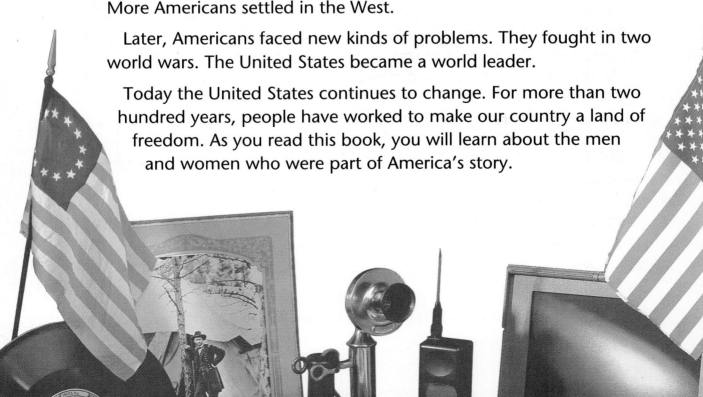

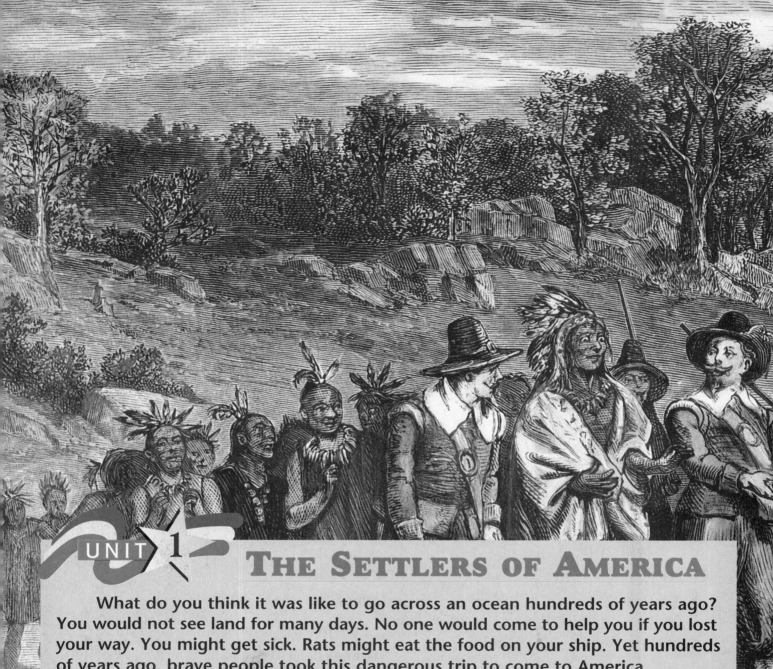

UNIT 1

THE SETTLERS OF AMERICA

What do you think it was like to go across an ocean hundreds of years ago? You would not see land for many days. No one would come to help you if you lost your way. You might get sick. Rats might eat the food on your ship. Yet hundreds of years ago, brave people took this dangerous trip to come to America.

About 500 years ago, people from Europe started coming to America. People came to America for different reasons. Some came to find gold. Others came because they wanted more freedom. Many people from Europe stayed to live in America. The Pilgrims came to live in America. But the people from Europe were not the first to live in America. Native Americans had been living in America for thousands of years. Some Native Americans helped settlers like the Pilgrims live in America.

How did Native Americans live their lives? Who were the people from Europe who explored and settled in America? As you read Unit 1, think about why different groups of people made the dangerous trip to America.

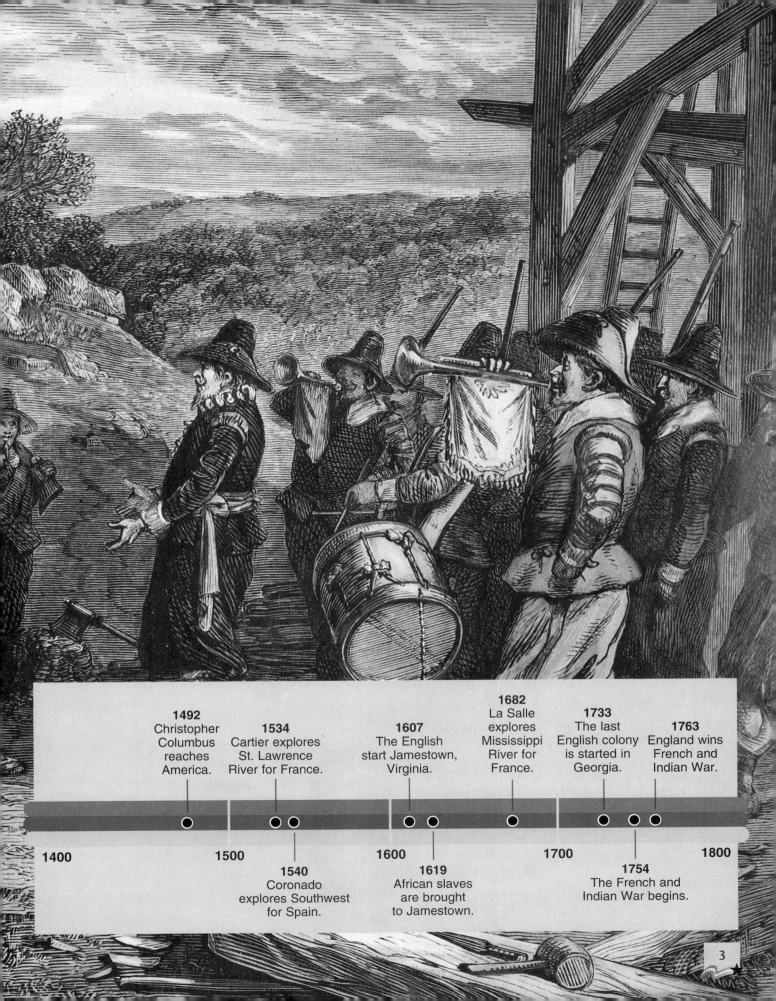

1492
Christopher Columbus reaches America.

1534
Cartier explores St. Lawrence River for France.

1607
The English start Jamestown, Virginia.

1682
La Salle explores Mississippi River for France.

1733
The last English colony is started in Georgia.

1763
England wins French and Indian War.

1400   1500   1600   1700   1800

1540
Coronado explores Southwest for Spain.

1619
African slaves are brought to Jamestown.

1754
The French and Indian War begins.

3

CHAPTER 1

THE FIRST AMERICANS

Think About As You Read

1. How did Native Americans live long ago?
2. Why did Native Americans live differently in different parts of the United States?
3. What have other people learned from Native Americans?

NEW WORDS

religions
cotton
buffalo

PEOPLE & PLACES

Native Americans
America
Asia
United States of America
United States
Northwest
Southwest
Midwest
Great Plains
East

Native Americans of the Northwest sometimes used nets to catch fish.

Native Americans were the first people to live in America. They may have lived in Asia before coming to this land. Native Americans are also known as Indians. They settled in different parts of America. Native Americans lived here for thousands of years. Then people from other lands started coming to America. About 220 years ago the name of our country became the United States of America. Native Americans lived in this land long before it was called the United States.

Native Americans in different parts of the United States spoke different languages. They also lived in different kinds of houses. They wore different kinds of clothes. They ate different kinds of food. They believed in different **religions**.

Regions of the
United States

Baskets made by
Native Americans
in the East

Many Native Americans lived in the Northwest of the
United States. In the Northwest, there were thick forests.
There were many fish in the ocean and rivers. The Native
Americans of the Northwest went fishing to get food. They
ate fish every day. They built houses and boats from trees
in the forests.

Some Native Americans lived in the Southwest. In the
Southwest, there was little rain. There were few trees. There
were very few fish and animals to eat. The Native Americans
of the Southwest became farmers. They used river water to
grow food. They grew corn and beans for food. They also
grew **cotton**. They made their clothes from cotton.

In the Midwest of the United States the land is very flat.
We call this flat land the Great Plains. Millions of **buffalo**
lived on the Great Plains. Many Native Americans lived on
the Great Plains. They became buffalo hunters. They used
every part of the buffalo that were killed. They ate buffalo
meat. They made clothes out of buffalo skins. They lived
in tents that were made of buffalo skins.

In the East of the United States there were many forests.
Animals lived in the forests. Many Native Americans lived
in these forests. They became hunters. They killed deer and
turkeys for food. They also became farmers. They grew corn,
pumpkins, and beans for their families.

Native Americans
who lived on the
Great Plains hunted
buffalo.

Native Americans who lived on the Great Plains made tents out of buffalo skins.

There were some ways that all Native Americans were alike. They loved beautiful plants and animals. They took good care of their land.

All Native Americans made their own tools. They needed tools for hunting, farming, and fishing. Native Americans made their tools out of stones and animal bones. They did not make metal tools. They made knives out of stones. Native Americans hunted with bows and arrows. They did not have guns.

Native Americans taught many things to people who later came to America. They taught them how to plant new foods like corn and potatoes. They taught people how to use special plants for medicine. Native American medicines helped sick people get well.

There are many Native Americans in the United States today. They still enjoy many songs, dances, and stories that their people enjoyed long ago. But Native Americans now work at many kinds of jobs. There are Native American doctors and teachers. Some Native Americans are farmers and builders. Native Americans today are proud that they were the first people to build our country. They are proud that they were the first Americans.

⭐ Read and Remember

Finish Up Number your paper from 1 to 7. Choose a word in blue print to finish each sentence. Write the correct answers on your paper.

Americans	**corn**	**fishing**	**hunters**
medicines	**East**	**buffalo**	

1. Native Americans were the first _____ .

2. Native Americans who lived in the Northwest went _____ for their food.

3. The Native American farmers of the Southwest grew beans and _____ .

4. Animals that lived on the Great Plains were the _____ .

5. Native Americans who lived on the Great Plains became _____ .

6. Native Americans who lived in forests in the _____ hunted deer.

7. Native Americans used special plants to make _____ .

Think and Apply ⭐

Fact or Opinion A **fact** is a true statement. An **opinion** is a statement that tells what a person thinks.

> **Fact** The land is very flat in the Midwest.
> **Opinion** The Midwest is the best place to live.

Number your paper from 1 to 5. Write **F** on your paper for each fact below. Write **O** for each opinion. You should find two sentences that are opinions.

1. Native Americans spoke different languages.

2. Millions of buffalo lived on the Great Plains.

3. It was easy to live on the Great Plains.

4. Native Americans made tools from stones and bones.

5. The best tools were made from stones.

Riddle Puzzle

Number your paper from 1 to 7. Then choose a word in blue print to finish each sentence. Write the correct answers on your paper.

food	animal	believed	ocean
lived	United	fishing	

1. Native Americans _____ in many religions.

2. Native Americans were the first people to live in the _____ States.

3. In the Southwest, Native Americans grew corn and beans for _____ .

4. Native Americans in the Northwest went _____ for their food.

5. Native Americans made tools out of _____ bones.

6. Native Americans _____ in many parts of the United States.

7. Native Americans in the Northwest lived near the _____ .

Now look at your answers. Circle the first letter of each answer you wrote on your paper. The first answer should look like this:

ⓑelieved

The letters you circled should spell a word. The word answers the riddle.

RIDDLE: What animal did Native Americans on the Great Plains use for food, tents, and clothing?

Write the answer to the riddle on your paper.

Journal Writing

Think about the different groups of Native Americans. Choose two groups. Write about where they lived. Then tell how they got food. Write four to six sentences in your journal.

Skill Builder

Understanding Continents   We live on Earth. Earth has large bodies of land called **continents**. There are seven continents. Most continents have many countries.

We live on the continent of North America. Our country, the United States, is in North America.

Here is a list of the continents in order of their size. The largest continent is first on the list.

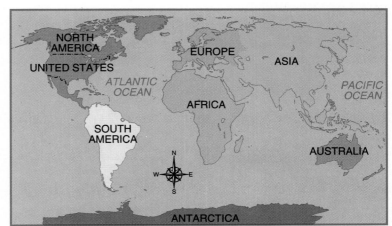

1. Asia
2. Africa
3. North America
4. South America
5. Antarctica
6. Europe
7. Australia

Look at the map above. Write a sentence on your paper to answer each question.

1. What are the seven continents?

2. Which continent has the United States?

3. Which is the largest continent?

4. Which is the smallest continent?

5. What are the names of the two oceans shown on the map?

6. Which ocean separates North America from Africa and Europe?

CHAPTER 2 CHRISTOPHER COLUMBUS

CHAPTER 2

Think About As You Read

1. Which people knew about America before Columbus took his trip?
2. Where did Columbus want to go?
3. Why did Queen Isabella help Columbus?

NEW WORDS

spices
claimed
New World

PEOPLE & PLACES

Christopher Columbus
Italy
Europe
India
Atlantic Ocean
Queen Isabella
Spain

After sailing for many days, Christopher Columbus and his crew reached an island in America.

Christopher Columbus lived a long time ago. Columbus was born in 1451 in Italy. Columbus became a sailor. He also made maps.

In the 1400s, people knew less about the world than we know today. Some people believed the world was flat. No one in Europe knew there was the land we now call America. Only the Native Americans knew about their land.

At that time, people from Europe went to India to get jewels, silks, and **spices**. They traveled thousands of miles to the east to reach India. Their route was long and dangerous.

Christopher Columbus

Queen Isabella

Christopher Columbus wanted to find an easier way to travel to India. Christopher Columbus thought the world was round. He believed he could go to India by sailing west across the Atlantic Ocean.

Many people did not believe Columbus. They laughed at him.

Columbus needed ships and sailors to sail across the Atlantic Ocean. Columbus went to see Isabella, the queen of Spain. Queen Isabella thought about Columbus's plan for six years. She believed he was right. She thought Columbus could reach India by sailing across the Atlantic Ocean. She wanted Columbus to find gold for Spain. So Queen Isabella decided to help him.

Queen Isabella gave Columbus three small ships. The names of the ships were the *Niña*, the *Pinta*, and the *Santa Maria*.

Columbus sailed with three ships—the *Niña*, the *Pinta*, and the *Santa Maria*.

Columbus and the sailors sailed west across the Atlantic Ocean. For many days the sailors could not see land. Many sailors were afraid. The sailors said, "Turn back for Spain, Columbus." Columbus was braver than the sailors. Columbus said, "I will not turn back. We will sail until we reach India."

On October 12, 1492, the sailors had not seen land for 33 days. On that day the three ships reached an island. The sailors were no longer afraid.

Columbus thought he was in India. He was not in India. Columbus was on an American island. People already lived on this island. Columbus called these people Indians because he thought he was in India. Now Indians are known as Native Americans.

Columbus **claimed** America for Spain. For the people of Europe, America was a **New World**. Of course, it was not a new world to the Native Americans who lived there. Soon after Columbus's trip, more people from Europe would come to America.

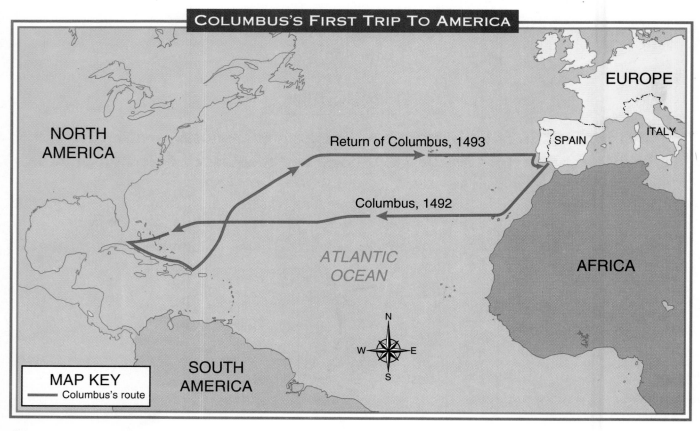

COLUMBUS'S FIRST TRIP TO AMERICA

EUROPE

NORTH AMERICA

Return of Columbus, 1493

SPAIN

ITALY

Columbus, 1492

ATLANTIC OCEAN

AFRICA

SOUTH AMERICA

N
W E
S

MAP KEY
Columbus's route

Read and Remember ★

Choose the Answer Number your paper from 1 to 7. Write the correct answers on your paper.

1. Where did Columbus want to go?
   America   India   Europe

2. Why did people from Europe want to go to India?
   to travel   to get jewels, silks, and spices   to see buffalo

3. What did Queen Isabella give to Columbus?
   jewels   ships   spices

4. What ocean did Columbus sail across?
   Pacific Ocean   Indian Ocean   Atlantic Ocean

5. When did Columbus reach America?
   1412   1451   1492

6. What did Columbus call the people he found in America?
   Indians   Americans   Asians

7. What did people in Europe call America?
   Old World   New World   Small World

★ Skill Builder

Using Map Directions The four main directions are **north**, **south**, **east**, and **west**. On maps, these directions are shown by a **compass rose**. Sometimes these directions are shortened to N, S, E, and W.

Draw a compass rose on your paper. Write the letters **N**, **S**, **E**, and **W** in the correct places on your compass rose.

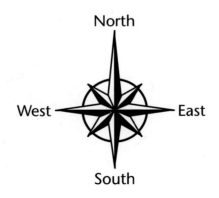

North

West — — East

South

Number your paper from 1 to 6. Look back at the map on page 9. Then finish each sentence with the word north, south, east, or west. Write the correct answers on your paper.

1. Europe is _____ of the Atlantic Ocean.

2. North America is _____ of the Atlantic Ocean.

3. South America is _____ of North America.

4. Europe is _____ of Africa.

5. Asia is _____ of Europe.

6. Antarctica is _____ of Africa.

Think and Apply

Finding the Main Idea   A **main idea** is an important idea in the chapter. Less important ideas support the main idea. Read each group of sentences below. One of the three sentences is a main idea. The other two sentences support the main idea. Number your paper from 1 to 4. Write the sentence that is the main idea in each group.

1. People wanted jewels from India.
   People wanted spices from India.
   People traveled to India to get jewels and spices.

2. The route to India was dangerous.
   Columbus wanted to find a better route to India.
   The route to India was very long.

3. In 1492 Columbus sailed for many days to reach America.
   Columbus sailed for 33 days.
   Columbus had three ships—the *Niña*, the *Pinta*, and the *Santa Maria*.

4. Columbus sailed west because he wanted to reach India.
   No one in Europe knew about America.
   When Columbus landed in America, he thought he was in India.

THE SPANISH EXPLORE AMERICA

CHAPTER 3

Think About As You Read

1. Why did the Spanish explore America?
2. Why did the Spanish build missions?
3. Why were some Native Americans unhappy at the Spanish missions?

NEW WORDS

slavery
Catholics
missions
priests

PEOPLE & PLACES

Mexico
South America
Spanish
Africa
Africans
Estevanico
Francisco Coronado
Hernando de Soto
Florida
Mississippi River
Texas
California
New Mexico
Santa Fe

Estevanico explored the Southwest to find the seven cities of gold for Spain.

Christopher Columbus claimed America for Spain in 1492. People from Spain settled in America. They settled in Mexico and South America. There they heard stories about seven cities that were made of gold. The Spanish wanted to find the seven cities of gold. They began to explore the land north of Mexico. Today this area is the Southwest of the United States.

The Spanish started **slavery** in America. They forced Native Americans to be slaves. In 1503 the Spanish started bringing people from Africa to work as slaves. Each year thousands of Africans became slaves in America. The Spanish forced the slaves to search for gold and silver.

15

Francisco Coronado

Hernando de Soto

The first person to explore the Southwest for Spain was Estevanico. He was an African. In 1539 he searched the Southwest for the seven cities of gold. He never found the seven cities of gold. During his search he was killed by Native Americans.

Francisco Coronado also wanted to find the seven cities of gold. In 1540 Coronado and 300 Spanish soldiers went to the Southwest of the United States. Coronado looked for gold in the Southwest for two years. Coronado found Native American farmers in the Southwest. He found Native American villages made of dried clay. But he never found the seven cities of gold. In 1542 Coronado went home to Mexico. Coronado had explored the Southwest. The king of Spain said that this land belonged to Spain.

Hernando de Soto also wanted to find the seven cities of gold for Spain. De Soto started in Florida with more than 700 people in 1539. While he was looking for gold, he came to a very wide river. It was the Mississippi River. He was the

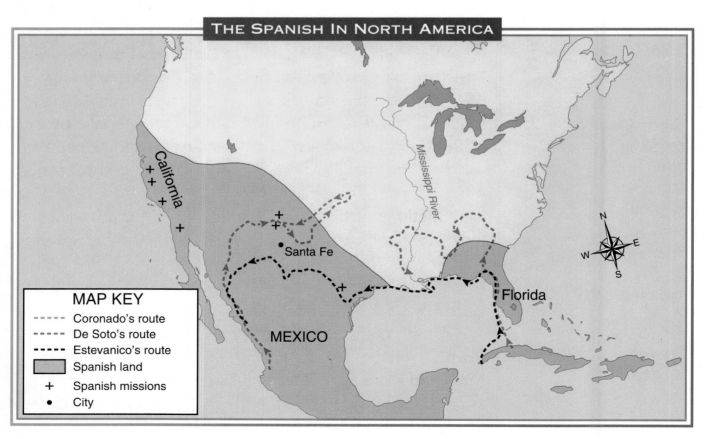

THE SPANISH IN NORTH AMERICA

California

Mississippi River

Santa Fe

MEXICO

Florida

N
W E
S

MAP KEY
- - - - Coronado's route
- - - - De Soto's route
- - - - Estevanico's route
☐ Spanish land
+ Spanish missions
• City

The Spanish built many missions in America to teach people how to be Catholics.

first person from Europe to see this river. De Soto never found the seven cities of gold. The Spanish king said that the area De Soto explored belonged to Spain, too.

Many Spanish people came to America to find gold. They did not find gold in the United States. Other Spanish people came to the Southwest of the United States. They came to teach the Native Americans how to be **Catholics**. That is why the Spanish built **missions** in Texas, California, and New Mexico. Every mission had a church. **Priests** worked in the missions. Priests taught the Native Americans to take care of cows, pigs, and sheep. Native Americans also helped the Spanish. They taught the Spanish how to grow tomatoes, potatoes, corn, and beans.

Sometimes Native Americans left the missions because they were not happy. They did not like living with the Spanish. They did not want to follow the Catholic religion. These Native Americans wanted to follow their own religions. Some missions closed when too many Native Americans left.

Other missions became very large. These missions became towns. Santa Fe was one Spanish mission in New Mexico. More and more people came to Santa Fe. Santa Fe became a town. Today Santa Fe is a city. For 300 years the Southwest and Florida belonged to Spain.

Read and Remember

Finish the Sentence   Number your paper from 1 to 7. Write on your paper the word or words that finish each sentence.

1. The first person to explore the Southwest for Spain was _____ .
   Estevanico   Columbus   De Soto

2. Coronado explored the _____ of the United States.
   Northwest   Southwest   Southeast

3. De Soto looked for gold in _____ .
   Florida   New Mexico   California

4. De Soto was the first person from Europe to see the _____ .
   Atlantic Ocean   Northeast   Mississippi River

5. Estevanico, Coronado, and De Soto tried to find the _____ cities of gold.
   five   six   seven

6. The Spanish built _____ for the Native Americans.
   farms   stores   missions

7. _____ taught Native Americans how to take care of cows, pigs, and sheep.
   De Soto   Priests   Estevanico

Think and Apply

Categories   Number your paper from 1 to 4. Read the words in each group. Decide how they are alike. Choose the best title in blue print for each group. Write the title on your paper.

Hernando de Soto	Explorers
Francisco Coronado	King of Spain

1. looked for seven cities of gold
   explored the Southwest
   found Native American villages

2. said the Southwest belonged to Spain
   said the Southeast belonged to Spain
   ruler of Spain

3. Estevanico
Francisco Coronado
Hernando de Soto

4. looked for seven cities of gold
explored Florida
explored the Mississippi River

Skill Builder

Using a Map Key Maps often show many things. Sometimes maps use little drawings to show what something on the map means. A **map key** tells what those drawings mean. Look at the map key below. Number your paper from 1 to 4. Write on your paper what each drawing means.

1. +

2. •

3. ▭

4. - - - - -

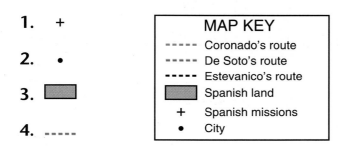

MAP KEY
- - - - - Coronado's route
- - - - - De Soto's route
- - - - - Estevanico's route
▭ Spanish land
+ Spanish missions
• City

Number your paper from 1 to 5. Use the map and map key on page 16 to finish these sentences. Write on your paper the number or word that finishes each sentence.

1. There are _____ missions on this map.
20   10   7

2. There were _____ missions in California.
4   7   15

3. The _____ River is on this map.
Mississippi   Florida   Santa Fe

4. De Soto's route began in the _____ .
east   north   west

5. Coronado's route began in the _____ .
north   south   east

CHAPTER 4 THE PILGRIMS' THANKSGIVING

Think About As You Read

1. Why did the Pilgrims want to go to America?
2. What happened to the Pilgrims during their first winter in America?
3. How did Native Americans help the Pilgrims?

NEW WORDS

Church of England
freedom of religion
Mayflower Compact
governor
peace treaty

PEOPLE & PLACES

Pilgrims
England
Holland
Dutch
English
Massachusetts
Plymouth
Massasoit
Squanto

The Pilgrims' trip to America took 66 days. They landed in Massachusetts in November 1620.

A long time ago, the Pilgrims lived in England. All the people in England had to pray in the king's church. This church was called the **Church of England**. The Pilgrims did not like the Church of England. They wanted to pray in their own church.

The Pilgrims left England and went to a small country called Holland. There was **freedom of religion** in Holland. The Pilgrims could pray in their own church in Holland.

The people of Holland are called the Dutch. They speak the Dutch language. The Pilgrims did not like living in Holland. They wanted to keep their English ways. They decided to go to America. In America they could live as they wanted and have freedom of religion.

In 1620 the Pilgrims left Holland for America. They had a ship. Their ship was the *Mayflower*. The trip took 66 days. The weather was rainy and cold. Many Pilgrims became sick during the long, cold trip.

At last the *Mayflower* reached America. It landed in Massachusetts. Before leaving their ship, the Pilgrims made a plan for a government. That plan was the **Mayflower Compact**. The plan said the Pilgrims would work together to make laws. The laws would be fair to all. The Pilgrims would not have a king in America. They would choose a **governor** and rule themselves. The Mayflower Compact was the first government in America that allowed people from Europe to rule themselves.

The Pilgrims landed in November. They started a town called Plymouth. The weather was very cold. It was too cold to grow food. The first winter in Plymouth was terrible. There was little food. Many Pilgrims became sick and died.

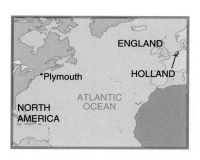

The Pilgrims' Journey to America

The *Mayflower*

Squanto taught the Pilgrims how to plant corn.

Native Americans lived in forests near Plymouth. They came and helped the Pilgrims. Their leader was Massasoit. He signed a **peace treaty** with the Pilgrims. The Pilgrims and Native Americans lived together in peace. Squanto was a Native American who taught the Pilgrims how to plant corn. He showed the Pilgrims where to find many fish. He taught the Pilgrims to hunt for deer and turkeys in the forests.

The Pilgrims worked hard in Plymouth. They planted seeds to grow food. They built a church. Then they built houses.

By November 1621 the Pilgrims had a lot of food. They would not be hungry that winter. The Pilgrims were very happy.

The Pilgrims had a Thanksgiving party in November 1621. They invited the Native Americans. The Native Americans brought deer to the party. The Pilgrims brought turkeys. This Thanksgiving party lasted three days. The Pilgrims gave thanks to God for helping them. They said "thank you" to the Native Americans for helping them. This was the Pilgrims' first Thanksgiving in America.

The Pilgrims and the Native Americans had their first Thanksgiving in 1621.

Read and Remember

Choose the Answer Write the correct answers on your paper.

1. Where did the Pilgrims first live?
   Holland   England   America

2. What was the name of the Pilgrims' ship?
   Niña   *Mayflower*   *Pinta*

3. Why did the Pilgrims come to America?
   to become farmers   to have freedom of religion
   to meet Native Americans

4. What town in America did the Pilgrims start?
   Massachusetts   Plymouth   Boston

Think and Apply

Cause and Effect A **cause** is something that makes something else happen. What happens is called the **effect**.

> **Cause** The Pilgrims planted corn and hunted deer,
> **Effect** so they had a lot of food that winter.

Write sentences on your paper by matching each cause on the left with an effect on the right.

Cause

1. The Pilgrims did not want to pray in the Church of England, so _____

2. The Pilgrims could not keep their English ways in Holland, so _____

3. The Pilgrims had little food for their first winter, so _____

4. The Native Americans wanted peace, so _____

5. The Pilgrims had a lot of food for their second winter, so _____

Effect

a. many Pilgrims died.

b. Massasoit signed a peace treaty with the Pilgrims.

c. they had a Thanksgiving party to thank God and the Native Americans.

d. they went to Holland.

e. they went to America.

Journal Writing

Write a paragraph in your journal that tells why the Pilgrims gave thanks. Give at least three reasons why they were thankful.

Riddle Puzzle

Choose a word in blue print to finish each sentence. Write the correct answers on your paper.

fair   ocean   religion   English

Dutch   Europe   Massasoit

1. The Mayflower Compact said that laws would be _____ to all.

2. The Pilgrims left England so they could follow their own _____ .

3. The Mayflower Compact was the first government in America that allowed people from _____ to rule themselves.

4. The Pilgrims wanted to keep their _____ ways in Holland.

5. The people in Holland are called the _____ .

6. The Pilgrims sailed across the _____ in the *Mayflower*.

7. The Native American who signed a peace treaty with the Pilgrims was _____ .

Now look at your answers. Circle the first letter of each answer you wrote on your paper.

The letters you circled should spell a word. The word answers the riddle.

RIDDLE: What was important to the Pilgrims that is still important to Americans today?

Write the answer to the riddle on your paper.

CHAPTER 5
THE ENGLISH SETTLE AMERICA

Think About As You Read

1. Why was the first winter in Jamestown very hard?
2. Which people came to America for freedom of religion?
3. Why did Roger Williams start Rhode Island?

NEW WORDS

colony
settlers
tobacco
religious
in debt

PEOPLE & PLACES

Jamestown
Virginia
Puritans
Roger Williams
Rhode Island
Providence
Anne Hutchinson
Maryland
Quakers
William Penn
Pennsylvania
James Oglethorpe
Georgia

In 1607 the English started Jamestown in Virginia.

The Pilgrims were not the first group of English people to live in America. The first group of English people came to America in 1585, but their **colony** failed.

Before long other English people moved to America. They came for three reasons. Some people came to get rich. Others wanted freedom of religion. Many people came because they thought they could have a better life in America.

In 1607 the English started Jamestown in America. This town was in the Virginia colony. The English came to Jamestown to find gold and become rich. The English did not find gold.

At first the Jamestown **settlers** did not want to grow food or build houses. The settlers were very hungry during the first winter. Many settlers died. More people came to

In 1619 the Jamestown settlers brought slaves from Africa to help them grow tobacco.

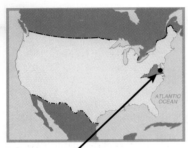

Jamestown, Virginia

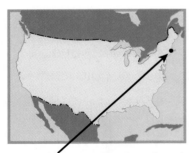

Providence, Rhode Island

live in Jamestown. Then the settlers began to work harder. They built farms and houses.

The settlers began to grow **tobacco** in Jamestown. People would smoke tobacco in pipes. The settlers sold their tobacco to England for a lot of money. Each year the settlers grew more and more tobacco. In 1619 the settlers brought slaves from Africa to help them grow tobacco. After that more Africans were brought to America. Africans were forced to work as slaves in the English colonies.

The Puritans were a group of people who did not want to pray in the Church of England. In 1628 a group of Puritans came to Massachusetts for freedom of religion. Later, more Puritans came. Everyone in Massachusetts had to pray in Puritan churches. The Puritans did not let other people have freedom of religion.

Roger Williams lived with the Puritans. He told them that everyone should have freedom of religion. He left Massachusetts and traveled through the forests. Roger Williams met Native Americans who helped him. He bought land from them. Roger Williams started the Rhode Island colony on that land in 1636. He started the city of Providence in Rhode Island. Providence was the first city in America where there was freedom of religion for all.

Anne Hutchinson was a woman who lived in Massachusetts. Her **religious** ideas were different from the Puritan ideas. Anne Hutchinson left Massachusetts. She went to Rhode Island in 1638 and started a new town.

William Penn

James Oglethorpe

Anne Hutchinson's ideas were different from the ideas of other Puritans.

More English people came to America for freedom of religion. Catholics were sent to jail if they prayed in Catholic churches in England. So 300 Catholics came to America in 1634. They started a colony called Maryland.

The Quakers were another group of people who would not pray in the Church of England. William Penn was a Quaker. In 1681 William Penn started the Pennsylvania colony. He bought the land for his colony from Native Americans. The Native Americans liked William Penn. There was peace in the Pennsylvania colony. Everyone had freedom of religion in Pennsylvania.

In England there were some people who did not have any money. People who were **in debt** were put into jail. These people could not work or help their families. James Oglethorpe started the Georgia colony to help these people. In 1733 James Oglethorpe went to Georgia with 120 of these people. They worked hard in Georgia. They started farms and built homes. Poor people from many countries in Europe came to live and work in the Georgia colony.

Each year more people came to live in the English colonies along the Atlantic Ocean. By 1753 there were 13 English colonies along the Atlantic Ocean.

Read and Remember

Write the Answer Write one or more sentences on your paper to answer each question.

1. What were three reasons English people came to America?

2. Why did the English come to Jamestown?

3. Why were African slaves brought to Jamestown?

4. Why did the Puritans come to America?

5. Which was the first city in America to allow freedom of religion for all?

6. Why did the Catholics come to America?

7. Who started the Pennsylvania colony?

8. Who did James Oglethorpe bring to Georgia?

True or False Number your paper from 1 to 10. Write **T** for each sentence that is true. Write **F** for each sentence that is false.

1. The Pilgrims were the first group of English people to live in America.

2. The English wanted to find gold in Jamestown.

3. The settlers in Jamestown brought African slaves to help them grow cotton.

4. Puritans let everyone have freedom of religion in Massachusetts.

5. Roger Williams thought that everyone should have freedom of religion.

6. The city of Providence was started in Virginia.

7. Anne Hutchinson started a town in Rhode Island.

8. William Penn was a Quaker.

9. James Oglethorpe started the Pennsylvania colony.

10. The Georgia colony was started to help people who were in debt.

Think and Apply

Drawing Conclusions   Read the first two sentences below. Then read the third sentence. Notice how it follows from the first two sentences. It is called a **conclusion**.

> There was no freedom of religion in England.
> The Pilgrims wanted to pray in their own church.
>
> **CONCLUSION**   The Pilgrims left England to find freedom of religion.

Number your paper from 1 to 5. Read each pair of sentences. Then look in the box for the conclusion you can make. Write the letter of the conclusion on your paper.

1. The Jamestown settlers did not want to grow food.
   They did not build houses.

2. The Puritans did not let people have freedom of religion.
   Roger Williams wanted freedom of religion.

3. The Puritans did not let people have freedom of religion.
   Anne Hutchinson's religious ideas were different from the Puritan ideas.

4. There was freedom of religion in Pennsylvania.
   The Native Americans liked William Penn.

5. Many English people were in jail for debt.
   James Oglethorpe wanted to help these people.

> **a.** She left Massachusetts.
> **b.** He started a colony with people from English jails.
> **c.** He left Massachusetts to start his own colony.
> **d.** They were hungry and cold the first winter.
> **e.** The colony was very peaceful.

⭐ Journal Writing

Which colony would you want to live in if you had moved to America in 1755? Write a paragraph in your journal that tells which colony you would choose. Explain your reasons.

Skill Builder

Reading a Historical Map A **historical map** shows how an area used to look. The historical map on this page shows the 13 English colonies in the year 1753.

The 13 colonies are numbered on the map in the order that they were started. Number your paper from 1 to 13. Write the name of the colony that matches each number.

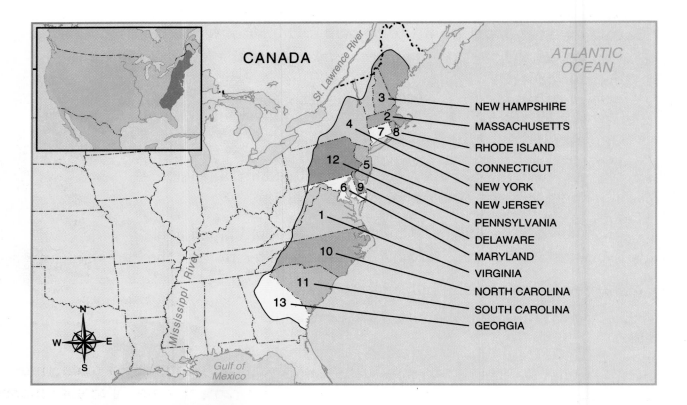

Write a sentence on your paper to answer each question about the map.

1. Which colony was started first?

2. Which colony was started last?

3. Which colony is west of New Jersey?

4. Which ocean is east of the colonies?

5. Which colony is north of Georgia?

6. Which colony is south of New Hampshire?

CHAPTER 6 THE FRENCH COME TO AMERICA

Think About As You Read

1. Why did the French come to America?
2. How did Native Americans help the French?
3. How did France lose its land in America?

NEW WORDS

short cut
body of water
snowshoes

PEOPLE & PLACES

France
King Louis
Jacques Cartier
Canada
St. Lawrence River
Sieur de la Salle
Gulf of Mexico
Louisiana
St. Louis
New Orleans
George Washington
Virginia
North America

Jacques Cartier explored the St. Lawrence River for France.

Many English people came to America for freedom of religion. Many poor people came to America to earn money. We learned that Spanish people came to America to find gold. People from France also came to America. People from France are called the French.

King Louis of France wanted to find a **short cut** to Asia. In 1534 the king sent Jacques Cartier to America. Cartier wanted to find a river in America that he could follow west all the way to Asia. Cartier sailed to Canada. Cartier could not find a river that went to Asia. He explored the St. Lawrence River. Look at the map on page 33. Find the St. Lawrence River. Cartier said that all the land around the St. Lawrence River belonged to France. French land in America was called New France.

La Salle called the land around the Mississippi River "Louisiana."

Sieur de la Salle

Jacques Cartier

Sieur de la Salle also explored America for France. In 1682 La Salle traveled from the St. Lawrence River to the Mississippi River. Then he paddled a canoe down the Mississippi River to the south. In the south there is a **body of water** called the Gulf of Mexico. La Salle was the first person we know of who traveled all the way down the Mississippi River to the Gulf of Mexico.

La Salle called the land near the Mississippi River "Louisiana." He put a big cross and a French flag on the land of Louisiana. La Salle said, "All the land around the Mississippi River belongs to King Louis of France. I am calling this land 'Louisiana'." The land around the Mississippi River and the land around the St. Lawrence River were part of New France.

The French king sent more people to America. The French started two cities on the Mississippi River. These two French cities were St. Louis and New Orleans. New Orleans was near the Gulf of Mexico.

The French owned much more land in America than the English. But not many French people wanted to move to America. They did not build many farms and towns in America. The French did not allow freedom of religion. Only Catholics were allowed to live in New France. The French colony grew very slowly.

French fur trapper wearing snowshoes

There were some French people who wanted to move to America. They came for two reasons. One reason was to find furs. Native Americans hunted many animals for their furs. The French traded with Native Americans for these furs. In France they sold these furs for a lot of money. The second reason the French came was to teach Native Americans how to be Catholics. French priests taught their religion to Native Americans.

Native Americans helped the French in many ways. They taught the French how to trap animals for furs. They taught the French how to use canoes to travel on rivers. They also showed the French how to make **snowshoes**. Many parts of New France had lots of snow in the winter. When they wore snowshoes, the French could walk on very deep snow.

Native Americans had fewer fights with the French than with the Spanish or the English. The Spanish had forced Native Americans to work as slaves. The French never treated them as slaves. The English took land away from the Native

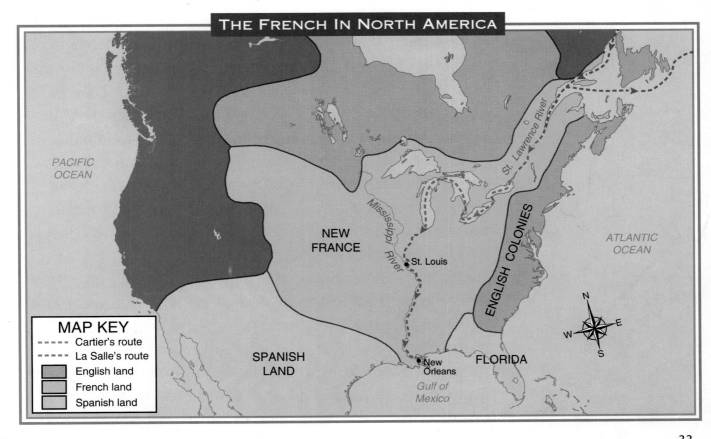

THE FRENCH IN NORTH AMERICA

PACIFIC OCEAN

NEW FRANCE

Mississippi River

St. Louis

St. Lawrence River

ENGLISH COLONIES

ATLANTIC OCEAN

SPANISH LAND

New Orleans

FLORIDA

Gulf of Mexico

MAP KEY
- - - - Cartier's route
- - - - La Salle's route
English land
French land
Spanish land

In 1763 France lost most of its land to England in the French and Indian War.

Americans in order to build farms and towns. The French did not take Native American lands.

England did not want France to own land in America. Many English people in the 13 colonies wanted to move west to Louisiana. France did not want English people to live in Louisiana. England and France had been enemies in Europe for many years. They became enemies in America. By 1754 England and France were fighting a war in America. This war was called the French and Indian War. Some Native Americans fought for the French, and some fought for the English. George Washington lived in the Virginia colony. He helped the English soldiers fight. The soldiers fought for many years.

The war ended in 1763. France lost the French and Indian War. England won the war. After the war, England owned Canada. England owned all the land that was east of the Mississippi River. Spain owned the land that was west of the Mississippi River. St. Louis and New Orleans belonged to Spain. France lost most of its land in America. France kept two small islands in Canada. In 1763 England and Spain owned most of the land in North America.

Read and Remember

Finish the Story   Number your paper from 1 to 6. Use the words in blue print to finish the story. Write the words you choose on your paper.

furs   Louisiana   Mississippi   canoes   Catholic   French

The French explorer La Salle traveled down the __(1)__ River. He paddled all the way to the Gulf of Mexico. La Salle called all the land around the Mississippi River "__(2)__." This land became part of the large French colony called New France. Some French people came to America to find __(3)__ . Others came to teach the __(4)__ religion to Native Americans. Native Americans taught the French how to use __(5)__ and snowshoes. In 1763 the __(6)__ lost the French and Indian War to England.

Think and Apply

Fact or Opinion   A **fact** is a true statement. An **opinion** is a statement that tells what a person thinks.

> **Fact**   The French explored America.
> **Opinion**   The French were the best explorers.

Number your paper from 1 to 8. Write **F** on your paper for each fact below. Write **O** for each opinion. You should find four sentences that are opinions.

1. The French king wanted to find a shortcut to Asia.

2. Jacques Cartier explored the St. Lawrence River.

3. La Salle was a smarter explorer than Cartier.

4. Before 1754 France owned more land in America than England.

5. New France was a better place to live than the English colonies.

6. The French were stronger soldiers than the English.

7. The Catholic religion was the best religion.

8. In 1763 England and Spain owned most of the land in America.

Skill Builder

Using Map Directions   In Chapter 2 you learned that there are four main directions on a map. They are north, south, east, and west. A compass rose also shows four in-between directions. They are **northeast**, **southeast**, **northwest**, and **southwest**. Southeast is between south and east. Southwest is between south and west. Sometimes the in-between directions are shortened to NE, SE, NW, and SW.

Draw a compass rose on your paper. Write the letters **NE**, **SE**, **NW**, and **SW** in the correct places on your compass rose.

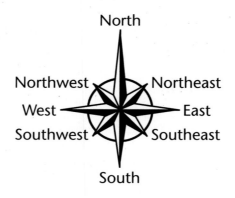

Number your paper from 1 to 6. Look at the map on page 37. Then write on your paper the word that finishes each sentence.

1. The St. Lawrence River is in the _____ .
   northeast   northwest   southwest

2. The English colonies were in the _____ .
   northwest   southwest   east

3. The Mississippi River was _____ of the English colonies.
   south   west   east

4. Florida is in the _____ .
   southeast   northeast   northwest

5. The Atlantic Ocean was to the _____ of the English colonies.
   north   south   east

6. New Orleans is in the _____ .
   east   north   south

The historical map on this page shows the Spanish, French, and English colonies in North America in 1754. Number your paper from 1 to 7. Then study the map. Use the words in blue print to finish the story. Write on your paper the words you choose.

**Atlantic Ocean   Gulf of Mexico   New Orleans   Florida
Southwest   St. Lawrence   Jamestown**

Spain had land in the Southeast called __(1)__ . Spain also had land in the __(2)__ . Then in 1607 the English started __(3)__ in the Virginia colony. All of the 13 English colonies were near the __(4)__ .

In 1534 Cartier explored a river in Canada called the __(5)__ River. La Salle traveled south on the Mississippi River to the __(6)__ . The French built the city of __(7)__ near the Gulf of Mexico.

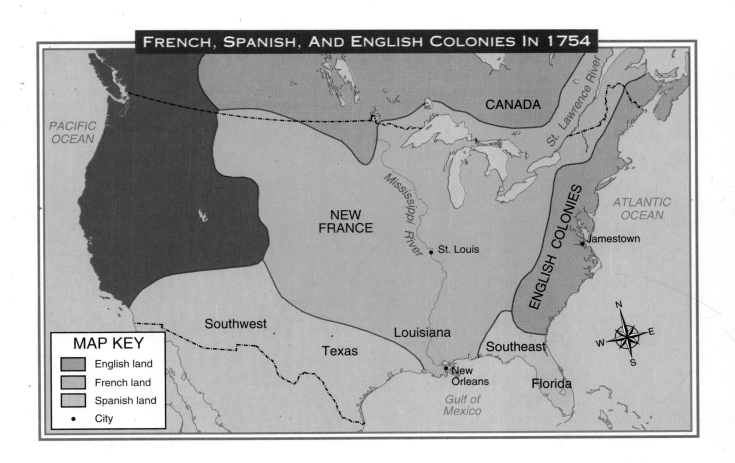

FRENCH, SPANISH, AND ENGLISH COLONIES IN 1754

PACIFIC OCEAN

CANADA

St. Lawrence River

NEW FRANCE

Mississippi River

St. Louis

ENGLISH COLONIES

ATLANTIC OCEAN

Jamestown

Southwest

Louisiana

Texas

Southeast

New Orleans

Florida

Gulf of Mexico

MAP KEY
English land
French land
Spanish land
• City

N E S W

BUILDING A NEW NATION

Imagine what it was like to live in America in 1776. Many Americans were angry at the British leaders who ruled over them. They were angry at unfair laws that the British leaders wrote for the colonies. Americans became so angry at these laws that they decided to fight.

Americans in the 13 colonies were not ready to fight. They did not have enough guns, money, or soldiers to fight for their freedom. The British army was much stronger. How could the Americans win? It would take the help of many different people, including George Washington.

What would you have done if you had lived in 1776? Would you have joined the fight to make the United States of America a free country? As you read Unit 2, think about how Americans built a new country.

1773
Americans throw tea into the Atlantic Ocean at the Boston Tea Party.

1776
Americans write and sign the Declaration of Independence.

1783
Great Britain and America sign a peace treaty.

1789
George Washington becomes America's first President.

1799
George Washington dies.

1760

1770

1780

1790

1800

1765
The British write the Stamp Act.

1775
The American Revolution begins.

1781
America wins the American Revolution.

1787
Americans write the Constitution.

1791
Americans write the Bill of Rights.

1797
George Washington finishes his work as President.

CHAPTER 7 ★ AMERICANS FIGHT FOR FREEDOM

British leaders made laws in a large building called Parliament.

Think About As You Read

1. Why did Americans think that the new laws from Great Britain were unfair?
2. What happened during the Boston Tea Party?
3. Why did Americans start to fight against Great Britain in 1775?

NEW WORDS

nation
tax
Stamp Act
Parliament
port
Boston Tea Party
American Revolution

PEOPLE & PLACES

Americans
Great Britain
British
King George III
Boston

Many people from England came to live in America. They came to live in the 13 colonies. The people who lived in the colonies were called Americans. Many people came to America because they wanted more freedom.

In 1707 England and three small countries became part of a larger **nation**. The larger nation was called Great Britain. People who lived in Great Britain were called the British. Great Britain ruled the 13 American colonies. The king of Great Britain was the king of the American colonies. From 1760 to 1820, King George III was the king of Great Britain.

In Chapter 6 you learned that the English, or British, won the French and Indian War. The war helped the American colonies. Americans felt safer because France no longer ruled Canada. Great Britain ruled Canada after this war. The British had spent a lot of money to fight the French. Great Britain paid for soldiers, guns, and food for its army. The British wanted the colonies to help pay for the French and Indian War.

The British made new laws. The laws said that Americans had to send some of their money to Great Britain. The money that Americans had to send was called **tax** money. This tax money would help Great Britain get back the money it had spent on the war.

In 1765 the British made a new tax law called the **Stamp Act**. The Stamp Act said that Americans had to pay a tax on things like newspapers. A special stamp was placed on the newspaper to show that the tax was paid.

Americans did not like the new tax law. Some Americans decided not to pay the new taxes. Some Americans burned stamps to show that they did not like the new law. They said the new law was not fair. It was not fair because Americans did not help write the tax law.

In Great Britain the British helped make their own laws. They did this by voting for leaders who would make laws for them. These British leaders met in a large building called **Parliament**. In Parliament the leaders wrote laws for Great Britain. Americans wanted to send their own leaders to help write laws in Parliament. The British would not let Americans write laws in Parliament.

King George III

Parliament Building

Americans burned stamps to show they did not like the Stamp Act.

The Parliament made more tax laws for the colonies. The British leaders did not let Americans help write any of these laws. Americans did not like the new laws that the British wrote for them.

In 1773 the British made another law. This law said that Americans must pay a tea tax. This meant that Americans had to pay a tax when they paid for their tea. Americans had to send the tax money to Great Britain. Americans were very angry because they did not help write the tea tax law.

Boston was a large **port** city in Massachusetts near the Atlantic Ocean. Three ships with boxes of tea came to Boston. The Americans did not want to pay a tea tax. They did not want the tea. They wanted to send the tea ships back to Great Britain. The British said that Americans had to pay for the tea.

Some Americans decided to throw the boxes of tea into the ocean. One night in 1773, they put on Native American clothes. They went on the tea ships. The Americans threw every box of tea into the Atlantic Ocean. This is known as the **Boston Tea Party**. The Boston Tea Party made King George very angry.

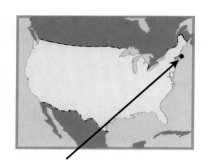

Boston, Massachusetts

At the Boston Tea Party, Americans threw British tea into the ocean.

The first battle of the American Revolution was in Massachusetts.

King George punished the people of Boston. He closed Boston's port. Ships could not come to or go from the port. He said the port would be closed until Americans paid for all the tea. He sent many British soldiers to Massachusetts.

The British had made another law that Americans did not like. This law said that Americans must give the British soldiers food and a place to sleep. The soldiers paid when they ate and slept in Americans' homes. But Americans did not like the British soldiers. They did not want the soldiers in their homes. And now King George sent more soldiers to Massachusetts. Americans were becoming angrier and angrier.

The angry Americans formed an army. In 1775 American soldiers began to fight Great Britain for freedom. The fighting began in Massachusetts. The British won the first battles. But the Americans would not stop fighting. Americans were fighting for the same freedom that people had in Great Britain. They wanted the freedom to write their own laws. A war had started in 1775 between Great Britain and America. Americans called this war the **American Revolution**.

Read and Remember

Match Up Finish each sentence in Group A with words from Group B. Write the letter of the correct answer on your paper.

Group A

1. Great Britain wanted the colonies to help pay for the _____

2. The new tax laws were not fair to Americans because _____

3. During the Boston Tea Party, the Americans went on three British ships and _____

4. After the Boston Tea Party, King George punished Americans by _____

5. In 1775 Americans began fighting a war with Great Britain that the Americans _____

Group B

a. closing the port of Boston.

b. called the American Revolution.

c. French and Indian War.

d. threw all the tea into the ocean.

e. Americans did not help write laws in Parliament.

Think and Apply

Understanding Different Points of View People can look in different ways at something that happens. Look at these two points of view about a math test.

The math test was very hard.
The math test was fair.

In 1775 the Americans and the British had different points of view about how to rule the 13 colonies. Number your paper from 1 to 6. Read each sentence below. Write **American** for each sentence that shows the American point of view. Write **British** for each sentence that shows the British point of view.

1. Only people in Great Britain should write laws in Parliament.

2. Americans should help write their laws in Parliament.

3. Americans should not pay a tea tax if they did not help write the tax law.

4. Americans should pay for all the tea they threw in the ocean.

5. Americans have enough freedom.

6. Americans should fight the British for more freedom.

★ Skill Builder

Reading a Time Line   A **time line** is a drawing that shows years on a line. Look at this time line. Read the time line from left to right.

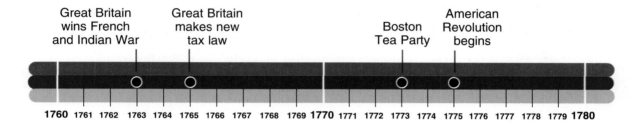

Great Britain wins French and Indian War

Great Britain makes new tax law

Boston Tea Party

American Revolution begins

1760 1761 1762 1763 1764 1765 1766 1767 1768 1769 1770 1771 1772 1773 1774 1775 1776 1777 1778 1779 1780

The year 1765 comes before 1766, and 1767 comes after 1766. Answer each question on your paper.

1. What year comes after 1774?

2. What year comes before 1775?

Events are sometimes placed on time lines. Read the events on the time line. Then write the answer to each question on your paper.

3. When did Great Britain win the French and Indian War?

4. When did Great Britain make a new tax law?

5. When was the Boston Tea Party?

Journal Writing ★

What would you do if you were an American living in the 13 colonies in 1775? Would you help the Americans or King George? Write a paragraph in your journal that tells what you would do and why.

CHAPTER 8

A NEW COUNTRY IS BORN

Think About As You Read

1. Why did Americans write the Declaration of Independence?
2. Why was George Washington an excellent army leader?
3. How did many different people help win the American Revolution?

NEW WORDS

independent
Declaration of Independence
equal
Loyalists
General

PEOPLE & PLACES

Thomas Jefferson
Philadelphia
Friedrich von Steuben
Germany
Thaddeus Kosciusko
Poland
African Americans
James Armistead
Molly Pitcher
Haym Salomon
Jewish American

In 1776 Thomas Jefferson and other leaders wrote the Declaration of Independence.

The American Revolution began in the year 1775. At first Americans were fighting the British because they wanted more freedom. American leaders wrote to King George. They asked him to let Americans write their own laws in Parliament. But King George would not give Americans more freedom. So in 1776 many Americans decided that they wanted the colonies to become **independent**. Independent means "to be free."

Americans decided to tell the world that the colonies no longer belonged to Great Britain. In 1776 Thomas Jefferson and a few other leaders were asked to write the **Declaration of Independence**. The Declaration of Independence was an important paper. It said, "All men are created **equal**."

Thomas Jefferson

The Declaration
of Independence

General Washington
was the leader of the
American army. He
is shown here with
his soldiers during
the cold winter.

This means that all people are just as important as a king. It also said all people should have freedom. The Declaration of Independence also said that the 13 colonies were an independent nation.

The leaders of the 13 colonies went to Philadelphia in the Pennsylvania colony. On July 4, 1776, the leaders signed the Declaration of Independence in Philadelphia.

Some Americans in the colonies did not want the colonies to be free. These people were called **Loyalists**. They fought for Great Britain during the American Revolution.

The American Revolution lasted six years. During that time George Washington was the leader of the American army. The soldiers called him **General** Washington. George Washington was a good leader. He tried to be fair to the soldiers, and he was a good fighter. The Americans lost many battles, or fights. They were often hungry and cold during the winters. But General Washington did not give up. The Americans continued to fight for independence.

Many people tried to help the Americans win the war. France sent French soldiers to America. French soldiers helped the Americans fight against the British.

James Armistead

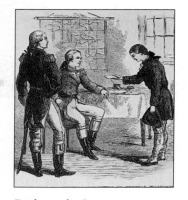

Deborah Sampson

People from other nations also helped Americans fight. Friedrich von Steuben came from Germany to help. He taught Americans how to be better soldiers. Thaddeus Kosciusko came from Poland to help Americans fight.

All kinds of Americans fought together in the war. Farmers, sailors, business owners, and teachers all became soldiers.

About five thousand African Americans fought against the British. They fought in every important battle. James Armistead was a brave African American soldier. He was a spy for the Americans.

Women also helped win the war. They did the farm work when the men were fighting. They grew food for the soldiers. They made clothes for the army. Women also cared for soldiers who were hurt during the war. Deborah Sampson and a few other women dressed like soldiers and fought in the war.

One woman, Molly Pitcher, brought water to American soldiers when they were fighting. Molly's husband, John, was a soldier. One day John was hurt during a battle. He could not fight. Molly took John's place in the battle against the British soldiers.

Molly Pitcher fought in the American Revolution.

Americans cheered for Washington and his soldiers when they won the American Revolution.

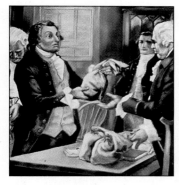

Haym Salomon

Haym Salomon was a Jewish American who helped the Americans win. He had left Poland to come to America for freedom of religion. Haym Salomon worked hard and became rich. He knew the American army had little money. The soldiers did not have enough food, clothes, or guns. Some soldiers did not even have shoes. Haym Salomon gave most of his money to the American army. The soldiers bought food, guns, shoes, and clothes with this money. Haym Salomon was a poor man when he died. He had given most of his money to help the Americans win.

The American Revolution ended in 1781. The Americans had won. Great Britain and the colonies signed a peace treaty in 1783. People in other countries learned how the Americans won their fight for freedom. Soon people in other countries would want more freedom, too.

Great Britain lost the American Revolution. When the war was over, the 13 colonies were independent. Now the 13 colonies were called 13 states. The Americans called their new country the United States of America.

Read and Remember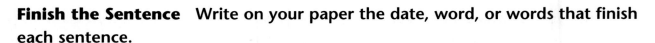

Finish the Sentence Write on your paper the date, word, or words that finish each sentence.

1. Americans in the 13 colonies told the world they were independent in _____ .
   1765   1776   1783

2. The Declaration of Independence said, "All men are created _____ ."
   smart   slow   equal

3. Americans signed the Declaration of Independence in _____ .
   Boston   Philadelphia   Jamestown

4. Many _____ soldiers helped the Americans fight.
   French   British   Russians

5. _____ taught Americans how to be better soldiers.
   King George   Friedrich von Steuben   Molly Pitcher

6. _____ was a brave African American soldier.
   Haym Salomon   James Armistead   Thomas Jefferson

7. The American Revolution ended in _____ .
   1765   1776   1781

True or False Write **T** on your paper for each sentence that is true. Write **F** for each sentence that is false.

1. The 13 colonies became independent in the French and Indian War.

2. Thomas Jefferson helped write the Declaration of Independence.

3. Some Americans who fought for Great Britain during the American Revolution were called Loyalists.

4. France sent French soldiers to help Americans fight.

5. Americans called their new country the United Colonies of America.

Think and Apply

Drawing Conclusions Read each pair of sentences. Then look in the box for the conclusion you can make. Write the letter of the conclusion on your paper.

1. Americans in the 13 colonies decided to become independent.
   Americans wanted to tell the world that they were independent.

2. Americans called Loyalists fought for Great Britain during the American Revolution.
   The Loyalists liked King George.

3. George Washington was fair to the soldiers.
   George Washington lost many battles but never gave up.

4. Many women made food and clothes for the army.
   Women took care of soldiers who were hurt.

5. Haym Salomon was a rich man.
   He knew the American army needed a lot of money.

Conclusions
   a. Americans asked Thomas Jefferson to write the Declaration of Independence.

   b. George Washington was an excellent army leader.

   c. Haym Salomon gave most of his money to the American army.

   d. Some Americans did not want the colonies to become independent.

   e. American women helped in many ways during the war.

Journal Writing

Imagine that you were working for a newspaper in 1776. Write a short news story about the signing of the Declaration of Independence. Tell why Americans wrote the Declaration, and write some of the things it said.

CHAPTER 9

THE CONSTITUTION

Think About As You Read

1. Why did the United States need a constitution after the American Revolution?
2. How do Americans write their own laws?
3. How does the Bill of Rights protect your freedom?

NEW WORDS

constitution
Congress
Senate
House of Representatives
senators
representatives
Supreme Court
judges
capital
freedom of the press
amendments
Bill of Rights

PEOPLE & PLACES

Capitol
White House
Washington, D.C.

Many leaders helped write the United States Constitution.

The American Revolution was won in 1781. The United States was now an independent country with 13 states. The new country needed new laws. A **constitution** is a group of laws. The leaders of the United States decided to write laws, or a constitution, for their new country. In 1787 leaders from 12 of the states went to Philadelphia. In Philadelphia the leaders wrote the United States Constitution.

Before the American Revolution, Great Britain made laws for the American colonies. Americans liked the way the British voted for leaders to write laws in Parliament. A group of men planned the Constitution so that Americans could help write their own laws. How do Americans do this?

The United States Constitution

The Constitution says that Americans should choose, or vote for, people to work for them in their government. Our country's laws are made by men and women in **Congress**. In some ways our Congress is like Great Britain's Parliament. Americans vote for people who will make laws for them in Congress. There are two houses, or parts, of Congress. The **Senate** and the **House of Representatives** are the two houses of Congress.

Men and women who write laws are called **senators** and **representatives**. Every state sends two senators to work in the Senate. States with many people send many representatives to work in the House of Representatives. States with fewer people send fewer representatives to work in the House of Representatives. The senators and representatives meet in a building called the Capitol. The Constitution says that Americans should vote for people to be their senators and representatives. Americans help write their own laws by voting for their senators and representatives.

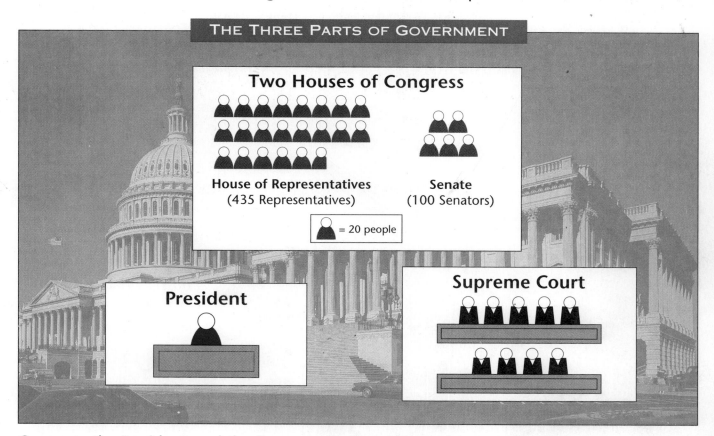

THE THREE PARTS OF GOVERNMENT

Two Houses of Congress

House of Representatives
(435 Representatives)

Senate
(100 Senators)

= 20 people

President

Supreme Court

Congress, the President, and the Supreme Court work together to make laws.

Bill of Rights

The White House

Americans vote for a President every four years. The President carries out the country's laws. The President helps make our laws. The White House is where the President lives and works.

The Constitution also gives the United States its **Supreme Court**. Nine **judges** work in the Supreme Court. In the Supreme Court, judges decide whether or not our laws agree with the Constitution.

The White House, the Capitol, and the Supreme Court buildings are in the city of Washington, D.C. It is the **capital** of our country.

Some of our leaders were not happy with the Constitution when it was written in 1787. The Constitution did not say that Americans had freedom of religion. The Constitution did not say that Americans had **freedom of the press**. "Freedom of the press" means the government cannot tell people what they can say in newspapers and books. British soldiers had often stayed in American homes. Americans wanted a law that said soldiers would no longer sleep in American homes.

Congress writes laws in the Capitol building in Washington, D.C. The two houses of Congress are the Senate and the House of Representatives.

The President sometimes meets with all the senators and representatives of Congress in the Capitol building.

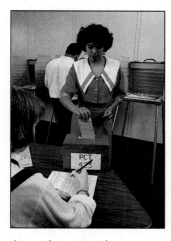

American voting

In 1791 our leaders added ten **amendments**, or new laws, to the Constitution. These ten amendments are called the **Bill of Rights**. The Bill of Rights is now part of our Constitution. What are some of these rights? Every American has freedom of religion. Every American has freedom of the press. Americans do not have to let soldiers sleep in their homes. The Bill of Rights gives every American many freedoms.

Since 1791, seventeen more amendments have been added to the Constitution. Our Constitution now has 27 amendments. These amendments were added because our leaders wanted laws to be fair to all Americans. As our country changes, more amendments may be added to the Constitution.

Today our Constitution is more than 200 years old. The leaders of 1787 gave us good laws. These laws helped America become a great country.

Read and Remember

Write the Answer   Write one or more sentences on your paper to answer each question.

1. Where did Americans write the Constitution?

2. How many states sent leaders to write the Constitution?

3. What do senators and representatives do in Congress?

4. How many senators does each state have in the United States Senate?

5. How do Americans help write their own laws?

6. What does the President do?

7. In what city are the White House, Capitol, and Supreme Court buildings?

8. Why did the leaders add the Bill of Rights to the Constitution?

9. What are some of the rights that the Bill of Rights added to the Constitution?

10. How many amendments does our Constitution now have?

 ## Think and Apply

Finding the Main Idea   Read each group of sentences below. One of the sentences is a main idea. Two sentences support the main idea. Write the sentence that is the main idea in each group.

1. Americans were angry when the British wrote laws for them.
   Americans made a constitution that said they could write their own laws.
   Americans wanted to make their own laws.

2. The Constitution says Americans can choose people to work in their government.
   Americans vote for their senators and representatives.
   Americans vote for their President every four years.

3. The Constitution did not say that Americans had freedom of the press.

   In 1791 America's leaders added the Bill of Rights to the Constitution.

   The Constitution did not say that Americans had freedom of religion.

4. The President and the Supreme Court are two parts of the government.

   The Senate and the House of Representatives make up one part of the government.

   The United States government has three parts.

5. Americans wrote the Constitution in 1787.

   The Constitution has helped our country for more than 200 years.

   Americans have added 27 amendments to the Constitution.

★ Journal Writing

After the American Revolution, Americans wanted their new Constitution to say that people could help write their own laws. Write a paragraph in your journal that explains how early American leaders set up our government so that Americans could help write laws.

Skill Builder ★

Reading a Diagram   A **diagram** is a picture that helps you understand something. The diagram on page 53 helps you understand our government. Number your paper from 1 to 5. Look back at the diagram. Then choose a word in blue print to finish each sentence. Write the correct answers on your paper.

   President   senators   nine   three   435

1. The United States government has _____ parts.

2. The government has one _____ .

3. The government has _____ Supreme Court judges.

4. There are fewer _____ than representatives.

5. There are _____ members of the House of Representatives.

When Ben was a young man, he worked in his brother's printing shop.

Think About As You Read

1. What kinds of work did Benjamin Franklin do in Boston and Philadelphia?
2. How did Benjamin Franklin help the city of Philadelphia?
3. How did Benjamin Franklin help the American colonies become independent?

NEW WORDS

printing shop
printer
published
electric sparks

PEOPLE & PLACES

Benjamin Franklin

Benjamin Franklin was born in Boston in 1706. He had 16 brothers and sisters. In those days, people used candles to light their homes. Ben's father earned money by making soap and candles.

Ben was a smart boy. He loved to read books. Ben went to school until he was ten years old. Then Ben made soap and candles with his father.

Ben had an older brother named James. James owned a **printing shop**. When Ben was 12 years old, he went to work for James. Ben became a **printer**. Ben and James **published** a newspaper together. Ben enjoyed his work, but he did not like working with James. Ben decided to run away from Boston.

Ben ran away. He went to Philadelphia. Ben worked in a printing shop in Philadelphia. When Ben was 24 years old, he published his own newspaper. People read Ben's newspaper in all 13 American colonies.

Ben wanted Philadelphia to be a better city. Ben started the city's first hospital. He started a fire department. He started a school in Philadelphia. Ben started Philadelphia's first public library.

Ben knew there was something called electricity. He wanted to learn more about electricity. One night there were rain and lightning outside. Ben tied a key to the end of a kite string. He flew the kite outside. Lightning hit the kite. **Electric sparks** jumped off the key. Then Ben knew that lightning is a kind of electricity. People all over America and Europe read about Ben's work with electricity. Ben became famous.

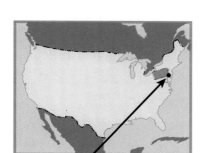

Philadelphia, Pennsylvania

Ben used a kite and a key to show that lightning is a kind of electricity.

Benjamin Franklin

Ben wanted the American colonies to become an independent country. He helped Thomas Jefferson write the Declaration of Independence in 1776. Ben was one of the men who signed the Declaration. Ben wanted to help his country win the American Revolution. He was then seventy years old. He was too old to be a soldier. Ben went to France. He asked the French people to help the Americans fight. The French people liked Ben Franklin. France sent soldiers and ships to the American colonies. France helped the Americans win the war.

In 1787 Ben was 81 years old. He had another job to do. He helped write the Constitution. Ben and the other leaders spent four months writing the Constitution in Philadelphia.

Benjamin Franklin died in Philadelphia when he was 84 years old. He was a very famous American. He helped Philadelphia become a great city, and he helped the United States become a free country.

Ben went to France to get help for the American soldiers.

Read and Remember

Find the Answers   Find the sentences below that tell how Ben helped Philadelphia and America. Write on your paper the sentences you find. You should find four sentences.

1. Ben started a hospital and a public library.

2. Ben started a police department.

3. Ben started a fire department.

4. Ben helped Thomas Jefferson write the Declaration of Independence.

5. Ben was a soldier in the American Revolution.

6. Ben helped Great Britain during the American Revolution.

7. Ben helped write the Constitution in 1787.

Think and Apply

Cause and Effect   Write sentences on your paper by matching each cause on the left with an effect on the right.

Cause

1. James and Ben did not get along well, so _____

2. Ben learned how to be a printer in Boston, so _____

3. Lightning hit Ben's kite and sparks flew off the key, so _____

4. Ben wanted the American colonies to become independent, so _____

5. Ben knew that America needed help during the American Revolution, so _____

Effect

a. he signed the Declaration of Independence.

b. he went to France to ask for help.

c. Ben learned that lightning is a kind of electricity.

d. Ben ran away to Philadelphia.

e. he found a job as a printer in Philadelphia.

Skill Builder

Reading a Bar Graph   Graphs are drawings that help you compare facts. The graph on this page is a **bar graph**. It uses bars of different lengths to show facts. The bar graph below shows the **population** of America's three largest cities in 1776. Population means the number of people.

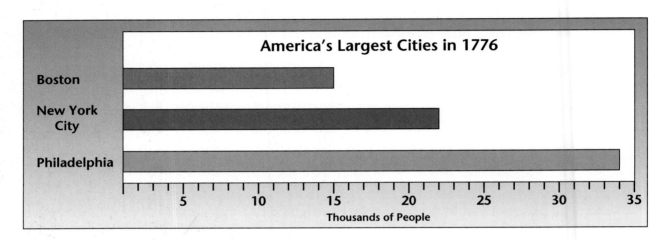

America's Largest Cities in 1776

Boston
New York City
Philadelphia

Thousands of People

Number your paper from 1 to 5. Use the bar graph to answer each question. Write the correct answers on your paper.

1. How many people lived in Boston?
   15,000   22,000   34,000

2. How many people lived in Philadelphia?
   15,000   22,000   34,000

3. What was the population of New York City in 1776?
   5,000   10,000   22,000

4. Which city had the largest population in 1776?
   Boston   New York City   Philadelphia

5. Which of these three cities had the smallest population in 1776?
   Boston   New York City   Philadelphia

Journal Writing

Write a paragraph telling why you think Benjamin Franklin was so important in American history.

11 GEORGE WASHINGTON

Think About As You Read

1. How did George Washington help win the American Revolution?
2. How did George Washington help his country after the American Revolution?
3. How did Martha Washington help her country?

NEW WORDS

manage
commander in chief
surrendered
First Lady
boundaries

PEOPLE & PLACES

Martha Washington
Mount Vernon
New York City
Trenton, New Jersey
Yorktown
Pierre L'Enfant
Benjamin Banneker

Many Americans call George Washington the "Father of our Country."

George Washington was born in the Virginia colony on February 22, 1732. George's parents owned a large house with a lot of farm land. George was a quiet, shy boy. His father died when George was 11 years old. George then helped his mother **manage** the family farm. He learned how to be a good farmer.

George was a soldier in Virginia. Do you remember that Great Britain and France were fighting for land in America in 1754? This fight was called the French and Indian War. George became a leader of the Virginia army. He was 22 years old. George and the Americans helped the British win the war.

In 1759 George married a wealthy woman named Martha. George and Martha Washington lived in a large, beautiful house in Virginia. They called their home Mount Vernon. There were large farms at Mount Vernon. George loved managing his farms.

In 1775 the American Revolution began. George wanted the American colonies to become independent. He became the **commander in chief** of the American army. This means that he was the leader of all the American soldiers. The soldiers called him General Washington.

George lost a battle in New York City. But he did not give up. He took his army south to Pennsylvania. On Christmas 1776 George took his army to Trenton, New Jersey. Find Trenton on the map on page 65. George knew that the British army would be having Christmas parties. They would not be ready to fight. So George and the Americans surprised the British army. The British army **surrendered**. General Washington won the Battle of Trenton, but the war was not over.

The British and the Americans continued to fight. The American army did not have enough food, clothes, or guns. Many soldiers became sick during the cold winters. Most soldiers liked George Washington. They stayed with him and helped him fight for American freedom.

Martha Washington

Mount Vernon was George and Martha's home in Virginia.

Martha Washington helped the American army during the war. Martha stayed with George during the six cold winters of the American Revolution. She sewed clothes for the soldiers. She fixed their torn shirts and pants. Martha took care of soldiers who became sick or hurt. During the summer Martha managed the home and farms at Mount Vernon.

In 1781 the Americans won an important battle at Yorktown, Virginia. The British army surrendered to George Washington at Yorktown. The American Revolution was over. In 1783 Great Britain and the colonies signed a peace treaty. Then General Washington said good-bye to the army. He was happy to go home to Mount Vernon.

Soon the American people needed George Washington again. They wanted him to help write the Constitution. George helped write the Constitution in Philadelphia in 1787. He wanted to return to Mount Vernon. But the United States needed a President. Americans voted for George Washington.

George Washington became our first President in 1789. Martha Washington became the **First Lady**. The government of the United States was in New York City. So George and

Important battles of the American Revolution

In 1781 British soldiers surrendered to General Washington in Yorktown, Virginia.

In 1789 George Washington became the first President of the United States.

Benjamin Banneker

Martha left Mount Vernon. They traveled to New York City. George was America's hero. As he traveled, crowds everywhere cheered for him.

George wanted the United States to have a new capital city. George found a beautiful place for the capital between Maryland and Virginia. George asked a Frenchman named Pierre L'Enfant to plan the new city.

Benjamin Banneker, a free African American, helped L'Enfant plan the new city. Banneker knew a lot about math and science. He used math and science to help plan the **boundaries** of the new capital. Banneker also wrote to American leaders about ending slavery in the new country. In 1800 the government moved to the new capital. The capital is now called Washington, D.C.

George Washington was President for eight years. As President, George helped the United States become a stronger nation. In 1797 George returned to Mount Vernon. He died at his home in 1799.

George Washington was one of our greatest American leaders. He led our country in war and in peace. Many people call him the "Father of our Country."

Read and Remember

Finish the Sentence Write on your paper the word or words that finish each sentence.

1. After his father died, George Washington helped his mother _____ the family farm.
   sell   manage   buy

2. George led the Virginia army in the _____ War.
   Revolutionary   Civil   French and Indian

3. George was the _____ of the American army.
   President   commander in chief   captain

4. George lost a battle in _____ .
   Boston   Philadelphia   New York City

5. George won a Christmas battle in _____ .
   New York City   Yorktown   Trenton

6. In 1787 George helped write the _____ .
   Constitution   Bill of Rights   Declaration of Independence

7. When George Washington was President, Martha Washington was _____ .
   Senator   First Lady   Judge

8. Pierre L'Enfant and _____ planned the capital city of Washington, D.C.
   Ben Franklin   James Armistead   Benjamin Banneker

Think and Apply

Sequencing Events Number your paper from 1 to 5. Write the sentences to show the correct order.

George Washington became the first President of the United States.

George was a leader of the Virginia army in the French and Indian War.

George won the Battle of Trenton on Christmas in 1776.

George helped write the Constitution.

George became the commander in chief of the American army.

Skill Builder

Understanding Decades on a Time Line Sometimes time lines show decades. A **decade** is ten years. This time line shows four decades.

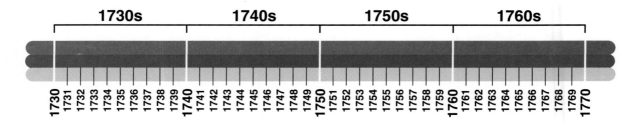

If something happened between 1730 and 1740, you say it happened in the 1730s. If something happened between 1750 and 1760, you say it happened in the 1750s. If something happened between 1760 and 1770, you say it happened in the 1760s.

Look at the events on the time line below. Write the correct decade on your paper for each of the sentences.

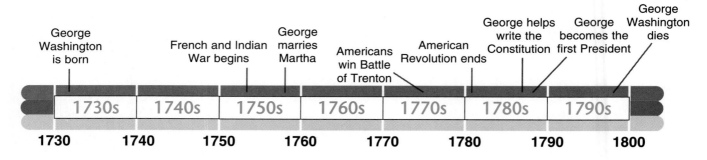

1. George Washington is born.

2. The French and Indian War begins.

3. Americans win the Battle of Trenton.

4. American Revolution ends.

5. George Washington helps write the Constitution.

6. George Washington becomes the first President.

7. George Washington dies.

The historical map on this page shows the United States when George Washington was President. Number your paper from 1 to 6. Then study the map. Use the words in blue print to finish the story. Write on your paper the words you choose.

Yorktown	**Philadelphia**	**Boston**
New York City	**Washington, D.C.**	**Trenton**

Americans were angry when the British said they had to pay a tax on tea. So Americans in __(1)__ threw tea into the Atlantic Ocean. In 1776 Americans signed the Declaration of Independence in __(2)__ .

During the American Revolution, George Washington won a Christmas battle at __(3)__ . In 1781 the British army surrendered to Washington at __(4)__ . In 1789 Washington went to __(5)__ to become the first President. As President he planned the country's new capital. The name of the capital is __(6)__ .

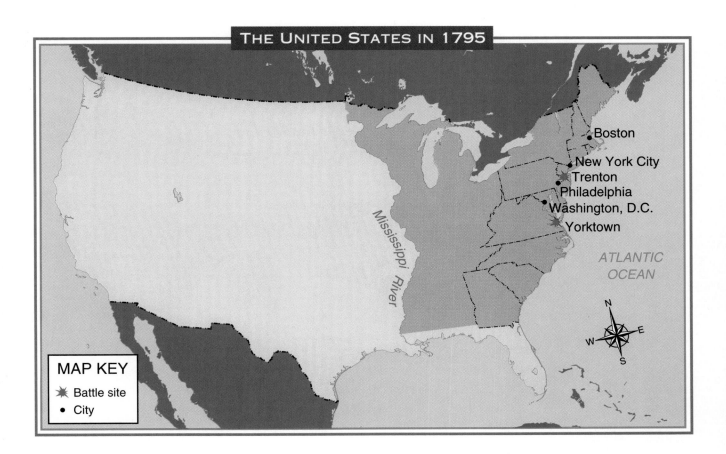

THE UNITED STATES IN 1795

Boston
New York City
Trenton
Philadelphia
Washington, D.C.
Yorktown

Mississippi River

ATLANTIC OCEAN

N
W   E
S

MAP KEY
✳ Battle site
• City

UNIT 3

THE UNITED STATES GROWS

Imagine you were an explorer in the year 1803. The United States has bought a large piece of a land west of the Mississippi River. Since Americans want to learn about this new land, President Thomas Jefferson wants to send people to explore it. The trip would be long and slow. You would have to cross wide rivers. You would have to climb over very tall mountains.

The United States grew much larger after Thomas Jefferson became President. The United States also became much stronger. From 1812 to 1814, Americans fought and won a second war against Great Britain. After the war more people moved west.

What would you have done if you lived between 1800 and 1840? Would you explore new lands in the West? As you read Unit 3, you will learn how the United States grew stronger and larger. While you read, think about what you would have done if you had lived in America before 1840.

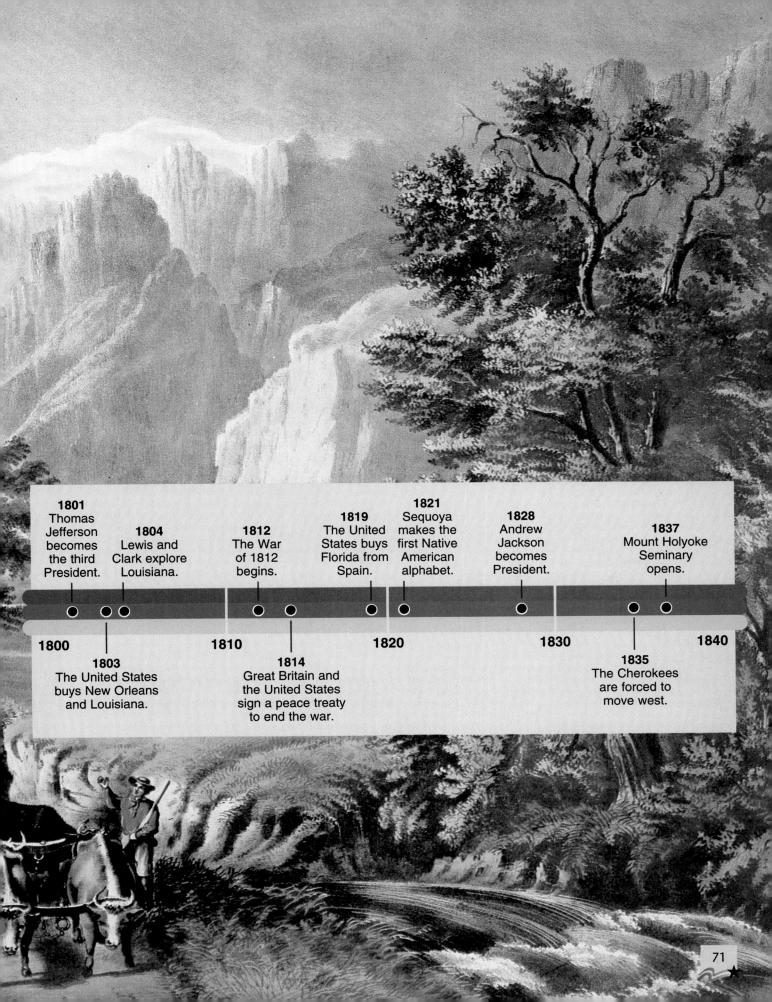

1801
Thomas Jefferson becomes the third President.

1804
Lewis and Clark explore Louisiana.

1812
The War of 1812 begins.

1819
The United States buys Florida from Spain.

1821
Sequoya makes the first Native American alphabet.

1828
Andrew Jackson becomes President.

1837
Mount Holyoke Seminary opens.

1800

1803
The United States buys New Orleans and Louisiana.

1810

1814
Great Britain and the United States sign a peace treaty to end the war.

1820

1830

1835
The Cherokees are forced to move west.

1840

CHAPTER 12

THE UNITED STATES DOUBLES IN SIZE

Think About As You Read

1. Why was New Orleans important to the United States?
2. How did the United States double in size in 1803?
3. How did Lewis and Clark help Thomas Jefferson?

NEW WORDS

crops
Louisiana Purchase
doubled

PEOPLE & PLACES

Napoleon
Meriwether Lewis
William Clark
York
Rocky Mountains
Pacific Ocean
Sacajawea
Oregon

A Native American woman named Sacajawea helped Lewis and Clark travel to the Pacific Ocean.

The man who wrote most of the Declaration of Independence became President of the United States in 1801. Americans voted for Thomas Jefferson to be their third President.

The American Revolution was over. The United States owned all the land east of the Mississippi River except Florida. At first, most Americans lived in the 13 states near the Atlantic Ocean. But every year more Americans moved to the West. By 1800 almost one million Americans lived on the land between the 13 states and the Mississippi River. They built homes and farms. They were starting new states for the United States. In 1803 the United States had 17 states.

Thomas Jefferson

Napoleon

Sometimes Americans moved to land that was being used by Native Americans. Then there were fights between Native Americans and settlers about who would use the land. Many Native Americans were forced to leave their lands.

New Orleans was an important port city near the Gulf of Mexico and the Mississippi River. Many American farmers lived near the Mississippi River. They sent their farm **crops** in boats down the Mississippi River to New Orleans. American farmers sold their farm crops in New Orleans. Ships from New Orleans carried the crops to port cities on the Atlantic Ocean.

Spain owned Louisiana and the city of New Orleans. You read about Louisiana in Chapter 6. Spain allowed American ships to use the port of New Orleans. In 1800 Spain gave New Orleans and Louisiana back to France. New Orleans was a French city again. President Jefferson was worried. Perhaps France would not allow Americans to use the port.

President Jefferson knew that American farmers needed the port of New Orleans. He wanted the United States to own New Orleans. Thomas Jefferson decided to offer to buy the city.

Napoleon was the ruler of France. France was fighting many wars in Europe. Napoleon needed money for the

The United States bought New Orleans from France as part of the Louisiana Purchase in 1803.

UNDER MY WINGS EVERY THING PROSPERS

French wars. Jefferson asked Napoleon to sell New Orleans to the United States. Napoleon said he would sell New Orleans and all of Louisiana to the United States for 15 million dollars. In 1803 the United States paid 15 million dollars for Louisiana. Look at the map of the **Louisiana Purchase** on this page. The United States now owned New Orleans and much land to the west of the Mississippi River. The United States **doubled** in size in 1803.

President Jefferson wanted to learn about the land, plants, and animals of Louisiana. He wanted to know about the Native Americans who lived on this land. Thomas Jefferson asked two men to explore Louisiana. Meriwether Lewis and William Clark became explorers for Thomas Jefferson.

Lewis and Clark started their trip across Louisiana in 1804. About forty men went with them. During the trip Lewis and Clark kept journals. They wrote about the people, plants, animals, and mountains.

An African American traveled with Lewis and Clark. His name was York. York was Clark's slave. He was an excellent

Clark's Journal

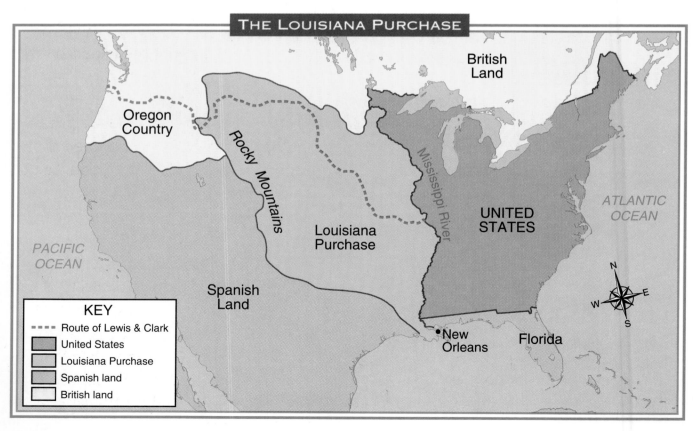

THE LOUISIANA PURCHASE

British Land

Oregon Country

Rocky Mountains

Mississippi River

Louisiana Purchase

UNITED STATES

ATLANTIC OCEAN

PACIFIC OCEAN

Spanish Land

New Orleans

Florida

KEY
- - - - Route of Lewis & Clark
United States
Louisiana Purchase
Spanish land
British land

Sacajawea and York helped Lewis and Clark get along with Native Americans.

hunter. York also knew how to get along well with Native Americans. He helped Lewis and Clark become friends with different groups of Native Americans. After the trip ended, Clark gave York his freedom.

During their trip Lewis and Clark reached the Rocky Mountains. Lewis and Clark wanted to cross these mountains and go to the Pacific Ocean. They did not know how to do this. They met a Native American woman who helped them. Her name was Sacajawea. Sacajawea had traveled to the Pacific Ocean before, and she knew the way.

Sacajawea and her husband led Lewis and Clark across the Rocky Mountains. She had a baby boy. She carried the baby on her back. She helped Lewis and Clark find food. Lewis and Clark met Sacajawea's family. Her family gave them horses. After many months, Lewis, Clark, and Sacajawea traveled through Oregon to the Pacific Ocean. The map on page 74 shows the way they traveled to the Pacific Ocean. In 1806 Lewis, Clark, and Sacajawea returned to their homes. They had explored 8,000 miles of land in the West.

Lewis and Clark told Thomas Jefferson about the beautiful land. They made new maps of the West. Thomas Jefferson helped the United States double in size. York, Sacajawea, Lewis, and Clark helped Americans learn about the land in the West.

Read and Remember

True or False   Write **T** on your paper for each sentence that is true. Write **F** for each sentence that is false.

1. Thomas Jefferson was the first President of the United States.

2. New Orleans was an important port for American farmers.

3. Few Americans moved west to the land between the first 13 states and the Mississippi River.

4. New Orleans always belonged to France.

5. Napoleon did not want to sell Louisiana to the United States.

6. America paid 15 thousand dollars for Louisiana and New Orleans.

7. The Rocky Mountains are in the West.

8. York helped Lewis and Clark get along with the Native Americans.

9. Sacajawea, a Native American woman, led Lewis and Clark across the Rocky Mountains.

Choose the Answer   Write the correct answers on your paper.

1. Which land east of the Mississippi River was not owned by the United States after the American Revolution?
   Florida   Oregon   Virginia

2. Which country gave Louisiana back to France in 1800?
   Great Britain   Germany   Spain

3. What city did the United States buy in the Louisiana Purchase?
   Boston   New Orleans   Jamestown

4. What did farmers sell in the port city of New Orleans?
   furs   horses   crops

5. Why did Napoleon need money?
   to buy crops   to pay for French wars   to travel west

Think and Apply

Categories   Read the words in each group. Decide how they are alike. Choose the best title in blue print for each group. Write the title on your paper.

Lewis and Clark   **Napoleon**   **York**
Thomas Jefferson   **Sacajawea**

1. helped write the Declaration of Independence
   third President of the United States
   bought Louisiana from France

2. ruler of France
   wanted to sell Louisiana
   needed money for wars in Europe

3. Native American
   helped Lewis and Clark
   knew how to cross the Rocky Mountains

4. African American slave
   excellent hunter
   friendly with Native Americans

5. explored Louisiana
   kept journals
   made maps of the West

Journal Writing

Look at the list below. If you had gone with Lewis and Clark, which things would you have taken? Choose the five things you think are most important. Then write a paragraph telling why you would have taken each one.

axe   rope   journal   matches   candles
soap   knife   blanket   animal trap   hat

Skill Builder

Reading a Chart This chart gives information about the groups or nations that have ruled Louisiana and New Orleans in America. The chart shows the year, the group or nation, and how it happened. Read the chart below.

Louisiana and New Orleans		
When?	**Which Group or Nation?**	**How Did It Happen?**
Before 1682	Native Americans	Native Americans lived in Louisiana and other areas of America before European settlers came.
1682	France	The French explorer Sieur de la Salle claimed Louisiana for France.
1762	Spain	Spain got Louisiana and New Orleans during the French and Indian War.
1800	France	Spain gave Louisiana and New Orleans back to France.
1803	United States	The United States paid 15 million dollars for the Louisiana Purchase.

Use the chart to answer each question below. Write a sentence on your paper to answer each question.

1. Which group lived in Louisiana before 1682?

2. Which French explorer claimed Louisiana for France in 1682?

3. Spain got Louisiana and New Orleans during which war?

4. When did Spain get Louisiana and New Orleans?

5. When did France get Louisiana and New Orleans back from Spain?

6. When did the United States buy the Louisiana Purchase?

7. How much did the United States pay for the Louisiana Purchase?

13 THE WAR OF 1812

Think About As You Read

1. Why did Americans fight a second war against Great Britain?
2. How did Tecumseh try to help Native Americans?
3. How did the War of 1812 help the United States?

NEW WORDS

captured
freedom of the seas
navy

PEOPLE & PLACES

James Madison
Tecumseh
Dolley Madison
Andrew Jackson

Americans fought the British in the War of 1812 for freedom of the seas.

America and Great Britain were fighting again in the year 1812. Why did Americans fight a second war against the British?

Napoleon, the ruler of France, started a war against Great Britain in 1803. The United States wanted to trade with both Great Britain and France. British ships **captured** many American ships that sailed to France. The French did the same thing to ships that sailed to Great Britain. This made the United States very angry. Americans wanted **freedom of the seas**. "Freedom of the seas" means that ships can sail wherever they want.

The British angered Americans in another way. British ships stopped American ships on the ocean. British captains went on the American ships. These captains said that some of the Americans were really British people. They forced these Americans to sail on the British ships. They had to work for the British **navy**. The British forced many Americans to work on British ships. Americans wanted to trade with France. They did not want their ships captured.

The French agreed to freedom of the seas. The British did not. In 1812 the United States began to fight Great Britain for freedom of the seas. This second war against Great Britain was called the War of 1812. James Madison was the President during the War of 1812. He thought the United States would win the war quickly. But the American army and navy were small. The war did not end quickly. Americans fought against the British for more than two years.

During the War of 1812, the United States tried to capture Canada. Canada belonged to Great Britain. American ships captured some of the lakes near Canada. The British army in Canada was strong. The United States could not capture Canada.

James Madison

Tecumseh was killed in a battle during the War of 1812.

A Native American leader named Tecumseh fought for the British during the War of 1812. Tecumseh lived on the land between the eastern states and the Mississippi River. He was angry because each year Americans took more land that belonged to Native Americans. The British promised Tecumseh that they would help the Native Americans get back their land. So Tecumseh and his people fought for Great Britain. He helped them win some battles in Canada. Tecumseh was killed in a battle during the War of 1812.

The American army had burned some buildings in Canada. The British army decided to burn the American capital city, Washington, D.C. President Madison was not in the city when the British army arrived. Dolley Madison, the First Lady, was at home in the White House when Washington, D.C., began to burn.

Dolley Madison stayed in the White House and packed important government papers in a trunk. A beautiful painting of George Washington was in the White House. Dolley asked someone to take it off the wall. The First Lady left Washington, D.C., with the painting and the government papers.

Dolley Madison

The British marched into Washington, D.C., and burned many government buildings.

Andrew Jackson and his soldiers won the Battle of New Orleans.

Important battles of the War of 1812

Very soon British soldiers came to the White House and burned everything inside. Dolley Madison had saved the painting of George Washington and the important government papers for the United States.

The British wanted to capture the port of New Orleans. Andrew Jackson was a general in the American army. He led 5,000 American soldiers in the Battle of New Orleans. These soldiers included people from Europe, Native Americans, slaves, and free African Americans. General Jackson won the Battle of New Orleans in January 1815. He did not know that two weeks before this battle Great Britain and the United States had signed a peace treaty.

Nothing really changed much because of the War of 1812. Both Great Britain and the United States had won and lost many battles. Neither country won new land in the war. But Great Britain never again fought against the United States. Great Britain and other countries now knew that the United States was strong enough to fight for what it wanted.

Read and Remember

Choose the Answer   Write the correct answers on your paper.

1. What country was Great Britain fighting in 1803?
   the United States   France   Spain

2. What did the United States fight Great Britain for in 1812?
   freedom of the seas   freedom of the press   freedom of religion

3. What did the British do to American ships that were sailing to France?
   captured them   burned them   traded with them

4. Who was President during the War of 1812?
   George Washington   Thomas Jefferson   James Madison

5. What did Tecumseh want?
   to be rich   to get back Native American lands   to go to France

6. Who fought for Great Britain during the War of 1812?
   Tecumseh   Andrew Jackson   James Madison

7. What city did the British burn?
   Boston   New Orleans   Washington, D.C.

8. Who saved the painting of George Washington when the British burned Washington, D.C.?
   Dolley Madison   Molly Pitcher   Martha Washington

9. Who won the Battle of New Orleans?
   James Armistead   Ben Franklin   Andrew Jackson

Journal Writing

It often took months for mail to get anywhere in the United States. Because of the slow mail, Andrew Jackson didn't know that the War of 1812 had ended. He and his soldiers fought the Battle of New Orleans. Imagine how he felt when he learned that the peace treaty had already been signed. Write four or five sentences in your journal that tell how Jackson must have felt.

Think and Apply

Drawing Conclusions   Read each pair of sentences. Then look in the box for the conclusion you can make. Write the letter of the conclusion on your paper.

1. British ships captured American ships.
   British captains forced American sailors to work on British ships.

2. Americans wanted Canada to be part of the United States.
   The British army in Canada was strong.

3. African Americans fought in the army.
   People from Europe fought for America.

4. Great Britain and the United States wanted peace.
   Both countries had won and lost many battles.

5. In December 1814 Great Britain and the United States signed a peace treaty.
   In January 1815 Jackson won the Battle of New Orleans.

   a. America could not capture Canada.

   b. Great Britain and the United States signed a peace treaty.

   c. Americans fought the British for freedom of the seas.

   d. Andrew Jackson did not know that the war was over.

   e. Many people helped the United States win the war.

Sequencing Events   Number your paper from 1 to 5. Write the sentences to show the correct order.

The British burned Washington, D.C.

The United States began to fight Great Britain for freedom of the seas.

The British forced many Americans to work on British ships.

Andrew Jackson won the Battle of New Orleans.

Great Britain and the United States signed a peace treaty.

Think About As You Read

1. How did Andrew Jackson become a hero?
2. How did Sequoya help the Cherokees?
3. Why did Osceola fight against the American army?

NEW WORDS

border
Trail of Tears
tariffs

PEOPLE & PLACES

North Carolina
South Carolina
Creeks
Cherokees
Alabama
Sequoya
Oklahoma
Osceola
Seminoles

Andrew Jackson became President in 1828. He was called the "People's President."

Andrew Jackson was the seventh President of our country. He was born near the **border** between North Carolina and South Carolina in 1767. Andrew's father died before Andrew was born. In 1780 Andrew fought for America during the American Revolution. He was 13 years old. Andrew's two brothers died during the American Revolution. His mother also died during the war. Andrew had to live by himself when he was only 14 years old. After the war Andrew studied law and became a lawyer.

Andrew Jackson wanted to help his country during the War of 1812. A large group of Native Americans called the Creeks lived in the South. The Creeks helped the British during the War of 1812. Andrew Jackson led his soldiers against the Creeks. Americans fought the Creeks for many months.

Another group of Native Americans was the Cherokees. They fought with Americans against the Creeks. In March 1814 the Creeks lost an important battle in Alabama. They surrendered to Andrew Jackson and stopped fighting the Americans. The Creeks had to give most of their land in Alabama and Georgia to the Americans. Jackson and his soldiers also fought Native Americans in Florida. Florida belonged to Spain. In 1819 Spain sold Florida to the United States for five million dollars.

Andrew Jackson became a hero. People liked him because he won the battle against the Creeks and the Battle of New Orleans. Andrew Jackson became President of the United States in 1828.

Sequoya was a Cherokee who helped Americans fight the Creeks. The Cherokees spoke their own language. They did not know how to write their language. The Cherokees, like other Native Americans, did not have an alphabet.

The United States fought many battles with Native Americans.

Sequoya decided to help his people learn to read and write. He carefully studied the Cherokee language. By 1821 Sequoya had made an alphabet for the Cherokee language. His alphabet had 86 letters.

Sequoya helped the Cherokees learn to read and write with his alphabet. The Cherokees started the first Native American newspaper. They printed books. The Cherokees started schools. Soon almost every Cherokee could read and write Sequoya's alphabet.

President Jackson believed that Native Americans should move to land west of the Mississippi River. People in the East wanted to have Native American lands. Jackson forced the Native Americans to move across the Mississippi River to Oklahoma in the West. Find Oklahoma on the map on page 276.

Starting in 1835, thousands of Native Americans were forced to move. The Cherokees were forced to move to Oklahoma. Sequoya also moved west. Americans in the East were happy because they had more land. The Native Americans were very unhappy. They did not want to leave their homes, farms,

Sequoya with his Cherokee alphabet

GWY JᏚᎪᎢᎣᎥᎯ.

CHEROKEE PHŒNIX.

VOL. I.   NEW ECHOTA, WEDNESDAY JUNE 4, 1828.   NO. 1

BY ELIAS BOUDINOTT
PRINTED WEEKLY BY
ISAAC H. HARRIS,
THE CHEROKEE NATION.

0 if paid in advance, $3 in six r $3 50 if paid at the end of the

cribers who can read only the language the price will be $2,00 , or $2,50 to be paid within the

ubscription will be considered as unless subscribers give notice to ry before the commencement of a

rson procuring six subscribers, hing responsible for the payment, ve a seventh gratis.

ements will be inserted at seven ts per square for the first inser thirty-seven and a half cents for

of said river opposite to Fort Strother, on said river; all north of said line is the Cherokee lands; all south of said line is the Creek lands.

ARTICLE 2. WE THE COMMISSION-ERS, do further agree that all the Creeks that are north of the said line above mentioned shall become sub-jects to the Cherokee nation.

ARTICLE 3. All Cherokees that are south of the said line shall become subjects of the Creek nation.

ARTICLE 4. If any chief or chiefs of the Cherokees, should fall within the Creek nation, such chief shall be continued as chief of said nation.

ARTICLE 5. If any chief or chiefs of the Creeks, should fall within the Cherokees, that is, north of said line,

William Hambly,   (Seal)
his
Big ⋈ Warrior,   (Seal)
mark.
WITNESSES.
Major Ridge,
Dan'l. Griffin.
A. M'COY, Clerk N. Com.
JOS. VANN, Cl'k. to the Commis-sioners.
Be it remembered, This day, that I have approved of the treaty of boun-dary, concluded on by the Cherokees, east of the Mississippi, and the Creek nation of Indians, on the eleventh day of December, 1821, and with the mod-ifications proposed by the committee and council, on the 28th day of March, in the current year. Given under my

mitting murder on the subjects of the other, is approved and adopted; but respecting thefts, it is hereby agreed that the following rule be substituted, and adopted; viz: Should the sub-jects of either nation go over the line and commit theft, and he, she or they be apprehended, they shall be tried and dealt with as the laws of that na-tion direct, but should the person or persons so offending, make their escape and return to his, her or their nation, then, the person or persons so aggriev-ed, shall make application to the pro-per authorities of that nation for re-dress, and justice shall be rendered as far as practicable, agreeably to proof and law, but in no case shall either na-tion be accountable.

The Cherokees started the first Native American newspaper. It was written in both English and Cherokee.

When Native Americans were forced to move west, their trip was called the Trail of Tears.

Osceola

and villages in the East. Their sad trip to the West was called the **Trail of Tears**. Many Native Americans became sick and died during the long, hard trip.

Osceola was a brave Native American who would not move west. Osceola was the leader of the Seminoles in Florida. He led his people in battles against the American army. After many battles Osceola was captured. He was sent to jail. He became very sick and died. After Osceola died most of the Seminoles moved west. Some Seminoles stayed in Florida.

While Jackson was President, some states did not want to obey laws made by Congress. People in South Carolina did not want to pay **tariffs**. A tariff is a tax on goods from other countries. Tariffs make goods from other countries cost more money. The southern states bought many goods from Europe. They did not want to pay tariffs for the goods. Andrew Jackson said that all states must obey the laws of the United States. He said that he would send warships to South Carolina. South Carolina obeyed the laws. The tariffs were paid.

Andrew Jackson was President for eight years. He was called the "People's President." He believed that all people, both rich and poor, should work for their country. Jackson died in 1845.

USING WHAT YOU'VE LEARNED

Read and Remember

Finish the Story Number your paper from 1 to 14. Use the words in the first box to finish the first paragraph. Use the words in the second box to finish the second paragraph. Write the words you choose on your paper.

Paragraph 1	Paragraph 2
Creeks	newspaper
Spain	west
five	Florida
Florida	army
Oklahoma	Osceola
Trail of Tears	alphabet
tariff	Mississippi

During the War of 1812, Jackson fought against the __(1)__ . After the war Jackson fought against Native Americans in __(2)__ . In 1819 __(3)__ sold Florida to the United States for __(4)__ million dollars. As President, Jackson said all states must obey the __(5)__ laws. President Jackson forced Native Americans to move west to __(6)__ . Their sad trip to the West was called the __(7)__ .

Two famous Native Americans lived during the time of Andrew Jackson. Sequoya was a Cherokee. He helped his people by making the first Native American __(8)__ . The Cherokees used this alphabet to print books and a __(9)__ . Sequoya was forced to move west across the __(10)__ River with the other Cherokees. The famous leader of Native Americans in Florida was __(11)__ . This brave leader would not move __(12)__ . He fought many battles against the United States __(13)__ . After Osceola died, most Native Americans in __(14)__ were forced to move west.

Think and Apply

Fact or Opinion   Read each sentence below. Write **F** on your paper for each sentence that tells a fact. Write **O** for each sentence that tells an opinion. You should find six opinions.

1. Andrew Jackson fought the Creeks.

2. Andrew Jackson was a kind man.

3. The United States paid too much money to Spain for Florida.

4. Sequoya was a Cherokee.

5. Sequoya spent too much time making the alphabet.

6. The Cherokees made the first Native American newspaper.

7. The Cherokee newspaper had many interesting stories.

8. The United States Congress can write tax laws.

9. States should not have to pay tariffs.

10. Andrew Jackson was a better President than Thomas Jefferson.

11. Jackson believed that Native Americans should move west of the Mississippi River.

12. The Cherokees moved to Oklahoma.

13. Osceola wanted to stay in Florida.

14. Many Native Americans died during the Trail of Tears.

 **Journal Writing**

Imagine that you and your family are Native Americans. You are forced to move west. Think about how you would feel. Write four or five sentences telling about your feelings. Be sure to tell why you feel the way you do.

Skill Builder

Understanding a Picture Pictures can help you learn about events. The picture below shows Native Americans moving west. Read each pair of sentences. Choose the sentence in each pair that explains the picture. Write the sentence on your paper.

1. Native Americans were happy to move west.

   Native Americans were sad about moving west.

2. Few Native Americans were forced to move west.

   Many Native Americans were forced to move west.

3. Native Americans took animals and other things with them.

   Native Americans did not take anything with them.

4. The trip was easy.

   The trip was very hard.

5. Native Americans of all ages moved west.

   Only Native American adults moved west.

Think About As You Read

1. What were some problems in American education in the 1830s and 1840s?
2. How did Mary Lyon help education for women?
3. How has education for women improved since Mary Lyon lived?

NEW WORDS

public schools
disabilities
education
subjects

PEOPLE & PLACES

Mary Lyon
Emma Willard
Connecticut
Mount Holyoke Seminary
Oberlin College
Ohio

Mary Lyon was an important leader in women's education.

How could the United States become a better country? Many people asked this question during the 1830s and 1840s. Some people believed they could help America by starting more schools for more people. At that time there were not enough **public schools** for the nation's children. There were few schools for children with **disabilities**. It was hard for women to get a good education. In this chapter you will learn how Mary Lyon worked for women's **education**.

Mary Lyon was born in 1797. She lived on a farm in Massachusetts. There were seven children in Mary Lyon's family. All the children in the family had to help with the farm work. Mary Lyon went to school near her house. She was a smart girl and an excellent student. She became a teacher when she was 17 years old.

At that time many people thought that women were not as smart as men. Most men thought women had enough education when they learned to read and write. Women did not study math and science in school. Women were not allowed to go to high school and college. Women could not become doctors or lawyers. Very few women were teachers. Men thought that women should cook, clean, and take care of their families.

One of the first people to work for better education for women was Emma Willard. At that time girls could not go to high school. Emma Willard started the first high school for girls.

Mary Lyon wanted women to have the same chance to learn that men had. She decided to start a college for women. She did not want women to pay a lot of money to be students at her school. She wanted all women to be able to study in her school. Lyon traveled through Massachusetts and Connecticut. Find these states on the

Emma Willard

Both boys and girls were taught to read and write. But girls were not allowed to go to high school or college.

map on page 276. She asked people to give her money to build a college for women. Lyon collected thousands of dollars in Massachusetts and Connecticut. In 1836 there was enough money to start building.

The college Mary Lyon built was in Massachusetts. She called it Mount Holyoke Seminary. Mount Holyoke opened in 1837. One hundred women began to study there. Some of the women were rich, but other women were poor. The women learned math, science, languages, and social studies. They studied the same **subjects** that men studied in college.

Mary Lyon was the principal of Mount Holyoke for 12 years. She helped 2,000 women study there. She died in 1849.

Many people learned about Mary Lyon's work. More colleges for women were started. Women were allowed to study in some colleges for men. Oberlin College in Ohio became the first college for men and women.

Today every girl can go to high school. Millions of American women go to college. Mount Holyoke Seminary is now called Mount Holyoke College. Hundreds of women study at Mount Holyoke each year. Mary Lyon was an important leader in women's education.

Mary Lyon opened the first college for women in 1837. It was called Mount Holyoke.

Read and Remember

Match Up   Finish each sentence in Group A with words from Group B. Write the letter of the correct answer on your paper.

Group A

1. In the 1830s there were not enough _____ .

2. There were few schools for children with _____ .

3. Women could not become doctors and _____ .

4. _____ were not allowed to study in colleges.

5. Lyon collected money for her school from people in Massachusetts and _____ .

6. Mary Lyon was _____ at Mount Holyoke Seminary.

Group B

a. Women

b. disabilities

c. the principal

d. lawyers

e. public schools

f. Connecticut

Think and Apply

Sequencing Events   Number your paper from 1 to 5. Write the sentences to show the correct order.

Mary Lyon collected money to start a college for women.

More colleges for women were started.

Mount Holyoke opened in 1837.

In 1836 there was enough money to build Mount Holyoke.

Mary Lyon became a teacher when she was 17 years old.

Riddle Puzzle

Choose a word in blue print to finish each sentence. Write the correct answers on your paper.

Oberlin	expensive	subjects	girls
education	languages	Connecticut	lawyers

1. Mary Lyon collected money in Massachusetts and _____ to start a college for women.

2. The first college for men and women was _____ College.

3. In the 1830s women could not become doctors or _____ .

4. Women could learn math, science, and _____ at Mount Holyoke Seminary.

5. Mary Lyon worked for better _____ for women.

6. Emma Willard started the first high school for _____ .

7. Mary Lyon did not want her college to be _____ .

8. Today women and men study the same _____ at school.

Now look at your answers. Circle the first letter of each answer you wrote on your paper.

The letters you circled should spell a word. The word answers the riddle.

RIDDLE: In what schools can both men and women study?

Write the answer to the riddle on your paper.

Journal Writing

What can women do today that they were not allowed to do in 1837? Write a paragraph in your journal that tells how women's lives have changed. Use at least three ideas from the chapter.

The historical map on this page shows how the United States had grown larger by 1819. Study the map. Then use the words in blue print to finish the story. Write the words you choose on your paper.

Canada   New Orleans   Oregon
Florida   Washington, D.C.   Louisiana

The United States bought __(1)__ and New Orleans from France in 1803. Lewis and Clark explored the area. They traveled through __(2)__ Country to the Pacific Ocean.

During the War of 1812, the United States tried to capture __(3)__ . The British burned the White House and other buildings in __(4)__ . Andrew Jackson won the Battle of __(5)__ at the end of the war. In 1819 the United States paid Spain five million dollars for __(6)__ .

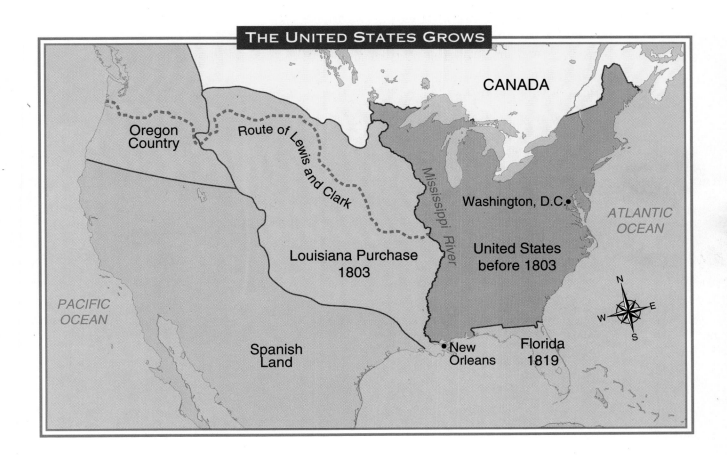

THE UNITED STATES GROWS

UNIT 4

THE NATION GROWS AND DIVIDES

Imagine living in the United States in 1860. Everyone believes there will be a war between the northern states and the southern states. You must choose a side to fight for in this war. You may have to fight against your own brothers during the war. You might fight against your best friend. Thousands will die during the Civil War.

The years between 1821 and 1865 were years of great change. The nation grew much larger. Many Americans moved west. The problem of slavery also grew. The northern states did not want slaves. The southern states said they needed slaves. In 1861 the terrible Civil War began.

What would you do if you lived between 1821 and 1865? Would you move west? Would you fight for the northern states or for the southern states? As you read Unit 4, think about what choices you would make.

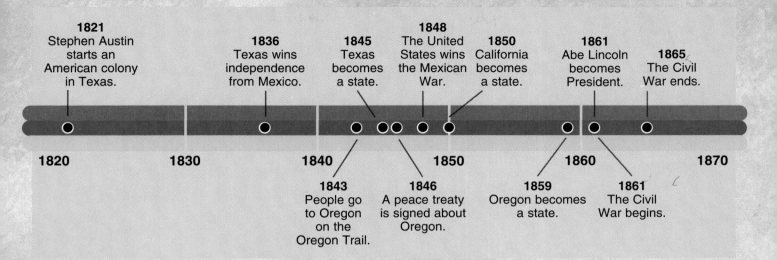

1821
Stephen Austin starts an American colony in Texas.

1836
Texas wins independence from Mexico.

1845
Texas becomes a state.

1848
The United States wins the Mexican War.

1850
California becomes a state.

1861
Abe Lincoln becomes President.

1865
The Civil War ends.

1820   1830   1840   1850   1860   1870

1843
People go to Oregon on the Oregon Trail.

1846
A peace treaty is signed about Oregon.

1859
Oregon becomes a state.

1861
The Civil War begins.

16 INDEPENDENCE FOR TEXAS

Many Americans and Mexicans moved to Texas in the 1800s.

Think About As You Read

1. Why did Americans want to settle in Texas?
2. What problems did Americans and Mexicans have in Texas?
3. How did Texas become free from Mexico?

NEW WORDS

fort
Texas Revolution
republic

PEOPLE & PLACES

Moses Austin
Stephen Austin
Mexicans
Texans
José Antonio Navarro
Lorenzo de Zavala
Santa Anna
Alamo
Suzanna Dickenson
Sam Houston
San Jacinto River
Republic of Texas

Mexico belonged to Spain for 300 years. In 1821 Mexico became an independent country. At that time, Texas was part of Mexico.

Moses Austin wanted to start a colony for Americans in Texas. He died before he could start the colony. His son, Stephen Austin, decided to continue his father's plan to settle Texas. Few Mexicans lived in Texas. So the leaders of Mexico wanted Americans to move to Texas.

Stephen Austin started an American colony in Texas in 1821. The settlers liked Texas. Land was cheaper there. African Americans, German Americans, and Asian Americans moved to Texas. Jewish Americans and new Americans from Europe also settled in Texas. More people from Mexico went to live in Texas. By 1830 there were many more Americans than Mexicans in Texas. People who live in Texas are called Texans.

Mexico's leaders were worried about Texas. They were afraid Americans might want Texas to become part of the United States. So in 1830 Mexico made a new law. The law said that Americans could no longer come to live in Texas. Americans in Texas did not like this law.

Texans did not like other Mexican laws. They did not like the tax laws. They did not like the law that said they could not bring slaves into Texas. Texans did not like the law that said they must speak Spanish. Another Mexican law said settlers must be Catholics. The Texans wanted to help write laws for Texas. Mexico would not let the settlers make laws for Texas.

Mexico was also angry with the new settlers. Mexico was angry because very few settlers had become Mexicans. The settlers brought slaves to Texas. Few Texans spoke Spanish. Many Texans were not Catholic. Mexican soldiers went to Texas to force the Texans to obey Mexican laws. This made

Stephen Austin

Austin sold land to many families who wanted to move to Texas.

José Antonio Navarro

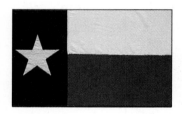

Lorenzo de Zavala

Texas flag

Santa Anna and his soldiers attacked the Texans at the Alamo.

the Texans angry and unhappy. They did not want Mexican soldiers in Texas.

The Texans decided that Texas should be independent from Mexico. In March 1836 the leaders of Texas wrote a declaration of independence. This declaration said that Texas was no longer part of Mexico.

American Texans were not the only people who wanted Texas to be independent. Some Mexican Texans also wanted an independent Texas. José Antonio Navarro was a Mexican who was born in Texas. He was a friend of Stephen Austin. He signed the Texas Declaration of Independence. He later helped write a new constitution for Texas. Lorenzo de Zavala was born in Mexico. He came to live in Texas with his family. De Zavala also signed the Texas Declaration of Independence. He told all Texans to fight for freedom.

Santa Anna, the Mexican president, did not want the Texans to be independent. He led his army against the Texans. There were about 180 Texan soldiers in a mission called the Alamo. The Texans used the Alamo as a **fort**. Santa Anna and 3,000 Mexican soldiers attacked the Alamo.

Santa Anna surrendered to Sam Houston after the battle at the San Jacinto River.

Santa Anna

Suzanna Dickenson

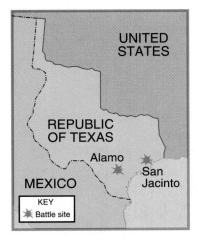

Republic of Texas

The Texans were brave and would not surrender. They fought for many days. Santa Anna won the Battle of the Alamo. Every Texan soldier was killed.

Some of the Texan soldiers had brought their wives and children to the Alamo. One of these wives was Suzanna Dickenson. After the battle, Santa Anna sent her to tell other Texans not to fight against Mexico.

Sam Houston became the commander in chief of the Texas army. He learned about the Battle of the Alamo from Dickenson. Sam told his soldiers to remember the brave people who died at the Alamo.

On April 21, 1836, the Texans fought Santa Anna again. They fought at the San Jacinto River. "Remember the Alamo!" Sam Houston's soldiers shouted as they fought the Mexicans. The battle lasted only 18 minutes. The Texans won. Santa Anna surrendered to Sam Houston. Texas was now free. The Texans called their war against Mexico the **Texas Revolution**.

Texas was no longer part of Mexico, and Texas was not part of the United States. Texas became a **republic**. A republic is an independent country. Sam Houston became the first president of the Republic of Texas.

Texans wanted Texas to become part of the United States. But they would have to wait almost ten more years before Texas would become a state.

Read and Remember

Finish Up Choose a word in blue print to finish each sentence. Write the word or words you choose on your paper.

republic   Sam Houston   Santa Anna   Texas Revolution
Alamo   San Jacinto   de Zavala   Stephen Austin

1. _____ started an American colony in Texas.

2. José Antonio Navarro and Lorenzo _____ were Mexican Texans who signed the Texas Declaration of Independence.

3. The commander in chief of the army and the first president of Texas was _____ .

4. The leader of the Mexican army was President _____ .

5. The war for Texan independence was called the _____ .

6. About 180 Texan soldiers died at the _____ .

7. Santa Anna surrendered at the _____ River.

8. After the war, Texas was an independent _____ .

True or False Write **T** on your paper for each sentence that is true. Write **F** for each sentence that is false.

1. In 1821 Mexico became an independent country.

2. José Antonio Navarro started an American colony in Texas.

3. By 1830 there were more Mexicans than Americans in Texas.

4. Texans were happy with the Mexican laws.

5. Mexico would not let the Texan settlers write laws.

6. Texans wrote a declaration of independence to say that Texas was no longer a part of Mexico.

7. Texans won the Battle of the Alamo.

8. Suzanna Dickenson told people about the Battle of the Alamo.

9. Texas became a republic after the Texas Revolution.

Think and Apply ★

Understanding Different Points of View   The Mexicans and the Americans had different points of view about Texas. Read each sentence below. Write **Texan** for each sentence that shows the Texan point of view. Write **Mexican** for each sentence that shows the Mexican point of view.

1. People in Texas should obey Mexican laws.

2. People in Texas should write their own laws.

3. Everyone in Texas must be Catholic.

4. Americans in Texas do not have to be Catholic.

5. Americans can bring slaves to Texas.

6. Americans cannot have slaves in Texas.

7. Americans should speak Spanish in Texas.

8. Americans can speak English in Texas.

9. Texas should be independent.

10. Texas must belong to Mexico.

★ Journal Writing

Read about the Texas Revolution again. Why was "Remember the Alamo!" a good thing to shout at the battle near the San Jacinto River? Write a paragraph that tells why. Include at least two reasons.

CHAPTER 17 THE UNITED STATES GROWS LARGER

Think About As You Read

1. What was Manifest Destiny?
2. How did the Mexican War help the United States grow larger?
3. How did Mexican Americans help the United States?

NEW WORDS

Manifest Destiny
citizens
Mexican Cession
Gadsden Purchase
property

PEOPLE & PLACES

James Polk
Rio Grande
Mexico City
Nevada
Utah
Arizona
Mexican Americans

When the flag of the Republic of Texas was lowered, Texas became the twenty-eighth state in the United States.

In Chapter 16 you read that Texans won their war against Mexico and started a republic. Santa Anna had surrendered to the Texans. But Mexican leaders did not accept his surrender. The Mexicans said that Texas was still part of Mexico. Texans wanted to become part of the United States. The Mexicans said there would be a war if Texas became part of the United States.

Many Americans wanted Texas to become a state. They believed in an idea called **Manifest Destiny**. Manifest Destiny meant the United States should rule all the land between the Atlantic Ocean and the Pacific Ocean. This idea also meant that the United States should become a larger and stronger country.

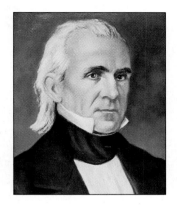

James Polk

Texas land claimed
by Mexico

In 1845 the United States Congress voted for Texas to become the twenty-eighth state. During that same year, James Polk became President. The new President believed in Manifest Destiny. He wanted the United States to own all the land to the Pacific Ocean.

In 1846 a war started between the United States and Mexico. The two countries did not agree on the border for Texas. The United States said a river called the Rio Grande was the southern border for Texas. Mexico said Texas should be smaller. The Mexicans said that much of the land northeast of the Rio Grande belonged to Mexico. Find the Rio Grande on the map on this page.

The United States and Mexico sent soldiers to the Rio Grande. The soldiers began to fight. This war was called the Mexican War. During the war American soldiers captured California and New Mexico. The Mexican soldiers were brave. They did not stop fighting. Americans and Mexicans continued to fight. American soldiers went into Mexico. They captured Mexico City, the capital of Mexico. In 1848 the Mexicans surrendered. The war was over.

American soldiers stand in the center of Mexico City after capturing this capital city of Mexico.

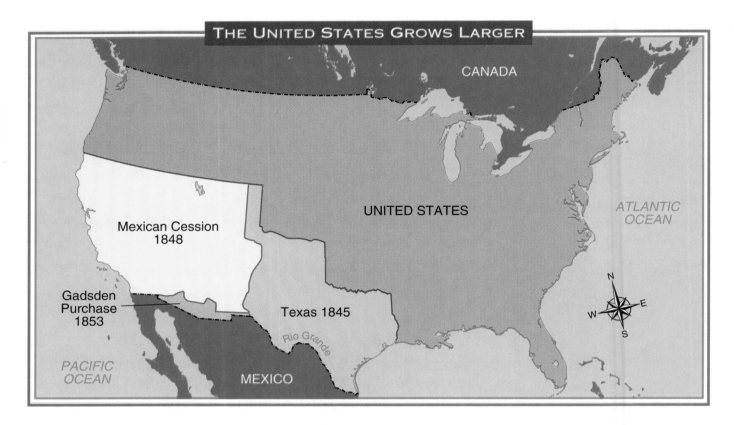

CANADA

UNITED STATES

ATLANTIC
OCEAN

Mexican Cession
1848

Gadsden
Purchase
1853

Texas 1845

Rio Grande

PACIFIC
OCEAN

MEXICO

The leaders of the United States and Mexico signed a peace treaty in 1848. The peace treaty said there was peace between the United States and Mexico. The treaty said that Texas belonged to the United States. Both countries agreed that the Rio Grande was the border between Texas and Mexico. The treaty also said that Mexicans in the Southwest could become American **citizens**. The United States gave Mexico 15 million dollars for land taken during the war.

The land that the United States got in 1848 was called the **Mexican Cession**. Find the Mexican Cession on the map above. California, Nevada, Utah, Arizona, and New Mexico were five new states made from the Mexican Cession. The United States now owned land from the Atlantic Ocean to the Pacific Ocean.

Americans wanted a railroad across the southern part of the United States. The land south of the Mexican Cession was a good place for a railroad. In 1853 the United States gave Mexico 10 million dollars for the land in the **Gadsden Purchase**. Find the Gadsden Purchase on the map above. Years later, Americans built a railroad across the Gadsden Purchase.

The Mexicans in the Southwest became American citizens after the Mexican War. They were called Mexican Americans.

Mexican Americans helped their new country. They taught Americans how to grow food on land where there was little rain. Mexican Americans helped build railroads for the United States. They helped other Americans look for gold and silver in the Southwest.

Mexican Americans helped the United States change a law that was unfair to women. Before the Mexican War, a married American woman could not own **property**. Her husband owned everything. Mexican law was fairer to women. Mexican women owned property together with their husbands. After the Mexican War, Americans changed their law so that women could own property with their husbands.

The land between the Atlantic Ocean and the Pacific Ocean belonged to the United States. The United States had become a strong country with a lot of new land and many new people.

Mexican Americans in the Southwest taught Americans many things, including how to be cowboys.

Read and Remember

Choose the Answer   Write the correct answers on your paper.

1. Which President believed in Manifest Destiny?
   James Madison   Andrew Jackson   James Polk

2. When did Texas become a state?
   1776   1845   1900

3. What city did the American soldiers capture?
   Rio Grande   Alamo   Mexico City

4. How much did the United States pay for the Mexican Cession?
   5 million dollars   15 million dollars   30 million dollars

5. Which three states were among the five made from the Mexican Cession?
   California, New Mexico, Arizona   New York, New Jersey, Florida
   Texas, Oregon, Oklahoma

6. Which river became the border for Texas?
   Mississippi River   St. Lawrence River   Rio Grande

7. What land did the United States buy in 1853?
   Louisiana Purchase   Gadsden Purchase   Florida

8. Why did the United States want the Gadsden Purchase?
   for oil   for a railroad   for a park

Skill Builder

Reviewing Map Directions   Look back at the map on page 108. Write the word that finishes each sentence on your paper.

1. The Gadsden Purchase is _____ of Mexico.
   east   south   north

2. The Pacific Ocean is _____ of the Mexican Cession.
   southeast   east   west

3. The Rio Grande is _____ of the Gadsden Purchase.
   south   southwest   east

4. The Mexican Cession is _____ of the Gadsden Purchase.

   south   southeast   north

5. Mexico is _____ of the United States.

   south   north   west

6. Texas is _____ of the Gadsden Purchase.

   east   southwest   west

7. Canada is _____ of Mexico.

   west   north   east

★ Think and Apply

Cause and Effect Write sentences on your paper by matching each cause on the left with an effect on the right.

Cause

1. In 1845 many Americans believed their country should be larger, so _____

2. Texas became a state, so _____

3. The United States captured Mexico City, so _____

4. In 1848 the United States got land in the Mexican Cession, so _____

5. Americans wanted to build a railroad across the southern part of the United States, so _____

Effect

a. they paid Mexico 10 million dollars for land in the Gadsden Purchase.

b. Mexico said there would be a war with the United States.

c. the country's borders went from the Atlantic Ocean to the Pacific Ocean.

d. the United States Congress voted for Texas to become the twenty-eighth state.

e. Mexico surrendered.

Journal Writing ★

Mexican Americans became citizens of the United States after the Mexican War. Write a paragraph in your journal that tells how Mexican Americans have helped the United States.

Riddle Puzzle

Choose a word in blue print to finish each sentence. Write the correct answers on your paper.

Texas	year	English	Purchase
republic	peace	Ocean	Rio Grande

1. The Gadsden _____ was in the Southwest of the United States.

2. All the land to the north of the _____ became part of Texas.

3. After 1853 the United States owned land from the Atlantic Ocean to the Pacific _____ .

4. The United States signed a _____ treaty with Mexico in 1848.

5. Americans wanted to speak _____ in Texas.

6. After the Texas Revolution, Texas became a _____ .

7. Mexicans said there would be a war if _____ became a part of the United States.

8. Texas became a state and James Polk became President in the same _____ .

Now look at your answers. Circle the first letter of each answer you wrote on your paper.

The letters you circled should spell a word. The word answers the riddle.

RIDDLE: What did American women in the 1800s want to own that Mexican women could own?

Write the answer to the riddle on your paper.

18 ON TO OREGON AND CALIFORNIA

Think About As You Read

1. Why did people want to go to Oregon?
2. How did people travel to Oregon in the 1840s?
3. What happened after gold was found in California?

NEW WORDS

covered wagons
oxen
wagon train
Oregon Trail
coast
gold rush
pass

PEOPLE & PLACES

Independence, Missouri
Washington
Idaho
James Marshall
China
James Beckwourth
Beckwourth Pass

Families that traveled to Oregon had to cross the Rocky Mountains.

"On to Oregon! Let's move to Oregon!" said thousands of Americans in the 1840s. Oregon had lots of trees for building new houses. Oregon had good land for farming. Soon thousands of Americans moved west to build new homes and farms in the Oregon country.

The trip to Oregon was long and slow. There were no roads across the United States to Oregon. Families traveled to Oregon in **covered wagons**. Horses and **oxen** pulled the covered wagons. In 1843 many families in 120 covered wagons met in Independence, Missouri. These 120 covered wagons made a **wagon train**. The covered wagons traveled together across the Great Plains and the Rocky Mountains to Oregon.

113

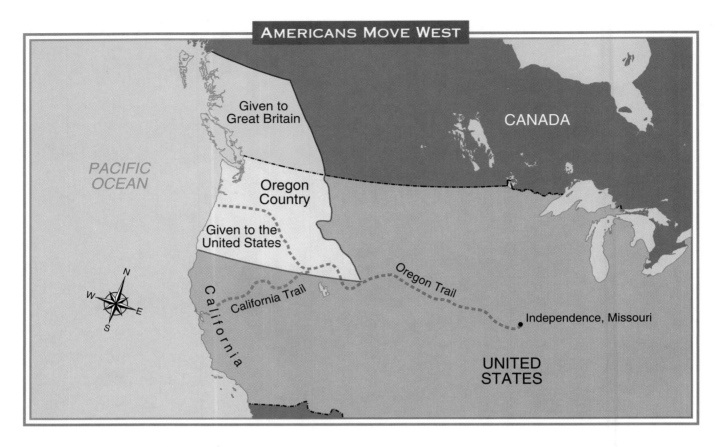

Given to
Great Britain

CANADA

PACIFIC
OCEAN

Oregon
Country

Given to the
United States

California

California Trail

Oregon Trail

Independence, Missouri

UNITED
STATES

N
W E
S

What was it like to travel on the wagon train? All families woke up very early every day. Then people traveled as many hours as they could. At night they slept on the floors of their covered wagons. When it rained, wagon wheels got stuck in mud. Sometimes wagons turned over. Then people inside the wagons were hurt or killed. It was hard to find food on the way to Oregon. Many families were hungry. The long trip to Oregon took about six months.

At last the families reached the Oregon country. They had traveled 2,000 miles. The families had followed a trail to Oregon. It became known as the **Oregon Trail**. Find the Oregon Trail on the map above. Thousands of people came to Oregon on the Oregon Trail. These people were some of the first Americans to settle along the Pacific **coast**.

The Oregon country was much bigger than our state of Oregon today. The Oregon country included part of Canada. Great Britain and the United States had shared the Oregon country for many years. The two nations could not decide on a way to divide Oregon. President Polk wanted

Oregon to be part of the United States. Many people thought Great Britain and the United States would fight for Oregon. This time the two nations did not fight. President Polk signed a peace treaty with Great Britain about Oregon in 1846.

The treaty said that northern Oregon was part of Canada. Canada and northern Oregon belonged to Great Britain. Southern Oregon became part of the United States. Later the states of Oregon, Washington, and Idaho were made from the southern part of the Oregon country.

The United States government gave free farm land to families that moved to the state of Oregon. Many Americans came to Oregon on the Oregon Trail for free land. In 1859 the United States Congress voted for Oregon to become a state.

While thousands of Americans were moving to the state of Oregon, other Americans were rushing to California. One day in 1848, a man named James Marshall found pieces of gold in a river in California. Soon everyone knew that James Marshall had found gold.

People from all over the United States began moving to California. "Gold! Gold! Gold! There's gold in California," said Americans as they traveled to California. They wanted

Many people moved to California to look for gold.

James Beckwourth found a mountain pass that made it easier for Americans to travel west.

to find gold and become rich. We say that California had a **gold rush** in 1848 and 1849 because thousands of people went to find gold.

The gold rush brought many kinds of people to California. Many people came from Europe to look for gold in California. People came from China to find gold. Free African Americans also moved to California.

James Beckwourth made it easier for many people to travel west to California. Beckwourth was an African American. He moved west and lived with Native Americans. Tall mountains in the West made it hard to go to California. Beckwourth looked and looked for an easier way to go across the mountains. At last Beckwourth found a **pass** through the mountains. Many people used this pass to reach California. Today that pass through the mountains is called the Beckwourth Pass.

Some people were lucky in California. They found gold and became rich. Most people did not find gold. Many people stayed in California. They built farms and factories. They started new cities. They built stores and houses. By 1850, 90,000 people were living in California. The United States Congress voted for California to become a state in 1850.

The California gold rush brought thousands of settlers to California. The Oregon Trail brought thousands of Americans to the Northwest. Every year more Americans moved west to California and Oregon.

Read and Remember ⭐

Finish the Sentence   Write on your paper the date, word, or words that finish each sentence.

1. Thousands of Americans went to the Oregon country in the _____ .
   1820s   1830s   1840s

2. In 1846 the northern part of the Oregon country became part of _____ .
   the United States   Canada   Washington

3. Families that moved to Oregon were given free _____ .
   wagons   houses   farm land

4. In 1848 and 1849, Americans rushed to California to find _____ .
   silver   gold   trees

5. California became a state in _____ .
   1850   1859   1860

6. The Oregon Trail began in _____ .
   Philadelphia   New Orleans   Independence

⭐ Think and Apply

Categories   Read the words in each group. Decide how they are alike. Find the best title in blue print for each group. Write the title for each group on your paper.

James Beckwourth   California   Oregon Trail   Gold Rush

1. 1848 and 1849
   people searched for gold
   thousands came to California

2. African American
   lived in the West
   found a pass

3. horses and oxen
   covered wagons
   went to Oregon

4. gold rush
   built farms
   started cities

Skill Builder

Reading a Historical Map   The map below shows how the United States became a large country. Study each area and when it became part of the United States.

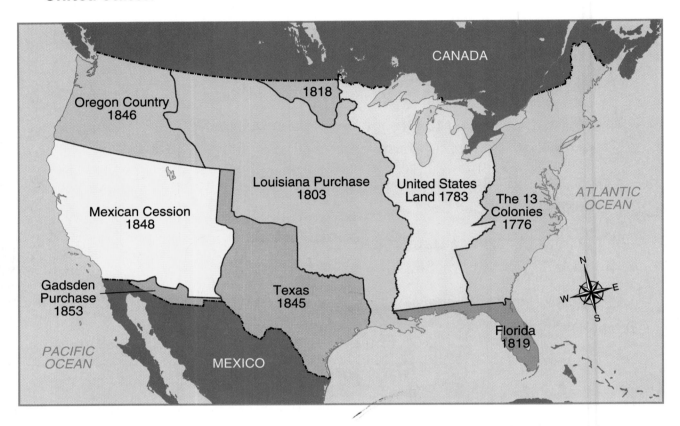

Use the map to answer each question. Write the correct answers on your paper.

1. What land made up the United States in 1776?
   Texas   The 13 Colonies   Louisiana

2. What southeast land belonged to Spain until 1819?
   Oregon Country   Texas   Florida

3. What land did the United States buy in 1803?
   Mexican Cession   Louisiana Purchase   Texas

4. Which northwest land became part of the United States in 1846?
   Oregon Country   Florida   Louisiana Purchase

5. Which land did the United States buy in 1853?
   Gadsden Purchase   Oregon Country   Texas

CHAPTER 19

THE SOUTHERN STATES LEAVE

Think About As You Read

1. Why were there more slaves in the South than in the North?
2. What were two reasons why the South became angry with the North?
3. What did the South do after Abraham Lincoln became President?

NEW WORDS

quarreling
plantations
sugar cane
escape
products
Confederate States of America

PEOPLE & PLACES

North
South
Harriet Tubman
Abraham Lincoln
Confederate States

On plantations in the South, slaves did most of the farm work.

The United States had become a large country after the Mexican War. But things were not going well in the United States. The northern states were **quarreling** with the southern states. The northern states were called the North, and the southern states were called the South. Why did the North and South quarrel?

In Chapter 5 you learned how the English started colonies in America. Do you remember that in 1619 the English brought African slaves to America? A slave is a person who belongs to another person. A slave is not free.

At first, there were slaves both in the North and in the South. But farms were small in the North. The North had many factories. Most people there did not need slaves to work on their farms and in factories. There were fewer slaves in the North.

119

In the South some people owned very large farms called **plantations**. The owners grew cotton, **sugar cane**, and tobacco on their plantations. Plantation owners needed many workers. They bought slaves to do the work. The plantation owners in the South thought they could not grow crops without slaves.

After the Mexican War, more Americans moved to the West. People from the South started new plantations in the West. They wanted to bring their slaves. The northern states did not want slavery in the West.

The North and South began to quarrel. In the North many people said that all people should be free. They said that it was not right for one person to own another person. In the South people said that the Constitution allowed slavery. People in the South said that people in the North should not tell them what to do. The people in the North wanted to make new laws against slavery in the West. This made the South very angry.

Plantation owners in the South bought and sold slaves.

Many slaves escaped to freedom in the North.

Harriet Tubman

The South was worried because many Americans were trying to end slavery. Some people wrote books and newspapers that told why slavery was wrong. Some people gave speeches against slavery. Other people helped slaves run away from their owners. Harriet Tubman was one of the people who helped slaves become free. Harriet Tubman had been a slave herself. She had run away to the North. In the North she became a free woman. She went back to the South and helped slaves **escape** to Canada. In Canada the slaves were free. Harriet Tubman helped hundreds of slaves get their freedom.

Southerners were also angry about a tariff law. You read about tariffs in Chapter 14. There were many factories in the North. People made shoes, clothes, and other things in factories. There were very few factories in the South. People in the South had to buy many things from the North and from Europe. Northerners wanted Southerners to pay extra money, or a tariff, for everything they bought from Europe. The tariff made things from Europe more expensive. Factories in the North also made their **products** more expensive. The South did not like paying more for things made in both Europe and the North.

Abraham Lincoln came from a poor family.

Abraham Lincoln

In 1861 a man named Abraham Lincoln became the President of the United States. What kind of man was Abe Lincoln? He came from a poor family. Abe lived very far from school when he was young. So he only went to school for about one year. He learned as much as he could by reading books. Abe grew up to be very tall, thin, and strong. He became a lawyer. Many people liked him because he was honest and smart.

Abe Lincoln believed that slavery was wrong. He said that slavery should not be allowed in the West. The North liked what Abe said, but the South did not. The South was afraid that Abe would work to end slavery everywhere.

Eleven southern states decided that they no longer wanted to be part of the United States. In 1861 they started a new country. They called their country the **Confederate States of America**.

Abe Lincoln was very unhappy. He said that the United States must be one country, not two. Would the United States and the Confederate States become one country again? Would it take a war to get them together? Chapter 20 will give you the answers.

Read and Remember

True or False   Write **T** on your paper for each sentence that is true. Write **F** for each sentence that is false.

1. The North had more factories than the South.

2. People grew cotton, sugar cane, and tobacco in the South.

3. Slaves worked on large plantations in the North.

4. Harriet Tubman only helped three slaves escape.

5. The North said that slavery should be allowed in the West.

6. Abe Lincoln became President in 1861.

7. Thirteen northern states left the United States and became the Confederate States of America.

Think and Apply

Fact or Opinion   Read each sentence below. Write **F** on your paper for each sentence that tells a fact. Write **O** for each sentence that tells an opinion. You should find three opinions.

1. The Constitution allowed slavery.

2. The North had more factories than the South.

3. It is wrong to own slaves.

4. The South had to pay a tariff on products from Europe.

5. The tariff laws were not fair.

6. Abe Lincoln did not want slavery in the West.

7. People in the South were the best farmers.

8. Harriet Tubman helped many slaves escape to Canada.

Skill Builder

Reading a Bar Graph   Graphs are drawings that help you compare facts. The graph on this page is a **bar graph**. It shows facts using bars of different lengths. The bar graph below shows the number of people who lived in the United States in 1860.

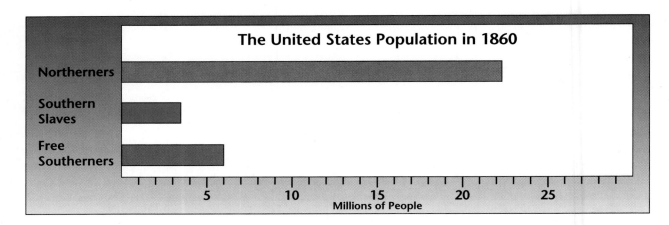

The United States Population in 1860

Use the bar graph to answer each question. Write the correct answers on your paper.

1. How many people lived in the North?
   $3\frac{1}{2}$ million   6 million   22 million

2. How many slaves lived in the South?
   $3\frac{1}{2}$ million   6 million   22 million

3. How many people were free Southerners?
   $3\frac{1}{2}$ million   6 million   22 million

4. Which group had the smallest population?
   Northerners   Free Southerners   Southern Slaves

5. Which group had the largest population?
   Northerners   Free Southerners   Southern Slaves

Journal Writing

Harriet Tubman helped slaves escape. Why do you think she helped them? Write a paragraph in your journal.

CHAPTER 20 THE CIVIL WAR

Think About As You Read

1. What did the South fight for during the Civil War?
2. What did the North fight for during the Civil War?
3. Why did Robert E. Lee surrender?

NEW WORDS

Union
Confederates
Civil War
goal
destroyed
rebuild

PEOPLE & PLACES

Fort Sumter
Robert E. Lee
Clara Barton
Ulysses S. Grant
Richmond

Many soldiers from both the North and the South were killed in the Civil War.

The South had started a new country called the Confederate States of America. President Lincoln did not want the North to fight against the South. He wanted the South to become part of the United States again. The **Union** is another name for the United States. The South did not want a war. But the South did not want to be part of the Union.

The United States Army owned a fort called Fort Sumter in South Carolina. South Carolina was one of the Confederate States. People who lived in the Confederate States were called **Confederates**. They said that the United States must give Fort Sumter to the Confederate States of America. But Union soldiers would not surrender Fort Sumter.

Confederate battle flag

Robert E. Lee

In 1861 Confederate soldiers began to shoot at Fort Sumter. A war between the North and South had begun. This war was called the **Civil War**. The Civil War lasted four years. People in the South fought to have their own country, the Confederate States of America. The North fought so that all states would remain in the Union.

The Confederates thought they would win. They had many good army generals and brave soldiers. But the North was stronger than the South. The North had more people and more soldiers. The North had more money to pay for a war. The North had more railroads. Union soldiers traveled on these railroads to many places. The North had more factories, too. Northern factories made guns for the war.

Robert E. Lee was the leader of the Confederate army. Robert E. Lee loved the United States. He did not like slavery. He also loved his own state of Virginia. President Lincoln wanted Robert E. Lee to lead the Union army. But Robert E. Lee would not fight against his family and friends in Virginia. Instead, he became the leader of the Confederate army. Lee was

UNION STATES AND CONFEDERATE STATES

CANADA

Maine

New Hampshire
Vermont
Massachusetts
Rhode Island
Connecticut

Oregon

Minnesota

Michigan

New York

Wisconsin

Pennsylvania   New Jersey

United States
Territories

Iowa

Ohio

Delaware

Illinois   Indiana   West
Virginia

Maryland

California

Kansas   Missouri

Virginia

Kentucky

North
Carolina

ATLANTIC
OCEAN

Tenessee

South
Carolina

Arkansas

Mississippi   Georgia

PACIFIC
OCEAN

Texas

Alabama

Louisiana

Florida

N
W   E
S

MAP KEY

Union states

Confederate states

MEXICO

Many African Americans joined the Union army and fought in the Civil War.

Clara Barton

Major Civil War battles

an excellent leader. He led the Confederate army for four long years.

President Lincoln had a **goal**. His goal was for the North and South to be one nation. He decided to help the Union win by working to end slavery. In 1863 he gave orders that said all slaves in the Confederate States were free. Many African American slaves left the South. Thousands of African Americans joined the Union army. They fought in many important battles of the Civil War.

Women in the North and South helped during the war. They took care of the farms and factories. Some women became spies. Many women became nurses. Clara Barton became one of the most famous Union nurses. She traveled to places where there were terrible battles. Clara Barton cared for soldiers who were hurt.

At the start of the Civil War, the South won many battles. After two years the South lost more and more battles. Most of the Civil War battles were fought in the South. The fighting **destroyed** houses, cities, and plantations in the South.

Ulysses S. Grant was the leader of the Union army. He won many battles. In 1865 the Union soldiers captured

President Abraham Lincoln was shot soon after the end of the Civil War.

Ulysses S. Grant

Richmond, Virginia. Richmond was the capital of the Confederate States. Then Robert E. Lee knew that the Confederates could not win the war. There was very little food to eat in the South. Lee's army was hungry and weak. He did not want more people to die in the war. Lee surrendered to Grant in April 1865. The war was over. Plans were made to return the Confederate States to the Union. Robert E. Lee returned to Virginia. He told the South to help the United States become a strong country.

President Lincoln was glad that the United States was one nation again. He was also sad. Almost 600,000 soldiers in the North and South had been killed. Thousands of other soldiers were badly hurt.

President Lincoln had new goals when the war ended. He wanted Americans to work together to **rebuild** the South. He wanted Americans in the North and South to like each other again.

President Lincoln never reached these goals. He was shot in the head five days after the Civil War ended. Abraham Lincoln died the next day. Americans in the North and South were sad because a great leader was dead.

People in the North and the South were united once again. It would take many more years to end the anger between the North and the South. But together they would continue to make the United States a great nation.

Read and Remember

Who Am I?   Read each sentence. Then look in the box for the person who might have said it. Write on your paper the name of the person you choose.

Clara Barton   Ulysses S. Grant   Robert E. Lee   Abe Lincoln

1. "I was President of the United States. I wanted the North and South to be one nation."

2. "I was the leader of the Confederate army. I surrendered to the Union."

3. "As a Union nurse, I cared for soldiers who were hurt during the Civil War."

4. "I led the Union army to win the Civil War."

Write the Answer   Write a sentence to answer each question.

1. What did the North fight for in the Civil War?

2. What did the South fight for in the Civil War?

3. Who led the Confederate army?

4. Who led the Union army?

5. How did women help during the Civil War?

6. What were Abraham Lincoln's goals after the Civil War?

★ Think and Apply

Sequencing Events   Number your paper from 1 to 4. Write the sentences to show the correct order.

In 1863 President Lincoln gave orders that slaves in the Confederate States were free.

In 1861 Confederate soldiers attacked Fort Sumter.

President Lincoln was killed after the war ended.

Robert E. Lee surrendered to Ulysses S. Grant.

Journal Writing

Write a paragraph about the Civil War in your journal. Tell how it began or how it ended. Write at least five sentences.

Skill Builder

Reading a Table A **table** lists a group of facts. You can compare facts by reading tables. Look at the table below. To learn facts about the North and the South, read the numbers listed beneath each heading. Read the table from left to right to find out what the numbers in the table stand for. Use the table to answer each question. Write a sentence to answer each question.

THE NORTH AND SOUTH BEFORE THE CIVIL WAR		
	North	South
Money	$330,000,000	$47,000,000
Number of factories and shops	111,000	21,000
Miles of railroad track	22,000	9,000

1. How much money did the North have?

2. How many factories and shops did the South have?

3. How many miles of railroad track did the North have?

4. Did the North or the South have less money?

5. Did the North or the South have more factories and shops?

6. Did the North or the South have more miles of railroad track?

Study the time line on this page. Then use the words in blue print to finish the story. Write the words you choose on your paper.

slaves	Abe Lincoln	state
Texas	California	Lee
Cession	Confederate	Civil War

In 1836 ___(1)___ won a war for independence from Mexico. In 1845 Texas became a ___(2)___ . The United States fought a war with Mexico. From that war the United States got the Mexican ___(3)___ . After the gold rush, ___(4)___ became a state in 1850.

As the nation grew larger, the North and the South quarreled about slavery. In 1861 southern states started a new nation called the ___(5)___ States of America. Later that year, the ___(6)___ began. In 1863 President Lincoln said that ___(7)___ in the Confederate States were free. In 1865 General ___(8)___ surrendered to General Grant. The North had won. A few days later, ___(9)___ was killed.

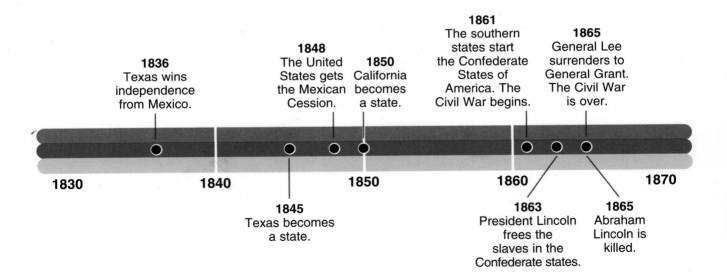

1836
Texas wins independence from Mexico.

1848
The United States gets the Mexican Cession.

1850
California becomes a state.

1861
The southern states start the Confederate States of America. The Civil War begins.

1865
General Lee surrenders to General Grant. The Civil War is over.

1830   1840   1850   1860   1870

1845
Texas becomes a state.

1863
President Lincoln frees the slaves in the Confederate states.

1865
Abraham Lincoln is killed.

UNIT 5 AFTER THE CIVIL WAR

What was it like to live in the United States after the Civil War? For the first time, you could travel across the western part of the country by train. You might move to the Great Plains. You might live in a small house that you helped your family build. All around your home you would see flat land and few trees. Your closest neighbor would be many miles away.

Life in America changed after the Civil War. In the North and in the South, people began to rebuild the country. People who had been slaves were now free. Many Americans moved west to the Great Plains. The United States got more land in 1867 and in 1898.

What would you have done if you had lived in the United States after the Civil War? Would you help build new railroads? Would you help rebuild the South? Would you fight in a war to win more land for your country? As you read Unit 5, think about what you would have done if you had lived in the United States after 1865.

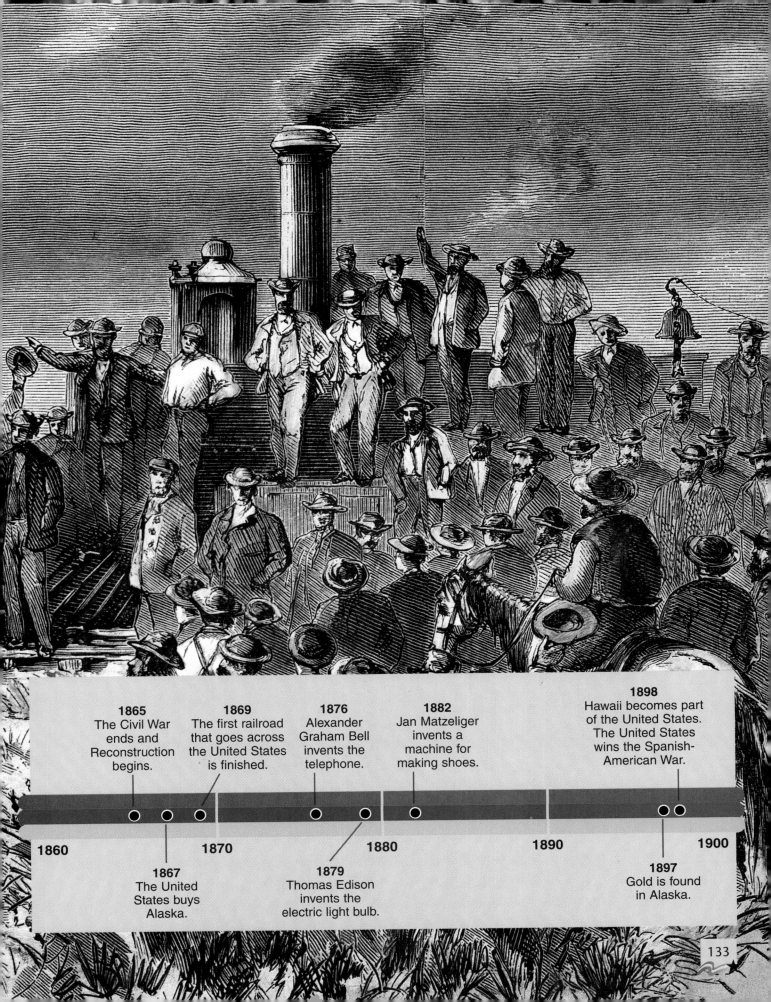

1865
The Civil War ends and Reconstruction begins.

1869
The first railroad that goes across the United States is finished.

1876
Alexander Graham Bell invents the telephone.

1882
Jan Matzeliger invents a machine for making shoes.

1898
Hawaii becomes part of the United States. The United States wins the Spanish-American War.

1860

1870

1880

1890

1900

1867
The United States buys Alaska.

1879
Thomas Edison invents the electric light bulb.

1897
Gold is found in Alaska.

21 RECONSTRUCTION

Think About As You Read

1. How was the South rebuilt?
2. How did life change for African Americans after the Civil War?
3. What laws were added to the Constitution to help African Americans?

NEW WORDS

Reconstruction
rejoined
equal rights

PEOPLE & PLACES

Booker T. Washington
Tuskegee Institute

Soldiers went home after the Civil War ended.

Americans in the North and South had hard work to do after the Civil War. Many cities and farms in the South were destroyed. The South had to be rebuilt. People in the North and South had to learn to like each other again. There was a lot of work to do.

The years after the Civil War were called the time of **Reconstruction**. During this time the southern states **rejoined** the United States. The South was slowly rebuilt. Cities, farms, and roads were rebuilt. New railroads and schools were built. There were few factories in the South before the Civil War. After the war the South began to build factories. Southern farmers began to grow cotton again.

There were many African American slaves in the South before the Civil War. After the war the slaves became free people. After the slaves became free, they had many problems. Most African Americans had never gone to school. Many of them did not know how to read or write. They had little money. After the Civil War, African Americans needed jobs to earn money. But it was often hard for them to find jobs.

After the Civil War, many African Americans still worked on large cotton plantations. The plantation owners paid African Americans for their work. Free schools were started for them. African American children and adults went to school. They wanted to learn. Many adults went to school at night because they worked all day. Sometimes teachers from the North came to teach the African Americans.

Booker T. Washington was a man who helped other African Americans get better jobs. Booker T. Washington had been a slave, but he became free after the Civil War. Washington went to school. He became a teacher. Booker T. Washington said that African Americans must learn to do many different kinds of jobs. He started a school for African Americans in Alabama. His school was called the Tuskegee Institute. People could learn to do many kinds of work at Tuskegee. Then they

Booker T. Washington

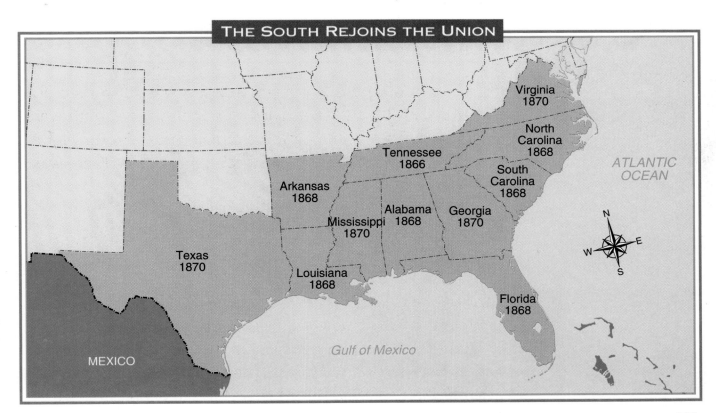

THE SOUTH REJOINS THE UNION

Virginia 1870

North Carolina 1868

Tennessee 1866

South Carolina 1868

Arkansas 1868

Alabama 1868

Georgia 1870

Mississippi 1870

Texas 1870

Louisiana 1868

Florida 1868

ATLANTIC OCEAN

Gulf of Mexico

MEXICO

could get better jobs. Tuskegee became a very large school. Thousands of students have studied at the Tuskegee Institute.

After the war United States senators and representatives wanted to help African Americans have better lives. So they added three laws, or amendments, to the Constitution. The first law was the Thirteenth Amendment. The Thirteenth Amendment said that no one in the United States could own slaves. Never again would there be slavery in America. The second law to help African Americans was the Fourteenth Amendment. This law said that African Americans were citizens. It also said all people have **equal rights**. The third law to help African Americans was the Fifteenth Amendment. This law said African American men could vote. At that time American women were not allowed to vote.

During Reconstruction African Americans voted for the first time. By 1900 more than twenty African Americans had become senators and representatives in Congress. But as time passed, laws were written in the South that were not fair to African Americans. Some laws made it hard for African Americans to vote.

Americans rebuilt the South. People in the North and South slowly began to like each other again.

Voting for the first time

These men were the first African American senators and representatives in Congress.

Read and Remember

Finish the Story   Use the words in blue print to finish the story. Write the words you choose on your paper.

Washington	equal rights	Constitution	vote
Amendment	plantations	Reconstruction	citizens

The years after the Civil War were called __(1)__ . During this time the South was rebuilt. Many African Americans got jobs on cotton __(2)__ . An African American teacher named Booker T. __(3)__ started a large school where African Americans could learn many kinds of jobs. Three amendments were added to the __(4)__ to help African Americans. The Thirteenth __(5)__ ended slavery. The Fourteenth Amendment said African Americans were __(6)__ . It also said all people have __(7)__ . The Fifteenth Amendment gave African American men the right to __(8)__ .

Write the Answer   Write one or two sentences on your paper to answer each question.

1. What problems did the United States have after the Civil War ended?

2. What was rebuilt in the South during Reconstruction?

3. What was Booker T. Washington's school called?

4. How many amendments were added during Reconstruction to help African Americans?

5. How many African Americans became United States senators and representatives by 1900?

Journal Writing

The United States changed after the Civil War. Write a paragraph in your journal that tells three ways the United States changed.

Think and Apply

Finding the Main Idea   Read each group of sentences below. One of the sentences is a main idea. Two sentences support the main idea. Write on your paper the sentence that is the main idea in each group.

1. There was a lot of hard work to do after the Civil War.

   Americans in the North and South had to learn to like each other again.

   Cities and farms had to be rebuilt in the South.

2. Southern cities and farms were rebuilt.

   New schools, factories, and railroads were built in the South.

   The South was rebuilt after the Civil War.

3. African Americans had many problems after they became free.

   Many African Americans had little money.

   It was hard for African Americans to get jobs.

4. African Americans wanted to go to school after the Civil War.

   Many African Americans went to school at night after they finished working.

   Many African American children and adults went to school together.

5. Booker T. Washington started the Tuskegee Institute for African Americans.

   Teachers from the North came to teach African Americans in the South.

   Many people wanted to help African Americans learn in schools.

6. Booker T. Washington said that African Americans must learn to do many different kinds of jobs.

   Booker T. Washington helped many African Americans get better jobs.

   Many African Americans went to Booker T. Washington's school to learn to do different kinds of jobs.

7. The Thirteenth Amendment ended slavery, and the Fifteenth Amendment said African American men could vote.

   Three amendments were added to the Constitution to help African Americans.

   The Fourteenth Amendment said all people have equal rights.

22 AMERICANS MOVE WEST

Think About As You Read

1. How did the Homestead Act help Americans settle in the West?
2. What problems did Native Americans have with the settlers of the Great Plains?
3. How did railroads help Americans move west?

NEW WORDS

Homestead Act
wheat
flour
weapons
reservations
immigrants
spike

PEOPLE & PLACES

Ireland
Chinese

Many settlers went to live on the Great Plains because of the Homestead Act.

The land between the Mississippi River and the Rocky Mountains is called the Great Plains. In the 1840s and 1850s, many Americans traveled west across the Great Plains and the Rocky Mountains to California and Oregon. Not many Americans wanted to live on the Great Plains. There was very little rain. The land was flat, and there were few trees. Americans did not think they could grow food on the Great Plains.

In 1862 the United States senators and representatives in Congress wrote a new law. It was called the **Homestead Act**. The Homestead Act gave land to settlers on the Great Plains for a very low price. The Homestead Act said settlers must live on the land they had paid for. The settlers had to build a house and a farm on the land.

Wheat

Buffalo

Thousands of poor Americans moved to the Great Plains because of the Homestead Act. After the Civil War, African Americans also moved west to get land at a low price. Many farms were started on the Great Plains. Some farmers grew corn. Other farmers grew **wheat**. **Flour** is made from wheat. Breads and cakes are made from flour.

It was hard work to be a wheat farmer on the Great Plains. Sometimes there was not enough rain for the wheat to grow. Many times there were bad windstorms. There were terrible snowstorms in the winter. People lived far apart on the Great Plains. Many people were lonely. The farmers worked hard. They learned better ways to grow wheat. Today most of our wheat comes from the Great Plains.

As Americans moved west, they settled on land where Native Americans lived. These Native Americans had always been buffalo hunters. Millions of buffalo lived on the Great Plains. The buffalo moved from place to place. The Native Americans moved from place to place as they hunted buffalo.

Native Americans used every part of the buffalo they killed. They ate the meat. They made clothes from the animal skins. They also made tents from the skins. They made tools and **weapons** from the horns and bones.

Farmers learned better ways to grow wheat on the Great Plains.

Native Americans were not happy when settlers built farms on the Great Plains. The settlers wanted Native Americans to live in one place. They did not want Native Americans to travel all over the Great Plains hunting for buffalo. There were many battles between the Native Americans and the settlers. Many settlers were killed. But many more Native Americans were killed.

The United States government told the Native Americans to stop moving from place to place. The government gave the Native Americans land to live on. These lands are called **reservations**. Many Native Americans became farmers on the reservations. They were not happy. Their land was not good for farming. They did not want to be farmers. They wanted to be buffalo hunters. They could not hunt buffalo on the reservations.

As Americans moved west, they needed better ways to travel. At first, people traveled with horses and covered wagons. Railroads would take Americans to the West faster. There were many railroads in the East. But there were no railroads across the West.

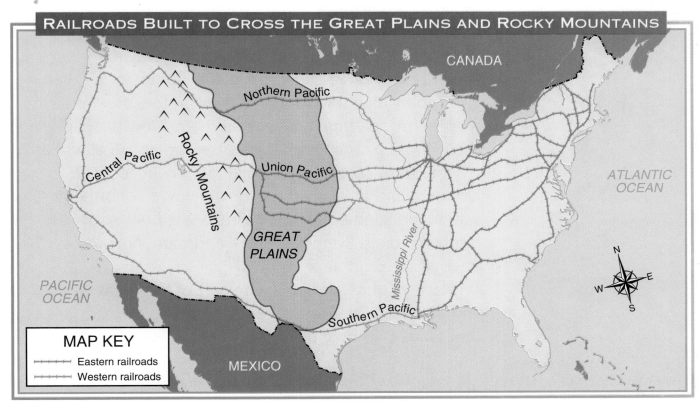

RAILROADS BUILT TO CROSS THE GREAT PLAINS AND ROCKY MOUNTAINS

CANADA

Northern Pacific

Central Pacific

Rocky Mountains

Union Pacific

GREAT PLAINS

Mississippi River

Southern Pacific

ATLANTIC OCEAN

PACIFIC OCEAN

MEXICO

MAP KEY
Eastern railroads
Western railroads

After 1869 more people traveled west on the new railroads.

After the Civil War, Americans started building railroad tracks across the West. Thousands of people helped build the railroads. African Americans and Mexican Americans worked on the railroads. **Immigrants** from Ireland also helped. Thousands of Chinese immigrants came to work on the railroads. They built railroads through the tall Rocky Mountains. The work was hard and dangerous.

In 1869 the first railroad tracks across the United States were finished. The Union Pacific Railroad was started in the East. The Central Pacific Railroad was started in the West. The two railroad tracks were connected together in Utah. A **spike** made of gold connected them. Now people could travel by train from the eastern states to California.

Americans continued to build more railroads. The Northern Pacific Railroad was built across the northern states. The Southern Pacific Railroad was built across the southern states. Every year more and more Americans traveled west in trains.

Many of our states today are part of the Great Plains and the West. The Homestead Act and the railroads helped thousands of people build the American West.

Read and Remember

Match Up   Each item in Group B tells about an item in Group A. Write the letter of the correct answer on your paper.

Group A

1. Homestead Act

2. buffalo

3. wheat

4. railroads

Group B

a. used to make flour for bread

b. made it easier for people to travel west

c. hunted by Native Americans

d. gave people land in the West at a low price

Think and Apply

Cause and Effect   Write sentences on your paper by matching each cause on the left with an effect on the right.

Cause

1. Americans did not want to live on the Great Plains, so _____

2. The Homestead Act gave settlers land at a low price, so _____

3. Buffalo moved from place to place, so _____

4. The United States government wanted Native Americans to live in one place, so _____

5. People needed better ways to travel to the West, so _____

Effect

a. Native Americans who hunted buffalo moved from place to place.

b. United States senators and representatives wrote the Homestead Act.

c. it told Native Americans to live on reservations.

d. railroads were built across the United States.

e. many Americans moved west to the Great Plains.

Journal Writing

Imagine that you were a poor factory worker in the 1860s. You dream about owning your own farm. You learn about the Homestead Act. Then you decide to move to the Great Plains. Write a paragraph in your journal that tells why you find it hard to live on the Great Plains.

Skill Builder

Reading a Flow Chart   A **flow chart** is a chart that shows you facts in the correct order they occur. The flow chart on this page shows how wheat becomes flour for bread. Wheat **kernels** are the seeds of the wheat plant. **Vitamins** are added to food to make it better for people to eat.

Read the flow chart. Then write on your paper the word that finishes each sentence below.

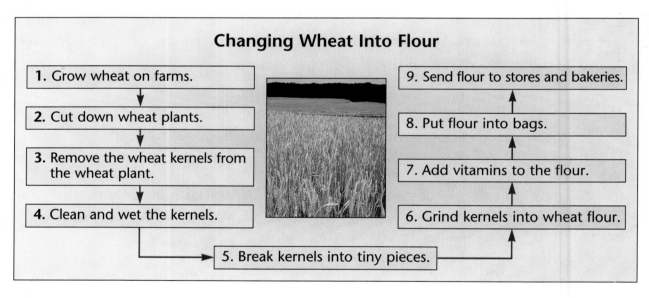

Changing Wheat Into Flour

1. Grow wheat on farms.
2. Cut down wheat plants.
3. Remove the wheat kernels from the wheat plant.
4. Clean and wet the kernels.
5. Break kernels into tiny pieces.
6. Grind kernels into wheat flour.
7. Add vitamins to the flour.
8. Put flour into bags.
9. Send flour to stores and bakeries.

1. The first step is to _____ wheat.
   cut   grow   shake

2. In Step 3 the wheat _____ are removed.
   leaves   flowers   kernels

3. After grinding the kernels into flour, _____ are added.
   vitamins   salt   colors

4. Step 8 is to put flour into _____ .
   balls   bags   barns

CHAPTER 23

THE UNITED STATES GETS MORE LAND

Think About As You Read

1. How did Alaska become part of the United States?
2. How did Hawaii become part of the United States?
3. How did the Spanish-American War help the United States get more land?

NEW WORDS

imperialism
icebox
oil
battleship
blew up
Spanish-American War

PEOPLE & PLACES

Alaska
Russia
Hawaiian Islands
Hawaii
Cuba
Puerto Rico
Guam
Philippines

The United States bought Alaska from Russia in 1867.

The United States owned land from the Atlantic Ocean to the Pacific Ocean. But the United States had not finished growing. In 1867 the United States bought more land. In 1898 the United States owned even more land. How did the United States get more land?

After the Civil War, the United States wanted to rule more land. People in many countries believed in an idea called **imperialism**. Imperialism means one country rules other countries or colonies. The United States wanted to rule other countries, too.

The United States decided that it wanted to rule Alaska. Alaska is a large piece of land near northwestern Canada. The weather in Alaska is very cold much of the year. There is a lot of snow. A country called Russia is very close to Alaska. Russia owned Alaska. Russia wanted to sell Alaska to the

145

United States. Some Native Americans lived in Alaska. Not many other people lived there.

In 1867 the United States bought Alaska from Russia for $7,200,000. Many Americans thought it was silly to buy Alaska. They said Alaska was a big **icebox**.

In 1897 gold was found in Alaska. Soon there was a gold rush in Alaska. Thousands of people rushed to Alaska to find gold. Many people did not find gold. They found other things there. Alaska has furs and good fish. Alaska has **oil**. Oil makes our cars go. Oil helps us make electricity.

People started towns and cities in Alaska. In 1959 Alaska became the forty-ninth state in the United States. It is also our largest state.

Many people wanted the United States to rule land in the Pacific Ocean, too. They became interested in the Hawaiian Islands. These beautiful islands are also called Hawaii. Hawaii is about two thousand miles from California. The weather is often sunny and warm. The land is good for farming.

Native Americans in Alaska

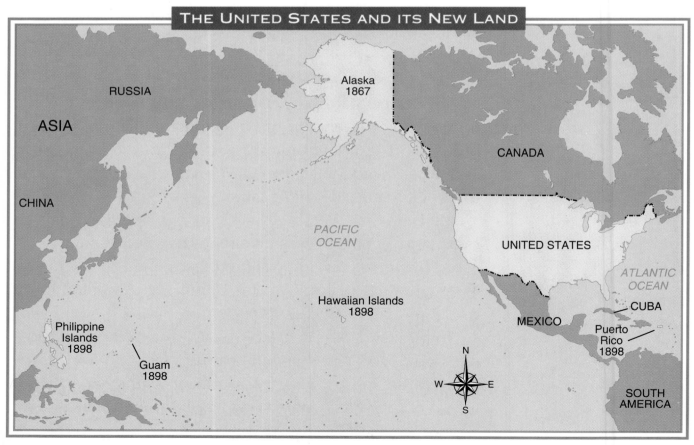

THE UNITED STATES AND ITS NEW LAND

RUSSIA

ASIA

CHINA

Alaska
1867

CANADA

PACIFIC
OCEAN

UNITED STATES

ATLANTIC
OCEAN

Hawaiian Islands
1898

CUBA

MEXICO

Puerto
Rico
1898

Philippine
Islands
1898

Guam
1898

N
W   E
S

SOUTH
AMERICA

The Hawaiian Islands have warm weather and good land for farming.

The *Maine* blowing up

In the 1820s many Americans went to Hawaii to build churches. Other Americans went to live and work in Hawaii. They grew sugar cane on large plantations. They wanted Hawaii to be part of the United States. Many of the Hawaiian people wanted Hawaii to belong to the United States, too. In 1898 the United States Congress decided to make Hawaii part of the United States. In 1959 Congress voted for Hawaii to become the fiftieth state.

The United States still had not finished growing. Cuba and Puerto Rico are island countries. Find them on the map on page 146. Both Cuba and Puerto Rico belonged to Spain.

The people of Cuba wanted their country to be free. They fought against Spain. Many Americans wanted the United States to help the people in Cuba fight for freedom. In 1898 the United States sent a **battleship**, the *Maine*, to Cuba. The ship **blew up**, and 260 Americans were killed. No one knew why the battleship blew up. Many people thought that Spanish soldiers had blown up the *Maine*. Today we know that the Spanish did not blow up the *Maine*.

Soldiers from the United States fought Spanish soldiers in Cuba.

Raising the American flag on Cuba

In 1898 the United States decided to fight against Spain to help the Cubans become free. This war was called the **Spanish-American War**. The United States won every battle. American soldiers fought the Spanish in Cuba. American soldiers captured Puerto Rico from Spain.

Americans also fought the Spanish in the Pacific Ocean. Guam and the Philippines are island nations in the Pacific Ocean. Guam and the Philippines had belonged to Spain. American soldiers helped Guam and the Philippines become free from Spain. After a few months, Spain surrendered to the United States.

At the end of the war, Spain gave Cuba, Puerto Rico, Guam, and the Philippines to the United States. Cuba became an independent country in 1902. The Philippines belonged to the United States for almost 50 years. Today the Philippines is an independent country. Guam and Puerto Rico belong to the United States, but they are not states. The people of Guam and Puerto Rico are American citizens.

The United States had a lot of new land in 1898. Other countries now knew that the United States had become a very strong nation.

Read and Remember

Choose the Answer   Write the correct answers on your paper.

1. What do we call the idea that one country should rule other countries?
   imperialism   reconstruction   government

2. What country sold Alaska to the United States?
   Cuba   France   Russia

3. What did people rush to find in Alaska in 1897?
   furs   gold   seals

4. How far is Hawaii from California?
   100 miles   2,000 miles   5,000 miles

5. When did Hawaii become a state of the United States?
   1867   1898   1959

6. What did people find in Alaska?
   bananas   oil   cotton

7. Which was the last state to become part of the United States?
   Georgia   Alaska   Hawaii

8. Where did people fight against Spain for freedom?
   Hawaii   Canada   Cuba

9. What country did the United States fight against in 1898?
   Great Britain   Russia   Spain

10. Which ship blew up near Cuba in 1898?
    Maine   *Mayflower*   *Pinta*

11. What island nation does not belong to the United States today?
    Guam   the Philippines   Puerto Rico

12. Where are people American citizens today?
    Guam and Puerto Rico   Cuba and the Philippines

Think and Apply

Fact or Opinion   Read each sentence below. Write **F** on your paper for each fact below. Write **O** for each opinion. You should find three sentences that are opinions.

1. The United States bought Alaska for $7,200,000.

2. Alaska is a big unfriendly icebox.

3. People rushed to Alaska to find gold.

4. Hawaii is about two thousand miles from California.

5. Hawaii is too far away to be part of the United States.

6. In 1898 American soldiers captured Puerto Rico from Spain.

7. The United States should rule Guam and Puerto Rico instead of Spain.

Skill Builder

Reading a Historical Map   A historical map shows the history of an area. The map on page 146 shows the United States in 1898.

Use the map to answer the questions below. Write a sentence on your paper to answer each question.

1. What new land did the United States get in 1867?

2. Which island nation near Guam did the United States own in 1898?

3. Which islands in the middle of the Pacific Ocean did the United States own in 1898?

4. Which island near Cuba did the United States own in 1898?

5. Which land owned by the United States was the farthest north?

 Journal Writing

Many Americans thought it was silly to buy Alaska from Russia. Why did they think it was silly? Write a paragraph in your journal that tells why Alaska was worth buying.

NEW INVENTIONS CHANGE THE UNITED STATES

CHAPTER 24

Think About As You Read

1. How have the electric light bulb and the telephone changed the United States?
2. How did Jan Matzeliger change the way shoes were made?
3. Why was the conveyor belt an important invention?

NEW WORDS

invention
invented
conveyor belt

PEOPLE & PLACES

Alexander Graham Bell
Scotland
Thomas Edison
Jan Matzeliger
Henry Ford
Garrett Morgan

Thomas Edison invented many things, including the electric light bulb.

The United States grew from a country with 13 states to a country with 50 states. America changed in other ways, too. At first most Americans lived on farms. The cities did not have many people. Today most Americans live and work in cities.

Americans had very few machines to help them with their work 200 years ago. There were no telephones, cars, or electric lights. People traveled on horses. People used candles to light their homes. Americans learned to make new machines. A new machine is called an **invention**. The new inventions made life easier and better for people in the United States and around the world.

Alexander Graham Bell worked for years on his invention, the telephone.

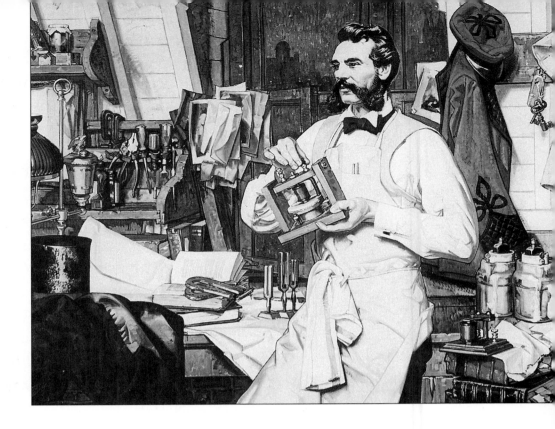

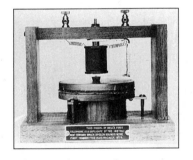

Alexander Graham Bell's telephone

Thomas Edison's light bulb

Alexander Graham Bell made, or **invented**, the first telephone. He was an immigrant from Scotland. Alexander was a teacher of children who were deaf. He taught them how to speak.

Alexander Graham Bell wanted to make a machine so that people who were far apart could talk to each other. Alexander worked on his machine for two years. In 1876 his machine worked. Alexander had made the world's first telephone. In a few years, there were telephones in most American cities.

A long time ago, American homes and streets were dark at night because there were no electric lights. Thomas Edison changed that. He invented the first electric light bulb. Thomas Edison started working on it in 1879. Finally, after many months, his bulb worked. It gave off light for a short time. Edison wanted his electric bulbs to burn for a long time. He continued to make different light bulbs. He learned how to make better bulbs that burned longer. The electric light bulb made our houses and streets bright at night.

A long time ago, people could not go to shoe stores to buy their shoes. Instead, most shoes were made by hand. Shoes were made to fit each person's feet. Jan Matzeliger,

Jan Matzeliger

an African American, changed the way shoes were made. In 1882 Matzeliger invented a special machine that could make shoes of many different sizes. Shoes could be made quickly in factories with Matzeliger's machine. Today most shoes are made in shoe factories with the kind of machine Matzeliger invented.

For hundreds of years, people traveled on horses. Henry Ford changed the way Americans traveled. In 1896 Henry Ford made one of the first cars in America. He started a factory that made cars. His factory was called the Ford Motor Company. He did not want his cars to be expensive. Ford wanted many Americans to be able to buy his cars.

Henry Ford invented a new way to make cars in his factory. In the Ford factory, a **conveyor belt** carried the body of each car past the workers. Each worker put one part on the body of each car. Each worker stayed in one place and did the same job all day. In less than two hours, a car was put together.

Henry Ford's cars replaced horses as the way to travel in this country and around the world.

The conveyor belt in the Ford factory helped to make cars quickly.

Henry Ford

Cars were made very quickly with the conveyor belt. Because cars were made quickly, they were less expensive. Millions of Americans bought Henry Ford's cars. The United States changed into a nation that traveled in cars and not on horses.

More and more Americans bought cars. Since there were many cars on the street, traffic became a problem. Drivers did not know when to stop and when to go. Police officers directed some of the traffic, but they could not direct all of it. In 1923 an African American named Garrett Morgan solved this problem. He invented the first traffic light in America.

Inventions have changed the way Americans live. People have better lives because of inventions like the telephone, the electric light bulb, and the traffic light. The conveyor belt changed America. Factories everywhere made products quickly by using conveyor belts. Today conveyor belts are used in almost every factory.

Read and Remember

Finish Up   Choose a word or words in blue print to finish each sentence. Write the correct answers on your paper.

telephone	expensive	shoes	bright
invention	conveyor belt	Edison	candles

1. Before Thomas Edison invented the light bulb, houses were lit with _____ .

2. A new machine is called an _____ .

3. Alexander Graham Bell invented the _____ , which allowed people who were far apart to talk to each other.

4. Thomas _____ tried to make electric light bulbs that would burn for a long time.

5. The electric light bulb makes houses and streets _____ at night.

6. Jan Matzeliger invented a machine to make _____ quickly in factories.

7. Henry Ford did not want his cars to be _____ .

8. At the Ford Motor Company, a _____ carried the bodies of cars past the workers.

Think and Apply

Sequencing Events   Number your paper from 1 to 5. Write the sentences to show the correct order.

In 1896 Henry Ford invented his first car.

In 1923 Garrett Morgan invented the traffic light to solve traffic problems.

Millions of Americans bought cars made in the Ford factory.

Henry Ford invented a way to make cars on a conveyor belt in the Ford factory.

For hundreds of years, people traveled on horses.

Skill Builder

Reading a Chart   A **chart** lists a group of facts. Charts help you learn facts quickly. Read the chart below to learn how inventions changed America.

Inventions Change America			
Inventor	**Invention**	**Date**	**How the Invention Changed America**
Alexander Graham Bell	telephone	1876	People who are far apart can talk to each other.
Thomas Edison	electric light bulb	1879	Electric lights are used to light homes, streets, schools, and offices.
Jan Matzeliger	shoe-making machine	1882	Shoes are made in shoe factories and sold in shoe stores.
Henry Ford	conveyor belt to make cars quickly	1896	People travel in cars instead of on horses.
Garrett Morgan	traffic light	1923	Traffic lights control traffic.

Write on your paper the word or words that finish each sentence.

1. To learn all the information you can about Henry Ford, read the chart from _____ .
   side to side   top to bottom

2. To learn all the information you can about how inventions changed America, read the chart from _____ .
   side to side   top to bottom

3. Alexander Graham Bell invented the _____ .
   car   telephone   light bulb

4. Using a conveyor belt to build cars was the idea of _____ .
   Henry Ford   Jan Matzeliger   Alexander Graham Bell

5. The traffic light was invented by _____ .
   Thomas Edison   Garrett Morgan   Henry Ford

Number your paper from 1 to 9. Study the time line on this page. Then use the words in blue print to finish the story. Write the words you choose on your paper.

Homestead Act   buffalo   shoes

reservations   Hawaii   Alaska

imperialism   Great Plains   Edison

In 1862 Congress passed the __(1)__ . This law allowed settlers to buy land on the __(2)__ for a low price. The settlers had fights with the Native Americans who were __(3)__ hunters. Many Native Americans were forced to move to __(4)__ .

Many Americans wanted the United States to own more land because they believed in __(5)__ . In 1867 the United States bought __(6)__ . Then in 1898 __(7)__ became part of the United States.

In 1879, Thomas __(8)__ invented the electric light bulb. In 1882 Jan Matzeliger invented a new machine for making __(9)__ .

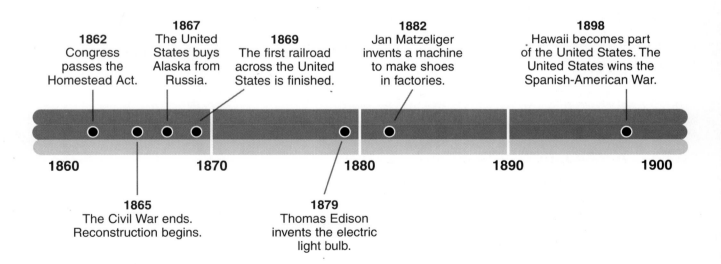

1862
Congress passes the Homestead Act.

1867
The United States buys Alaska from Russia.

1869
The first railroad across the United States is finished.

1882
Jan Matzeliger invents a machine to make shoes in factories.

1898
Hawaii becomes part of the United States. The United States wins the Spanish-American War.

1860   1870   1880   1890   1900

1865
The Civil War ends. Reconstruction begins.

1879
Thomas Edison invents the electric light bulb.

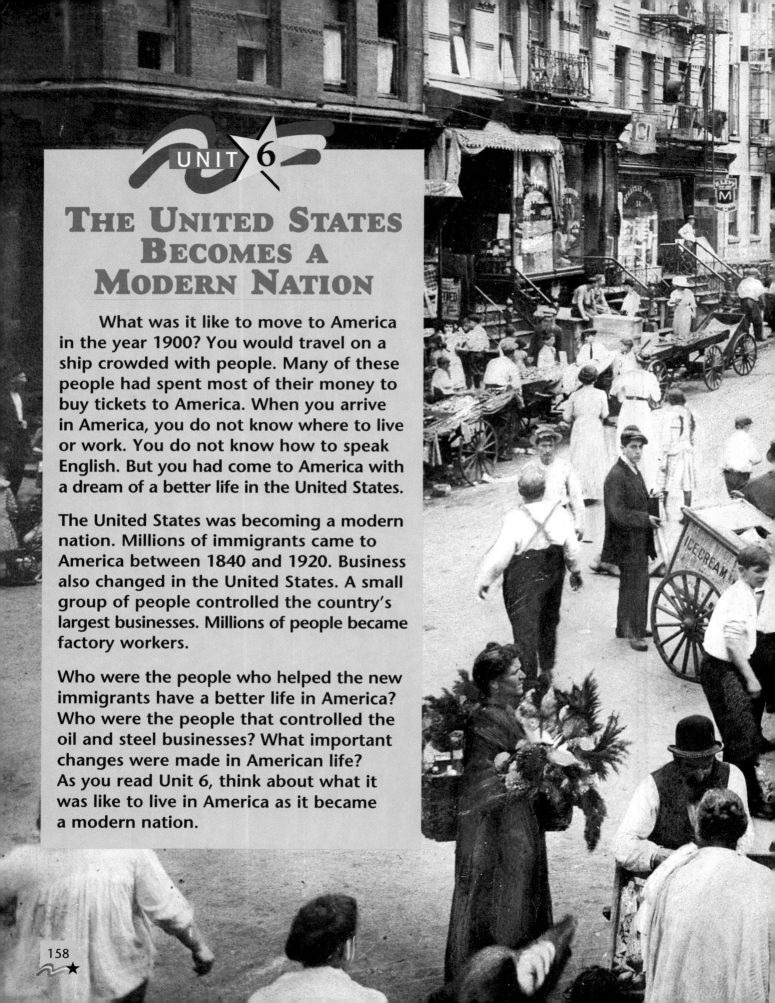

THE UNITED STATES BECOMES A MODERN NATION

What was it like to move to America in the year 1900? You would travel on a ship crowded with people. Many of these people had spent most of their money to buy tickets to America. When you arrive in America, you do not know where to live or work. You do not know how to speak English. But you had come to America with a dream of a better life in the United States.

The United States was becoming a modern nation. Millions of immigrants came to America between 1840 and 1920. Business also changed in the United States. A small group of people controlled the country's largest businesses. Millions of people became factory workers.

Who were the people who helped the new immigrants have a better life in America? Who were the people that controlled the oil and steel businesses? What important changes were made in American life? As you read Unit 6, think about what it was like to live in America as it became a modern nation.

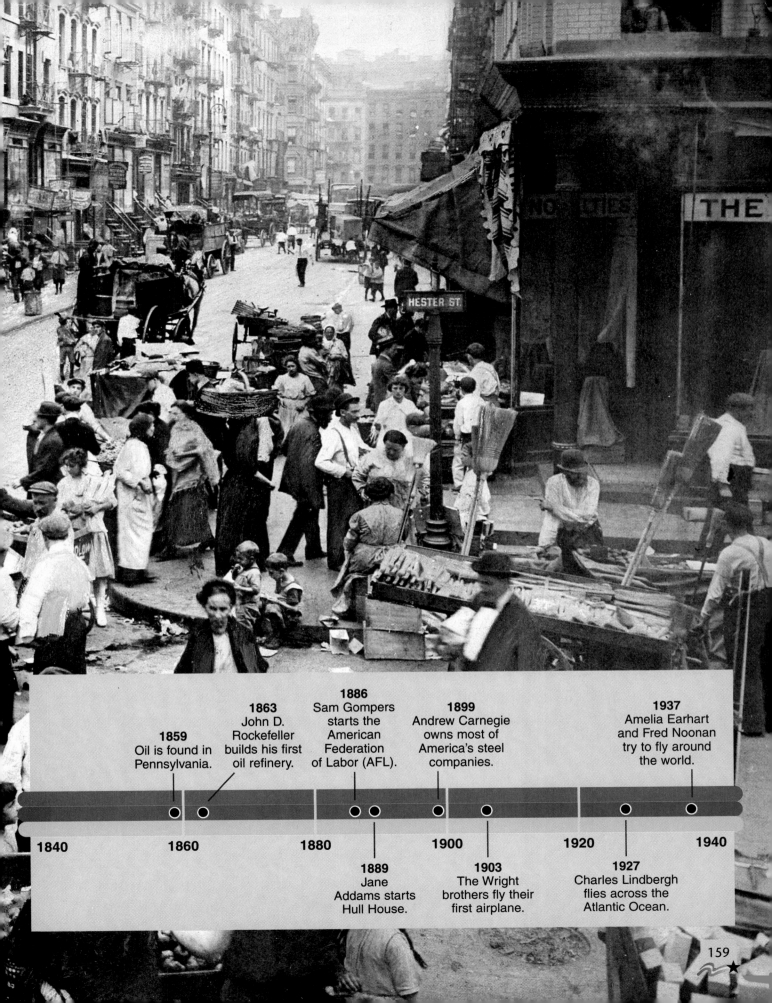

1859
Oil is found in Pennsylvania.

1863
John D. Rockefeller builds his first oil refinery.

1886
Sam Gompers starts the American Federation of Labor (AFL).

1899
Andrew Carnegie owns most of America's steel companies.

1937
Amelia Earhart and Fred Noonan try to fly around the world.

1889
Jane Addams starts Hull House.

1903
The Wright brothers fly their first airplane.

1927
Charles Lindbergh flies across the Atlantic Ocean.

1840   1860   1880   1900   1920   1940

CHAPTER 25 STARTING A NEW LIFE IN AMERICA

Think About As You Read

1. Why did people want to come to America?
2. Which groups of people came to America?
3. What was it like to be an immigrant in America?

NEW WORDS

starving
reporter
photographs

PEOPLE & PLACES

Irish
John F. Kennedy
Jacob Riis
Denmark

Many immigrants arrived from Europe to start a new life in the United States.

For hundreds of years, people have moved to America from other countries. Millions of immigrants have come to the United States. They have come from every part of the world. Native Americans are the only Americans who lived in the United States long before other immigrants came to America. Perhaps you, your parents, or your grandparents were immigrants. Why did immigrants come to America?

At first most immigrants came to America from Great Britain and other countries in Europe. Many people came to America for freedom of religion. Others came because they did not like the laws of their country. Many people were poor in western Europe. They thought they could earn more money in America.

John F. Kennedy

In the 1840s many people in Ireland were **starving**. Irish farmers could not grow enough food. So thousands of Irish people came to the United States. They were hungry and poor. In America they helped build railroads. They worked in factories. John F. Kennedy was an Irish American who became the President of the United States in 1961. His great-grandfather had been an Irish immigrant.

Thousands of immigrants from China came to America after the Civil War. The Chinese helped build railroads in the West. Many of the Chinese immigrants settled in the West. Some Chinese Americans became farmers and store owners. Others made their living by fishing.

African Americans were different from other groups of immigrants. They were forced to come to America as slaves. In 1619 the first African slaves were brought to the Virginia colony. Each year more Africans were forced to be slaves. Most slaves lived in the South. The slaves became free after the Civil War. Many of the free African Americans continued to work on plantations in the South. Many African Americans thought they could get better jobs in the North and in the West. From 1860 to 1920, thousands of African Americans moved to the North and to the West.

Many immigrants helped build our country's railroads.

Before the 1880s many people from Germany and northern Europe came to America. Many had been farmers in Europe. They became farmers in the United States. From the 1880s to 1920s, other immigrant groups came to America. Millions of people left Italy, Russia, and Poland. They did not have enough food in Europe. They traveled to America on large, crowded ships. Most of these immigrants were very poor.

Many of the immigrants from Russia and Poland were Jewish. They did not have freedom of religion in Russia and Poland. They had religious freedom and better jobs in the United States.

Most of the immigrants from Italy, Russia, and Poland lived in large cities in America. Many of them settled in New York City. The immigrants had many problems in America. They had to learn to read, write, and speak English. They lived in small, crowded houses. Many immigrants worked in dirty factories. Often they were paid very little for their hard work. Many of their children had to work all day in factories.

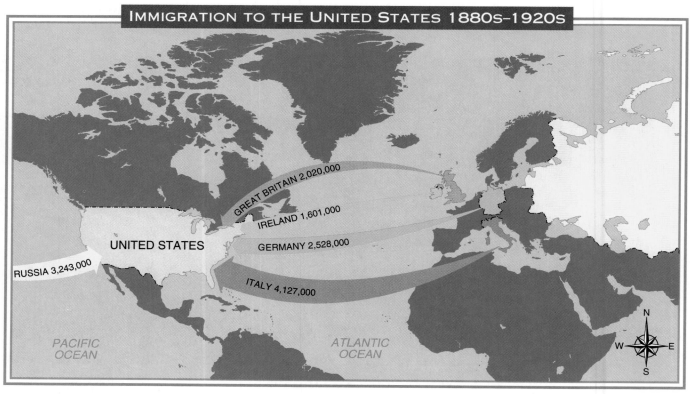

IMMIGRATION TO THE UNITED STATES 1880s–1920s

GREAT BRITAIN 2,020,000
IRELAND 1,601,000
GERMANY 2,528,000
RUSSIA 3,243,000
ITALY 4,127,000
UNITED STATES
PACIFIC OCEAN
ATLANTIC OCEAN

Immigrant families in New York City often lived crowded together. Children had only narrow streets to play in.

Jacob Riis

Jacob Riis took this photograph of immigrant children sleeping outside.

Immigrant children went to free schools in America. Their parents studied English in schools at night. Schools helped the immigrants become Americans. After they lived in the United States for five years, they could become American citizens. Then they were allowed to vote like other American citizens.

Jacob Riis was an immigrant from Denmark. He became a newspaper **reporter** in New York City. Jacob Riis loved being an American. He wanted to help the many poor immigrants in American cities.

Riis wrote newspaper stories and a book about the new immigrants. He took **photographs** for his stories. His pictures showed the ugly, crowded houses where immigrants lived. His stories said that there were no parks where immigrant children could play. People learned about immigrant life from Riis's work. They wanted to help the immigrants. Better houses were built. Parks and playgrounds were built.

Millions of immigrants helped build America. They became store owners and farmers. Some became very rich. Some immigrants became government leaders. Others became teachers and doctors. Many immigrants built our factories and railroads.

Today our laws allow several hundred thousand immigrants to come to America every year. This year and every year, thousands of people from other countries will start a new life in America.

⭐ Read and Remember

Find the Answers   Find the sentences below that tell why people came to America. Write on your paper the sentences you find. You should find three sentences.

1. People wanted to live near the ocean.

2. People wanted freedom of religion.

3. People wanted to earn more money.

4. People wanted to live in crowded houses.

5. People did not like the laws of their own country.

6. People liked to travel on large, crowded ships.

7. People wanted to work hard in dirty factories.

Think and Apply ⭐

Categories   Read the words in each group. Decide how they are alike. Choose the best title in blue print for each group. Write the title on your paper.

Immigrant Life
Jacob Riis

African Americans
Irish Immigrants

1. starved in Ireland
    built railroads
    factory workers

3. children worked in factories
    went to schools
    crowded homes

2. came from Africa
    forced to be slaves
    moved north and west

4. immigrant from Denmark
    newspaper reporter
    wrote stories about immigrants

⭐ Journal Writing

Immigrants came to the United States to find a better life in America. But many immigrants had problems in America. Write a paragraph in your journal that tells about the problems that immigrants had.

Skill Builder

Reading a Bar Graph   A **bar graph** shows information by using bars. You can compare information on a bar graph.

Study this bar graph. It shows how many immigrants came to the United States from five countries in 1900. The Soviet Union is one of the countries on the graph. Russia and some smaller countries later became the Soviet Union.

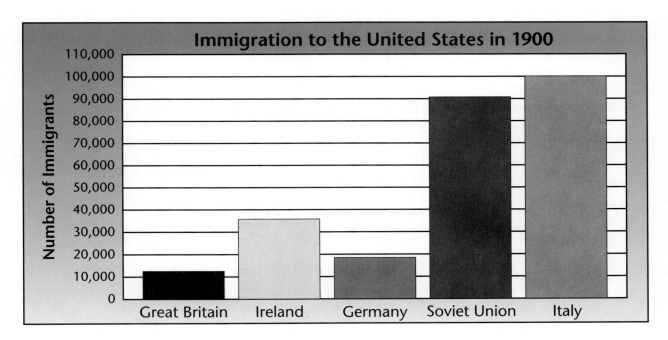

Write on your paper the word or words that finish each sentence.

1. The largest number of immigrants in 1900 came from _____ .
   Ireland   Germany   Italy

2. The smallest number of immigrants came from _____ .
   Great Britain   Soviet Union   Italy

3. There were more German immigrants than _____ immigrants.
   Irish   British   Italian

4. There were about _____ immigrants from Italy.
   10,000   50,000   100,000

5. There were _____ 30,000 immigrants from Ireland.
   more than   less than

26 BIG BUSINESS GROWS BIGGER

Think About As You Read

1. What big business did Andrew Carnegie control?
2. What big business did John D. Rockefeller control?
3. Why did Congress write new laws about big business?

NEW WORDS

big business
ore
steel mills
millionaire
drilled
oil refineries

PEOPLE & PLACES

Andrew Carnegie
Minnesota
John D. Rockefeller

Making steel was one big business that changed life in America.

Life in America changed after the Civil War. More and more Americans lived and worked in cities. Thousands of Americans worked for factories, railroads, stores, and other kinds of businesses.

Sometimes one business owned many factories or smaller businesses. This is called **big business**. Sometimes one person would control a very large business. Railroads were an example of big business. At one time, one man controlled most of the railroads in the United States. This person could decide how much money to charge people to use the railroads.

Before the Civil War, most machines were made of a metal called iron. Railroad tracks were made of iron. Iron is made from an **ore** found in the earth. Iron is not very strong. A man in Great Britain found a way to make iron stronger. This new, stronger iron was called steel. Railroad tracks and cars are now made of steel.

Andrew Carnegie was an immigrant from Scotland. He moved to America when he was a young boy. When he grew up, he built factories in Pennsylvania for making steel. These factories are called **steel mills**. He called his steel mills the Carnegie Steel Company. Andrew Carnegie became very rich. He used his money to buy other steel companies. By 1899 Andrew Carnegie owned most of the steel mills in the United States. He became a **millionaire**.

Andrew Carnegie also owned railroads and ships for sending his steel to different places. He owned land in Minnesota where much of the iron for making steel was found. Andrew Carnegie was the "steel king."

In 1859 oil was found deep in the earth in Pennsylvania. Soon people **drilled** for oil all over the United States. Oil had to be cleaned before it could be used. Oil was cleaned in factories called **oil refineries**. In 1863 John D. Rockefeller built his first oil refinery. His business did well. He used his money to build more refineries. He called his business the Standard Oil Company.

Andrew Carnegie

The steel mills of the Carnegie Steel Company were large and had many workers.

John D. Rockefeller

Rockefeller sold his oil for less money than other oil companies. The other companies tried to sell their oil for less money, too. The other companies were soon losing money and not earning money. John D. Rockefeller bought the other oil companies. Soon Rockefeller owned almost all the oil companies in America. He also became a millionaire.

John D. Rockefeller and Andrew Carnegie used their money to help other people. They gave money to schools and churches. Andrew Carnegie used his money to build many libraries. He built over 2,500 libraries.

The big businesses of railroads, steel, and oil helped America become a nation with tall buildings and many factories.

Many Americans thought that it was not right for a few companies to control all the oil, steel, and railroads in America. It was not right for a few people to decide how much Americans should pay for their oil, steel, and railroads. New laws were written in Congress. These laws said that a few companies could not control all the big business in the United States.

Tall wooden towers were used to drill deep into the ground to get to the oil.

Read and Remember

True or False   Write **T** on your paper for each sentence that is true. Write **F** for each sentence that is false.

1. When one business owns many factories or small businesses, it is called big business.

2. Railroad tracks and cars are now made of iron.

3. Andrew Carnegie gave money to build libraries.

4. In 1859 oil was found in Hawaii.

5. Oil is cleaned in a refinery.

6. John D. Rockefeller owned almost all the oil companies in the United States.

Think and Apply

Cause and Effect   Write sentences on your paper by matching each cause on the left with an effect on the right.

Cause

1. Steel is stronger than iron, so _____

2. Andrew Carnegie owned most of the steel mills in America, so _____

3. Oil had to be cleaned before it could be used, so _____

4. Rockefeller and Carnegie wanted to help people, so _____

5. Many people said a few companies should not control all the oil, steel, and railroads in America, so _____

Effect

a. they gave money to schools, churches, and libraries.

b. Congress wrote laws to prevent a few companies from owning all of America's big business.

c. he became a millionaire.

d. oil refineries were built to clean the oil.

e. it is used for making railroad tracks and cars.

Using a Map Key to Read a Resource Map   A **resource map** shows where **natural resources** are found. Natural resources are things we get from the earth. Coal, iron ore, and oil are natural resources. A resource map uses little drawings to show different natural resources. A **map key** tells you what each drawing means. This resource map shows where some natural resources are found that are used in making oil and steel. Find the map key below.

Use the map and map key to answer the questions. Write the answers on your paper.

1. What natural resource is shown as squares on the map?

2. Name three states that have coal.

3. What natural resource is shown as triangles on the map?

4. Name three states that have iron ore.

5. What natural resource is shown as circles on the map?

6. Name three states that have oil.

7. Name one state that has coal, iron ore, and oil.

CHAPTER 27

UNIONS HELP THE WORKING PEOPLE

Think About As You Read

1. What problems did factory workers have by the year 1900?
2. How did labor unions help workers?
3. What kinds of laws were written to help workers?

NEW WORDS

employers
labor unions
salaries
strike
American Federation of Labor (AFL)
photographer

PEOPLE & PLACES

Samuel Gompers
Mary Jones
Lewis Hine

Many people worked long hours in dangerous factories. Most factory workers were immigrants.

Should small children work all day in dirty factories? "Yes," said factory owners. "No," said factory workers. Should factory workers work 12 or 15 hours every day? "Yes," said factory owners. "No," said factory workers.

By 1900 millions of Americans were working in factories. Many factory workers were immigrants. They spoke little English. There were not many kinds of jobs they could do. They had to work 12 to 15 hours each day in dirty, dangerous factories. Most workers could not earn enough money for their families. Their young children had to work in factories, too. These children could not go to school. They had no time to play. Factory workers were afraid to ask their bosses,

171

Many children worked in factories.

or **employers**, for more money. They were afraid of losing their jobs. Then they would have no money for their families at all.

Factory workers decided to help themselves. They started **labor unions**. A labor union is a group of workers who work together to get better **salaries** from their employer. Every union has leaders. The union leaders can ask the employers for better salaries. The employer can say "no" to the union leaders. Then the union members can decide to stop working until they get better salaries. This is called a **strike**.

When union workers will not work because they want more money, we say that they are "on strike." Factory owners do not like strikes. Their factories cannot make things when workers are on strike. Often employers will pay workers better salaries because the employers do not want their workers on strike. Labor unions have helped workers get better salaries.

Samuel Gompers was a famous union leader. He was a Jewish immigrant from England. Sam Gompers started working in a factory when he was 13 years old because his family was very poor. Later he became a leader of the union in his factory.

Samuel Gompers

Sam Gompers felt that workers all over America needed unions. He felt that new laws were needed to help working people. Gompers wanted laws that would not allow children to work. He wanted a law that said workers should work only eight hours a day. Many times the government would not allow workers to go on strike. Gompers wanted laws that would allow strikes.

In 1886 Gompers helped start the **American Federation of Labor (AFL)**. Many unions joined the AFL. Gompers was the president of the AFL for 37 years. Gompers and the AFL tried to have new laws made to help workers. Sam Gompers and the AFL helped unions go on strike for better salaries.

Most businesses did not want their workers to join unions. Many employers said they did not have enough money to pay better salaries. Employers refused to talk to union leaders. Slowly the AFL changed things. After many years employers learned to work together with union leaders. Workers worked fewer hours and were paid better salaries. As the years passed, more workers joined unions.

Union workers sometimes had to go on strike to get better salaries. A "scab" is someone who works when the union is on strike.

Many Americans learned from photographs about the problems children had working in factories like this coal factory.

Mother Jones

Mary Jones was an Irish immigrant who also helped the factory workers. Many people called her "Mother Jones" because she was more than seventy years old. She traveled around America and helped workers start unions. She told workers to go on strike for better salaries. She told workers to strike for a shorter working day. People read about Mary Jones in their newspapers. They were told that new laws to help workers were needed. Mother Jones lived to be 100 years old. She died in 1930.

Lewis Hine wanted to help the children who worked in factories. Hine was a **photographer**. He went into factories and took photographs. His pictures showed how terrible it was for children to be factory workers. His pictures were published in magazines and books. Many Americans learned from Hine's photographs about the problems children had. As time passed, new laws were written. These laws said children could not be factory workers.

Today we have many laws that help working people. Our laws allow union workers to go on strike. Most workers work only eight hours a day. Today millions of workers belong to labor unions.

Read and Remember

Finish the Sentence   Write on your paper the word or words that finish each sentence.

1. To get better salaries, factory workers started _____ .
   labor unions   schools   libraries

2. Union workers who stop working because they want more money are _____ .
   on vacation   on strike   on sick leave

3. In 1886 Sam Gompers started the _____ .
   AFL   NFL   ABC

4. Mother Jones helped workers start _____ .
   schools   playgrounds   unions

5. Lewis Hine used _____ to help children who worked in factories.
   photographs   strikes   playgrounds

Think and Apply

Drawing Conclusions   Read each pair of sentences. Then look in the box for the conclusion you can make. Write the letter of the conclusion on your paper.

1. Factory workers worked 12 to 15 hours a day.
   Factories were dirty and dangerous.

2. Factory workers wanted safe factories.
   Factory owners would not make changes when the workers asked.

3. Factory workers sometimes asked for better salaries.
   The employers did not always listen to the labor union leaders.

> **a.** Factory workers started labor unions to help them get safe factories.
>
> **b.** Factory workers had a hard life.
>
> **c.** Factory workers went on strike to get better salaries.

Skill Builder

Reading a Line Graph   A **line graph** is another type of graph. It is used to show change over time. The line graph on this page shows how many workers belonged to unions from 1900 to 1990. Study the graph.

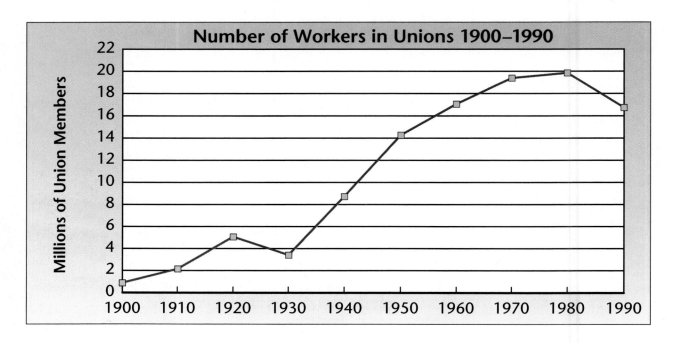

Write on your paper the words or the numbers that finish each sentence.

1. The numbers on the left stand for _____ of union members.
   hundreds   thousands   millions

2. The smallest number of people belonged to unions in the year _____ .
   1900   1940   1980

3. The largest number of workers belonged to unions in _____ .
   1910   1930   1980

4. In 1980 about _____ people belonged to unions.
   5 million   17 million   20 million

5. From 1930 to 1980, the number of people in unions became _____ .
   larger   smaller

6. From 1980 to 1990, the number of people in unions became _____ .
   larger   smaller

CHAPTER 28 WOMEN WORK FOR A BETTER AMERICA

Think About As You Read

1. How did Jane Addams help people?
2. How did Lillian Wald help people in New York City?
3. How did Alice Hamilton help factory workers?

NEW WORDS

kindergarten
lead
lead poisoning

PEOPLE & PLACES

Jane Addams
Chicago, Illinois
Hull House
Janie Porter Barrett
Locust Street Social
    Settlement House
Lillian Wald
Henry Street
    Settlement House
Dr. Alice Hamilton

Jane Addams took care of neighborhood children at Hull House.

How can we help the new immigrants in our country? How can we help men, women, and children who work all day in factories? Many people asked these questions after 1880. Four women found ways to help many other Americans.

Jane Addams helped people in a neighborhood of immigrants in Chicago, Illinois. In 1889 she bought a large old house called Hull House. She bought Hull House with her own money and with money from other people.

Hull House helped the people of the neighborhood in many ways. Hull House workers took care of small children

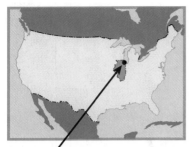

Chicago, Illinois

Jane Addams

Lillian Wald

Hull House is still helping neighborhood people in Chicago, Illinois.

while their mothers were at work. Immigrants learned to speak English at Hull House. Addams helped them become American citizens. Addams started clubs and a summer camp for children. She started the first playground in Chicago.

Jane Addams worked to get new laws that would help immigrants, factory workers, and children. As time passed, new laws were written that helped these people.

People in other cities wanted to start houses like Hull House. Janie Porter Barrett was one of these people. In 1890 she started the Locust Street Social Settlement House in Virginia. At this house Barrett helped African American women learn better ways to care for their homes and children.

Lillian Wald was a nurse who started a house like Hull House. Her parents were Jewish immigrants. In 1895 Wald started the Henry Street Settlement House. This house was in a crowded neighborhood in New York City. The Henry Street Settlement House had a **kindergarten**, clubs, English classes, and a library.

Lillian Wald also helped sick people. She thought nurses should visit sick people at home if they were too poor or too sick to go to a hospital. So she started a visiting nurse program in New York City. Many nurses began helping sick people at home. Lillian Wald also thought there should be

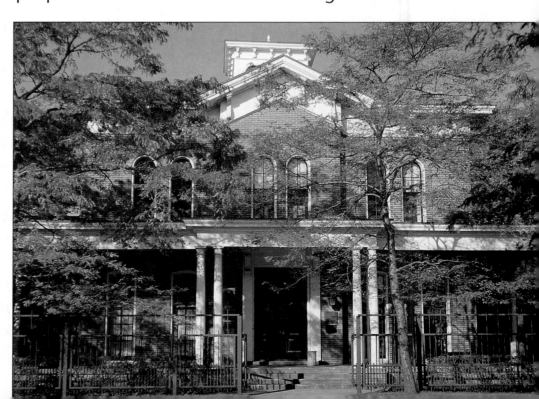

Lillian Wald started a kindergarten at the Henry Street Settlement House.

Dr. Alice Hamilton

nurses in schools to help sick children. Other people liked Wald's idea. Soon there were nurses in New York's schools.

Alice Hamilton was a doctor who helped factory workers. At first Dr. Hamilton lived and worked at Hull House. She took care of sick children there. She wanted to help factory workers. The air in many factories was dirty. Dr. Hamilton said that workers became sick from breathing dirty air.

Alice Hamilton visited paint factories. Paint had **lead** in it. She proved that many workers in paint factories had **lead poisoning**. Lead poisoning made workers very weak. Many of these workers died. Dr. Hamilton had a big job to do. She taught factory owners how to make their factories safer. She taught them how to keep the factory air clean.

Alice Hamilton also worked to get new laws for factory workers. One new law said that workers should be paid if they got hurt while working and could not work afterward. Another law said that factories must be clean and safe. Today our factories are cleaner and safer because of Dr. Hamilton's work.

Jane Addams, Janie Porter Barrett, Lillian Wald, Alice Hamilton, and other women proved that women could make important changes in America.

Read and Remember

Who Am I? Read each sentence. Then look in the box for the person who might have said it. Write on your paper the name of the person you choose.

Alice Hamilton   Jane Addams   Janie Porter Barrett   Lillian Wald

---

1. "I started the Locust Street Social Settlement House to help African American women in Virginia."

2. "I started the Henry Street Settlement House and the visiting nurse program in New York City."

3. "I started Hull House and worked for new laws to help immigrants, workers, and children."

4. "I worked to stop lead poisoning in paint factories and to get laws passed for safer factories."

Think and Apply

Fact or Opinion Read each sentence below. Write **F** on your paper for each sentence that tells a fact. Write **O** for each sentence that tells an opinion. You should find three opinions.

1. Jane Addams started a playground, clubs, and a summer camp at Hull House.

2. The Locust Street Social Settlement House had better workers than Hull House.

3. Lillian Wald started a program for nurses to help sick children in New York's schools.

4. It was silly to have nurses work in schools.

5. The Henry Street Settlement House had clubs, a kindergarten, and English classes.

6. Alice Hamilton should not have left Hull House.

7. Dr. Hamilton taught factory owners how to make their factories safer.

Riddle Puzzle

Choose a word in blue print to finish each sentence. Write the correct answers on your paper.

read   crowded   American
first   taught   immigrants
other   English   Settlement

1. Jane Addams started the _____ playground in Chicago.

2. People learned to be _____ citizens at Hull House.

3. The Henry Street Settlement House was in a _____ neighborhood.

4. Janie Porter Barrett _____ African American women better ways to care for their homes and children.

5. Jane Addams bought Hull House with her own money and with money from _____ people.

6. At settlement houses immigrants could learn to _____ , write, and speak English.

7. Jane Addams helped _____ become American citizens.

8. Immigrants learned how to speak _____ at Hull House.

9. Lillian Wald started a kindergarten at Henry Street _____ House.

Now look at your answers. Circle the first letter of each answer you wrote on your paper.

The letters you circled should spell a word. The word answers the riddle.

RIDDLE: What places became safer for workers because of Dr. Hamilton's work?

Write the answer to the riddle on your paper.

CHAPTER 29

AMERICANS LEARN TO FLY

Think About As You Read

1. Why did the Wright brothers become famous?
2. What made Charles Lindbergh famous in 1927?
3. What did Amelia Earhart do that made her famous?

NEW WORDS

motorized
gasoline engine
pilot
flight

PEOPLE & PLACES

Orville Wright
Wilbur Wright
Kitty Hawk, North Carolina
Charles Lindbergh
Paris
Amelia Earhart
Fred Noonan

The Wright brothers' airplane first flew at Kitty Hawk, North Carolina.

For hundreds of years, people all over the world wanted to travel through the sky. Until 1903 no one knew how to make an airplane that could fly well. Americans became leaders in inventing and flying airplanes.

Orville Wright and Wilbur Wright were brothers. They were called the Wright brothers. When they finished high school, the Wright brothers opened a bicycle store.

The Wright brothers wanted to make a machine that a person could fly. No one had ever before made a **motorized** airplane that a person could fly. The two brothers worked on their machine for several years. They made a **gasoline engine** for their airplane. They made

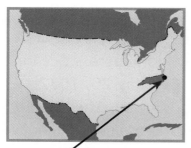

Kitty Hawk, North Carolina

Orville and Wilbur Wright

Charles Lindbergh's plane

Charles Lindbergh was the first person to fly alone across the Atlantic Ocean.

many kinds of wings. At last they thought their airplane had the right kind of wings. The Wright brothers were ready to fly.

Orville and Wilbur Wright took their airplane to Kitty Hawk, North Carolina. They called their plane the *Flyer*. The brothers decided to fly their airplane on December 17, 1903. On that day the *Flyer* flew through the sky. The plane worked. The Wright brothers had made the world's first motorized airplane.

The Wright brothers and other people tried to build better airplanes. The first planes could not stay in the air for more than a few minutes. Planes were soon built that could fly for many hours.

Could people fly across the Atlantic Ocean in an airplane? Many people said it was impossible to fly across the Atlantic Ocean. A **pilot** named Charles Lindbergh decided to fly alone across the Atlantic Ocean. He had a new plane built for the **flight** across the ocean. He wanted to fly alone from New York to Paris, the capital city of France.

On May 20, 1927, Charles Lindbergh's plane left New York. Lindbergh flew all day and all night. He was cold and tired in the plane. But he could not go to sleep. During the night Lindbergh could not see where he was flying.

Lindbergh and
Earhart's flights

Amelia Earhart and
Fred Noonan

He continued to move through the sky. After 33 hours Lindbergh landed safely in Paris. Charles Lindbergh became a hero. He proved that pilots could fly alone across oceans.

Women also wanted to be pilots. On May 20, 1932, Amelia Earhart flew across the Atlantic Ocean. She landed safely in Ireland. Earhart became the first woman to fly alone across the Atlantic Ocean. She returned to the United States. Earhart was famous. She taught other people how to be airplane pilots.

In 1937 Amelia Earhart decided to fly around the world. She asked Fred Noonan, another pilot, to fly with her. First they flew over South America, Africa, and India. Then they flew over the Pacific Ocean. Earhart and Noonan never returned to the United States. Their plane was lost over the Pacific Ocean. No one knows what happened to Amelia Earhart and Fred Noonan. Many people believe they died in the Pacific Ocean.

In the 1800s it took Americans many months to travel in wagons from New York to California. Today we can fly from New York to California in less than six hours. Airplanes have greatly improved since the Wright brothers' first flight at Kitty Hawk.

Amelia Earhart was the first woman to fly alone across the Atlantic Ocean.

Read and Remember

True or False   Write **T** on your paper for each sentence that is true. Write **F** for each sentence that is false.

1. Charles Lindbergh built the first motorized airplane.

2. The Wright brothers made a gasoline engine and wings for their plane.

3. The Wright brothers called their plane the *Flyer*.

4. The *Flyer* could stay in the air for many hours.

5. Charles Lindbergh flew from New York to Paris in 6 hours.

6. Charles Lindbergh proved that pilots could fly alone across oceans.

7. Amelia Earhart flew across the Atlantic Ocean to Ireland.

8. Amelia Earhart wanted to fly around the world.

9. Amelia Earhart and Fred Noonan's plane was lost over the Gulf of Mexico.

Write the Answer   Write a sentence on your paper to answer each question.

1. Where did the Wright brothers fly their plane?

2. What two things did the Wright brothers make for their plane?

3. How many hours did Charles Lindbergh's trip to Paris take?

4. Why did Charles Lindbergh become a hero?

5. What country did Amelia Earhart fly to in 1932?

6. Why did Amelia Earhart become famous?

7. How long does it take to fly from New York to California today?

Journal Writing

Write a paragraph about what either the Wright brothers, Charles Lindbergh, or Amelia Earhart did. Then tell why it was important.

Think and Apply

Sequencing Events   Number your paper from 1 to 5. Write the sentences to show the correct order.

Amelia Earhart flew alone across the Atlantic Ocean in 1932.

In 1903 the Wright brothers flew the first motorized airplane.

The Wright brothers spent many years inventing an airplane.

In 1937 Amelia Earhart and Fred Noonan were lost in a plane flying over the Pacific Ocean.

Charles Lindbergh flew alone from New York to Paris in 1927.

Skill Builder

Reading a Chart   This chart gives information about American leaders in airplane travel. Read the chart.

American Leaders in Airplane Travel				
Leader	Leader's Work	Date	What Did the Person Do?	What Did the Person Prove?
Orville and Wilbur Wright	inventors	1903	Invented and flew the first motorized airplane at Kitty Hawk	Proved motorized planes could fly
Charles Lindbergh	pilot	1927	First man to fly alone across the Atlantic Ocean	Proved people could fly alone across oceans
Amelia Earhart	pilot	1932	First woman to fly alone across the Atlantic Ocean	Proved women could be good pilots

Write a sentence on your paper to answer each question.

1. When did the Wright brothers invent their airplane?

2. When did Charles Lindbergh fly across the Atlantic Ocean?

3. What did Charles Lindbergh prove?

4. Who was the first woman to fly alone across the Atlantic Ocean?

Finish the Story   Number your paper from 1 to 13. Use the words in the first box to finish the first paragraph. Use the words in the second box to finish the second paragraph. Write the words you choose on your paper.

Paragraph 1
reporter
big business
steel
immigrants
Italy
labor unions
oil

Paragraph 2
Hull House
Amelia Earhart
Lillian Wald
Atlantic
lead
Wright

From the 1880s to 1920, millions of immigrants came to America from Russia, Poland, and __(1)__ . Jacob Riis was a newspaper __(2)__ . He wanted to help poor __(3)__ . Andrew Carnegie was an immigrant from Scotland. By 1899 Carnegie owned most of the __(4)__ mills in the United States. John D. Rockefeller helped __(5)__ grow bigger. His company owned many __(6)__ refineries. Most factory workers did not earn much money. Factory workers started __(7)__ to get better salaries.

In 1889 Jane Addams started __(8)__ to help people in Chicago. __(9)__ started the Henry Street Settlement House. Dr. Alice Hamilton worked to make factory workers safe from __(10)__ poisoning. In 1903 the __(11)__ brothers became the first men to fly a motorized plane. Charles Lindbergh flew alone across the __(12)__ Ocean in 1927. Later, __(13)__ became the first woman to fly alone across the Atlantic Ocean.

UNIT 7

PROBLEMS AT HOME AND ACROSS THE SEA

What was it like to live during World War II? If you were in the United States, you would read about battles being fought. American soldiers were fighting all over the world. There were battles on islands in the Pacific Ocean. There were battles in Europe and in the deserts of Africa.

The United States had to solve big problems between 1914 and 1945. One problem was World War I. Then in 1929 the Great Depression began. Millions of people became very poor. Finally World War II began. Thousands of Americans would die during this long terrible war.

What would you have done if you had lived in America between 1914 and 1945? Would you work for an amendment that would allow women to vote? Would you stand on a bread line to get food for your family during the Great Depression? Would you join the army and fight in World War II? As you read Unit 7, think about the many problems Americans tried to solve between 1914 and 1945.

1914
World War I begins.

1918
World War I ends.

1920
An amendment is added to the Constitution that allows women to vote.

1929
The stock market crashes. The Great Depression begins.

1939
World War II begins.

1941
Japan attacks the United States at Pearl Harbor. The United States begins to fight in World War II.

1910

1917
The United States begins to fight in World War I.

1920

1930

1933
Adolf Hitler becomes the leader of Germany.

1940

1945
World War II ends.

1950

30 WORLD WAR I

Think About As You Read

1. What were the causes of World War I?
2. How did Americans help the Allies during the war?
3. Which side won World War I?

NEW WORDS

building armies
Allies
Central Powers
neutral
sunk
Liberty Bonds

PEOPLE & PLACES

Serbia
Austria-Hungary
Woodrow Wilson
German Americans

Americans joined the Allies during World War I.

In 1914 a war began in Europe. Millions of soldiers from many countries fought in this war. This war was called the Great War then. It is now known as World War I. How did this war begin?

Many countries in Europe were **building armies**. Each country wanted to have the strongest army with the most soldiers. Imperialism became important, too. You read about imperialism in Chapter 23. Countries like Germany and Great Britain wanted to win control over other countries.

There were two groups of countries in Europe. One group was called the **Allies**. Great Britain, France, Russia, Serbia, and some other countries were the Allies. These countries promised to help each other during a war.

The other group of countries was called the **Central Powers**. Germany, Austria-Hungary, and some other countries were part of the Central Powers. The Central Powers promised to help each other during a war.

Some countries did not want to help the Allies or the Central Powers. These countries were **neutral**. During the war the neutral countries did not fight for the Allies or for the Central Powers. The map below shows the Allies, Central Powers, and the neutral countries during World War I.

One day in 1914, the prince of Austria-Hungary was shot and killed by a person from Serbia. The people of Austria-Hungary were very angry. Their army attacked Serbia. Serbia was one of the Allies. Now the Allies had to keep their promise to help Serbia fight. All the Central Powers had to keep their promise to help Austria-Hungary fight. World War I had begun.

The United States did not want to fight in World War I. Most Americans did not want to fight in a war that was across the Atlantic Ocean. The United States had become good friends with Great Britain and France. Great Britain and France

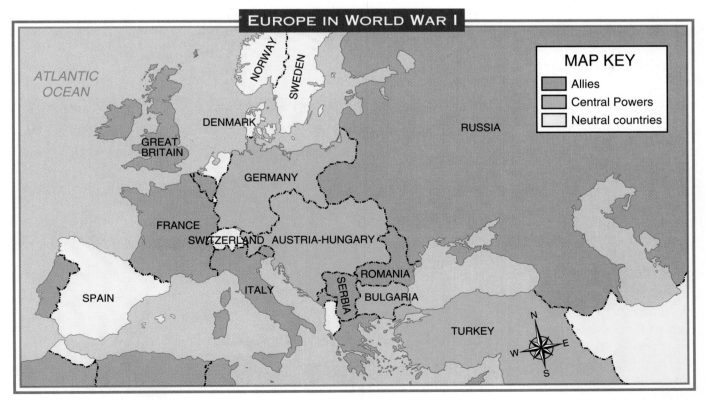

EUROPE IN WORLD WAR I

MAP KEY
- Allies
- Central Powers
- Neutral countries

ATLANTIC OCEAN

NORWAY

SWEDEN

DENMARK

RUSSIA

GREAT BRITAIN

GERMANY

FRANCE

SWITZERLAND   AUSTRIA-HUNGARY

SPAIN

ITALY

SERBIA

ROMANIA

BULGARIA

TURKEY

Woodrow Wilson

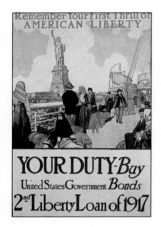

A poster asking people to buy Liberty Bonds

African Americans were among the two million soldiers from the United States who fought in World War I.

were part of the Allies. The United States did not want to fight, but most Americans wanted the Allies to win. The Allies did not have enough food or weapons. The United States sent ships filled with food and weapons to the Allies.

Germany did not want the United States to help the Allies. In 1917 German ships attacked American ships. Many American ships were **sunk**. Many Americans were killed. The United States was angry that Germans killed Americans at sea. Woodrow Wilson was the President of the United States. He decided that it was time to fight. He wanted Americans to help the Allies win the war. Congress voted to fight against Germany. In 1917 the United States began to fight in World War I.

During the war many Americans began to hate the people and the language of Germany. There were millions of German Americans who were good American citizens. But many other people were unfair to German Americans during World War I. Many German Americans lost their jobs. Many high schools stopped teaching the German language.

Americans in every part of the country wanted to help during the war. The government did not have enough money to pay for the war. President Wilson asked Americans to buy **Liberty Bonds**. Millions of people bought these bonds. Bond money helped pay for the war.

American soldiers marched through Paris after helping the Allies save the city.

World War I poster

Americans also knew that the Allies needed a lot more food. So Americans ate less wheat, meat, and sugar. They sent wheat, meat, and sugar to the Allies.

About two million American soldiers went to fight in Europe. They helped the Allies win the war. The German soldiers were fighting in France. They tried to capture Paris. They came closer and closer to Paris. The Allies could not stop the German soldiers by themselves. The Americans helped the Allies. Together they pushed the German army away from Paris. Paris was saved.

The Allies and the Americans continued to fight against the German army. The German army became weaker and weaker. Finally, Germany and the Central Powers surrendered. World War I ended on November 11, 1918. The Allies had won. The American soldiers crossed the Atlantic Ocean and went home to America.

Americans were happy that the world had peace. They were also sad because more than 100,000 American soldiers had been killed during the war. President Wilson wanted the world to have peace for a long time. He went to France to help write a peace treaty. He wanted Americans to work for world peace.

Would there be another terrible war? Would American soldiers fight for the Allies again? Chapter 33 will give you the answers.

Read and Remember

Finish the Story   Use the words in blue print to finish the story. Write the words you choose on your paper.

German Americans	1917	surrendered	Allies
Woodrow Wilson	Paris	American	1914

World War I began in ___(1)___ . During the war ___(2)___ was the President of the United States. Americans wanted the ___(3)___ to win. Many people were unfair to ___(4)___ during the war. German ships sank ___(5)___ ships that were sailing to the Allies. The United States went to war against the Central Powers in ___(6)___ . Americans fought with the Allies to save the city of ___(7)___ . In 1918 Germany and the Central Powers ___(8)___ .

Think and Apply

Finding the Main Idea   Read each group of sentences below. One of the sentences is a main idea. Two sentences support the main idea. Write on your paper the sentence that is the main idea.

1. Some nations in Europe promised to fight for each other during a war.

    Germany and Austria-Hungary were part of the Central Powers.

    Great Britain, France, Serbia, and Russia were some of the Allies.

2. World War I began after a person from Serbia killed the prince of Austria-Hungary.

    Austria-Hungary and the Central Powers went to war against Serbia.

    The Allies began to fight for Serbia.

3. Switzerland was a neutral country.

    Some countries did not fight for the Allies or the Central Powers.

    Sweden and Norway were neutral and did not fight.

4. The United States sent food to the Allies.

   The United States sent weapons to the Allies.

   The United States wanted to help the Allies.

5. German ships attacked many American ships.

   America entered World War I to help the Allies win against Germany and the Central Powers.

   The United States was angry that Germans killed Americans.

6. The United States helped the Allies win World War I.

   The Allies needed help to push the German army away from Paris.

   The United States sent wheat, meat, and sugar to the Allies.

Skill Builder

Reading a Historical Map The **historical map** on page 191 shows Europe during World War I. Study the map and the map key. Write a sentence on your paper to answer each question.

1. Name four countries on the map that were Allies.

2. Name three countries on the map that were Central Powers.

3. What country is north of Serbia?

4. Name four neutral countries.

5. Which of the Allies was the largest country?

Journal Writing

Many Americans did not like Germany and the German language during World War I. Many German Americans who were good American citizens lost their jobs. Write four to five sentences in your journal that tell why it was unfair for German Americans to lose their jobs.

CHAPTER 31

WOMEN WIN THE RIGHT TO VOTE

Think About As You Read

1. How did American women help the United States during World War I?
2. What were the goals of Susan B. Anthony?
3. How did women get the right to vote?

NEW WORDS

tanks
spend her life
women's rights
supervisors

PEOPLE & PLACES

Susan B. Anthony
Elizabeth Cady Stanton

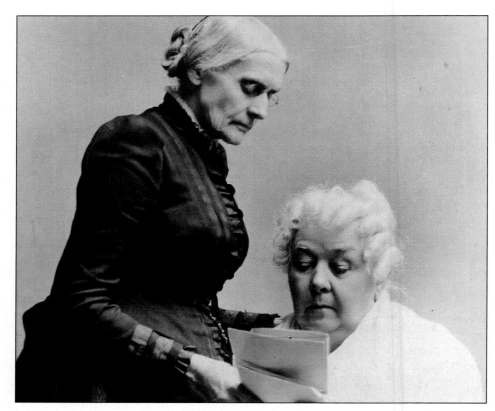

Susan B. Anthony and Elizabeth Cady Stanton worked together to help women get the right to vote.

During World War I, American men helped the Allies fight the war in Europe. At the same time, American women worked for their country at home. Women did the jobs that men usually did because the men were fighting in the war. Women worked in factories to make guns. They built warships and **tanks**. Women sold Liberty Bonds. Women worked hard to help the United States win the war.

Many women were angry. They were angry because in most states women were not allowed to vote. Women helped the United States win the war, but they could not vote for their country's leaders. The United States Constitution needed a new amendment that would give women the right to vote.

Susan B. Anthony

Elizabeth Cady
Stanton

Many years before World War I, Susan B. Anthony wanted women to have the right to vote. Anthony was born in 1820. She became a teacher. At that time male teachers were paid better salaries than female teachers. Susan B. Anthony said it was not fair that women were paid less than men for doing the same work.

Susan B. Anthony felt that women were not treated fairly in other ways. Married women often could not own their own property. Many women wanted to study in colleges with men. Men did not allow women to study in most colleges. Susan B. Anthony stopped teaching. She decided to **spend her life** working for **women's rights**.

Elizabeth Cady Stanton was another woman who wanted women to have equal rights. Elizabeth Cady Stanton and Susan B. Anthony were good friends. Together they worked for a new amendment that would allow women to vote. Many senators and representatives in Congress did not want this new amendment.

Anthony and Stanton traveled throughout the United States. They made many speeches. They told men and women that the Constitution needed an amendment that

During World War I, women worked in factories making airplanes.

Women marched in parades to show that they wanted the right to vote.

would allow women to vote. The two women also started a newspaper. Their newspaper stories said that women should have the same rights as men.

Anthony and Stanton worked together for many years. Some laws were changed because of their work. Women were allowed to own property. Women were allowed to study in many colleges. Elizabeth Cady Stanton died in 1902. Susan B. Anthony died in 1906. When they died the Constitution still did not allow women to vote.

Other women continued to work for an amendment that would allow women to vote. In 1920 the Nineteenth Amendment was added to the Constitution. It said that women could vote. The amendment is often called the Susan B. Anthony Amendment. In 1920 women voted for the President of the United States for the first time.

Today many Americans feel that women still do not have the same rights that men have. Most working women do not earn as much as men. It is harder for women to get jobs as **supervisors**. Most doctors, bus drivers, and police officers are men. But today more women are doctors, bus drivers, and police officers than ever before. Now there are female senators and representatives in Congress. American men and women will continue to work for women's rights.

Women in Congress

Read and Remember

Match Up Finish each sentence in Group A with words from Group B. Write the letter of the correct answer on your paper.

Group A

1. During World War I, women built warships and _____ .

2. Laws were changed to allow women to own _____ .

3. In 1920 an amendment was added to the Constitution that gave women the _____ .

4. Today many working women are paid _____ than working men.

Group B

a. less money

b. right to vote

c. tanks

d. property

Think and Apply

Understanding Different Points of View People can look in different ways at problems and events. Look at these two points of view.

Women should be allowed to study in colleges.
Women should not study in colleges.

Read each pair of sentences below. Write **For** on your paper for each sentence that is for women's rights. Write **Against** for each sentence that is against women's rights.

1. Women should be allowed to own property.

2. Women should not own property.

3. Women should not have the right to vote.

4. The Constitution needs an amendment that allows women to vote.

5. Women should be paid the same salaries as men.

6. Men should have higher salaries than women.

Journal Writing

Women have more rights now than they did in 1820. Write a paragraph in your journal that tells about the rights women have earned since 1820.

Riddle Puzzle

Choose a word in blue print to finish each sentence. Write the correct answers on your paper.

Anthony	equal	tanks
newspaper	married	male
drivers	nation	earn

1. Susan B. _____ spent her life working for women's rights.

2. Most _____ teachers earned better salaries than female teachers earned.

3. Many people wanted men and women to have _____ rights.

4. Susan B. Anthony and Elizabeth Cady Stanton wrote _____ stories about women's rights.

5. Today most doctors, police officers, and bus _____ are men.

6. _____ women often could not own property.

7. Most working women do not _____ as much as men.

8. Our _____ has passed new laws that are more fair to women.

9. During World War I, American women built _____ for the army.

Now look at your answers. Circle the first letter of each answer you wrote on your paper.

The letters you circled should spell a word. The word answers the riddle.

RIDDLE: What kind of law was added to the Constitution so that women would have the right to vote?

Write the answer to the riddle on your paper.

CHAPTER 32 THE GREAT DEPRESSION

CHAPTER 32

Think About As You Read

1. How did the Great Depression hurt Americans?
2. What were the causes of the Great Depression?
3. How did Franklin D. Roosevelt try to end the depression?

NEW WORDS

Great Depression
depression
shares of stock
stock
stock market
crashed
popular
elected
New Deal

PEOPLE & PLACES

Herbert Hoover
Franklin D. Roosevelt

Many people lost everything they owned after the stock market crash that started the Great Depression.

The year was 1930. Most Americans had little money. Many people did not have money to buy bread, even though a loaf of bread cost only five cents. Americans were living through the years of the **Great Depression**.

The Great Depression was not the nation's first **depression**. But it was the longest and hardest depression. It lasted more than ten years. It started in the United States. Then the depression spread to Europe and other countries. During those years millions of Americans lost their jobs. Many people did not have enough money to pay for food, clothes, or homes.

The Great Depression began in 1929. At that time many Americans had been buying **shares of stock**. Buying a

The stock market is where shares are bought and sold.

Many people lost their homes.

share of stock means owning a small part of a business. When the business makes money, your **stock** makes money. Then you can sell your stock and get back more money than you paid for it. Sometimes the businesses don't do well. Then the owners of the stock sell the stock for less money than they paid for it.

Americans bought stock in many businesses. They bought and sold stock on the **stock market**. Many Americans did not have enough money to buy the stock they wanted. So they borrowed money from banks to buy stocks. The banks bought stocks, too.

On October 29, 1929, the stock market **crashed**. The price of most stocks on the stock market became very, very low. On that day almost everyone wanted to sell their shares of stock. No one wanted to buy shares. Shares were sold for much less money than people had paid for them. People lost millions of dollars. They couldn't pay back the money they had borrowed from banks. So banks could not get the money people had borrowed to buy stocks. Banks lost more money because they had bought stocks, too. The money that banks lost was the money that people had saved in the bank. Suddenly, many people became very poor when the stock market crashed.

Three other problems helped cause the Great Depression. The first problem was that farmers grew more crops than they could sell after World War I. Then farmers had to sell their crops at very low prices. They sold the crops for less than they had spent to plant the crops. So many farmers did not earn enough to pay for their farms.

The second problem was that factories were making too many products. Americans could not buy all the things that were being made. Factory owners sold their products for less and less money. Many factories were forced to close. Many workers lost their jobs.

Low salaries were the third problem. Workers were not earning enough money. They could not buy the farm crops and factory products. Everything became cheaper and cheaper. Soon almost everyone was losing lots of money.

Herbert Hoover

Herbert Hoover was President of the United States when the depression started. He thought the depression would end quickly. The depression grew worse each year. Hoover was not **popular**. Americans felt he did not do enough to end the depression. In 1932 Americans **elected** a new President.

Franklin D. Roosevelt became President in 1933. Roosevelt promised a "**New Deal**" for America. He promised to try to end the depression.

People did not have money to buy food, so they were given free food at soup kitchens.

The New Deal put people back to work.

Franklin D. Roosevelt

Roosevelt and the New Deal helped America. When Roosevelt became President, 13 million workers had lost their jobs. Roosevelt wrote laws with Congress to make new jobs for Americans. The government paid people to build roads, bridges, and parks. Americans built new schools and buildings. Millions of trees were planted across the nation.

Roosevelt also helped the farmers. New laws helped the farmers borrow money to pay for their farms. Farmers were paid to grow less food. Food prices grew higher because there was less food to buy. Slowly many farmers began to earn more money.

President Roosevelt knew the United States needed strong, safe banks. Roosevelt forced all the banks to close for a bank holiday. After a few days, only safe banks were allowed to open. Americans began to put money in banks again.

Franklin D. Roosevelt was a very popular President. He was the only President to be elected four times. He was President for twelve years. Most Americans felt Roosevelt worked hard to end the depression.

The depression ended when World War II began. There were new jobs because of the war. Men became soldiers. Men and women worked in factories making guns, warships, tanks, and other things for war. The depression slowly ended. Americans would never forget the hard, hungry years of the Great Depression.

Read and Remember ⭐

True or False   Write **T** on your paper for each sentence that is true. Write **F** for each sentence that is false.

1. When you buy a share of stock, you own a small part of a business.

2. One cause of the depression was that factories were making too many products.

3. One cause of the depression was low salaries.

4. Americans loved President Hoover.

5. President Roosevelt's plan for ending the depression was the New Deal.

6. The depression ended in one year.

7. President Roosevelt was elected only once.

8. The depression ended when World War II began.

⭐ Think and Apply

Cause and Effect   Write sentences on your paper by matching each cause on the left with an effect on the right.

Cause

1. Too many people decided to sell their stocks on October 29, 1929, so _____

2. Farmers grew more crops than they could sell, so _____

3. During the depression most Americans had very little money, so _____

4. The depression grew worse when Hoover was President, so _____

Effect

a. it was hard to pay for food, clothes, and homes.

b. the stock market crashed.

c. crops were sold at very low prices.

d. Americans felt Hoover did not do enough to end the depression.

Skill Builder

Using a Map Key   President Roosevelt started the **Tennessee Valley Authority**, or **TVA**, to help end the depression. There had been many floods on the Tennessee River. The TVA built forty dams on rivers to control the floods. Thousands of people had jobs while they built the dams. The dams made electricity for many people in nearby states.

Study the map on this page. Use the **map key** to learn where dams were built and where people got electricity. Find the sentences below that tell about the TVA map. Write on your paper the sentences you find. You should find 3 sentences.

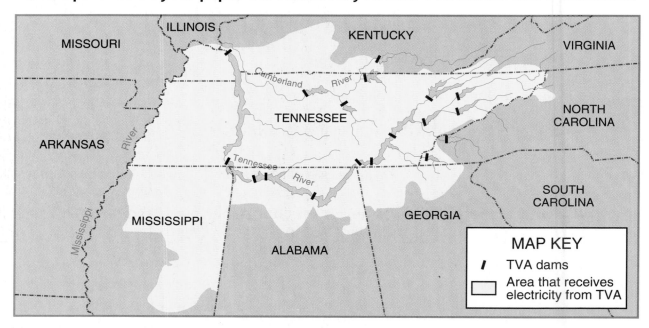

1. Florida and New York receive electricity from the TVA.

2. Tennessee, Mississippi, and Alabama receive electricity from the TVA.

3. Kentucky, Virginia, and Georgia receive electricity from the TVA.

4. The TVA has dams on the Colorado and St. Lawrence rivers.

5. The TVA has dams on the Cumberland and Tennessee rivers.

Journal Writing

Study the photograph at the bottom of page 203. Write one or two sentences that tell about the photograph. Then write two or three sentences that tell what the photograph shows about the Great Depression.

CHAPTER 33

WORLD WAR II BEGINS

Think About As You Read

1. **What happened to the Allies at the beginning of World War II?**
2. **What was the Holocaust?**
3. **What happened at Pearl Harbor in 1941?**

NEW WORDS

dictator
conquer
bombs
Axis countries
concentration camps
Holocaust
naval base
declared war

PEOPLE & PLACES

Adolf Hitler
Japan
Jews
Winston Churchill
Japanese
Pearl Harbor

Adolf Hitler was the ruler of Germany during World War II.

World War I ended in 1918. Twenty-one years later, in 1939, World War II began. What caused the war to begin? What did Americans do during World War II?

Great Britain and France punished Germany after World War I. Great Britain and France made Germany pay large amounts of money to them after the war. The Great Depression brought hard years to Germany and other countries in Europe. The German people were unhappy. They wanted a new leader to help them. In 1933 Adolf Hitler became the leader of Germany.

Adolf Hitler was a **dictator**. He had full power to rule Germany. People who spoke against Hitler were killed. Hitler said many things that the German people liked. He

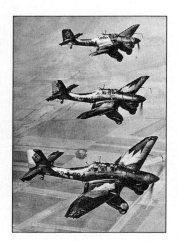

German airplanes

said he would help Germany become a strong country again. He told the Germans to fight in another war. He said that Germany would **conquer** and rule much of Europe. Many German people liked what Hitler said. They wanted Germany to be strong and powerful again. The Germans got ready for another war. They built airplanes, **bombs**, tanks, and ships.

Italy and Japan also wanted to conquer and rule other countries. Germany, Italy, and Japan were called the **Axis countries**. They promised to help each other during a war. Great Britain, France, and some smaller countries were called the Allies. Some countries were neutral countries. They did not fight for the Axis countries or for the Allies.

World War II began in September 1939. Germany attacked Poland. The armies of the Allies were not ready for war. But they sent their soldiers to help Poland. The German army was very strong. In a few weeks, Germany captured Poland. German soldiers then captured more countries in Europe.

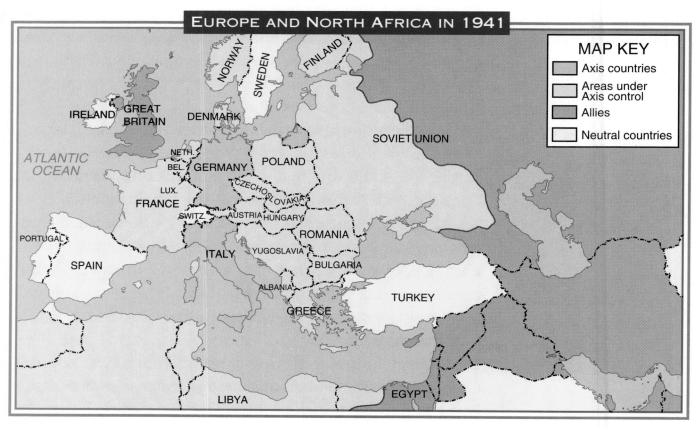

EUROPE AND NORTH AFRICA IN 1941

MAP KEY

Axis countries

Areas under Axis control

Allies

Neutral countries

NORWAY
SWEDEN
FINLAND
IRELAND
GREAT BRITAIN
DENMARK
SOVIET UNION
ATLANTIC OCEAN
NETH.
BEL.
GERMANY
POLAND
LUX.
FRANCE
CZECHOSLOVAKIA
SWITZ.
AUSTRIA
HUNGARY
PORTUGAL
ROMANIA
SPAIN
ITALY
YUGOSLAVIA
BULGARIA
ALBANIA
TURKEY
GREECE
LIBYA
EGYPT

Children were among the millions killed in the Holocaust.

Adolf Hitler

Great Britain and France tried to stop the German army. Their armies were not strong enough. Then Germany attacked France. The Germans quickly captured the city of Paris. Thousands of British and French soldiers escaped from France in small boats. They went to Great Britain. These soldiers would continue to fight against Hitler. In 1940 Germany ruled all of France.

The years 1940 and 1941 were very bad years for the Allies. Italy was trying to capture northern Africa. Japan was attacking countries in Asia. Germany had conquered many countries in Europe.

Hitler brought fear to all of Europe. People who said they did not like Hitler's government were killed in death camps. These death camps were called **concentration camps**. Hitler did not like Jewish people, or Jews. His goal was to kill all the Jewish people in Europe. German soldiers forced Jews in most conquered countries to leave their homes. They forced millions of Jews to go on special trains to concentration camps. Many Jews wanted to escape. But few governments would allow Jews to come and live in their countries. So about six million Jewish people were killed in concentration camps. This killing of millions of Jews and other people is now called the **Holocaust**. Never before had so many people been killed because of one leader.

209

Winston Churchill

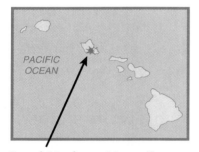

Pearl Harbor, Hawaii

Great Britain was the only country in Europe that could fight against Hitler. The British had an excellent leader. His name was Winston Churchill. He believed that people in many nations would lose their freedom if Hitler won the war. Churchill said that Great Britain would never surrender to Hitler. In 1940 Germany tried to capture Great Britain. German planes dropped thousands of bombs on British cities. The brave British pilots shot down hundreds of German planes. Great Britain remained free.

Franklin D. Roosevelt was the President of the United States. He knew that Great Britain needed help to fight against Germany. He told Americans to help the British people. American factories made guns, planes, bombs, tanks, and ships. The United States also gave loans to Great Britain. The United States sent food, weapons, and money to Great Britain.

Suddenly the United States had to fight. On December 7, 1941, the Japanese attacked American planes, ships, and soldiers at Pearl Harbor. Pearl Harbor was an American **naval base** in Hawaii. The Japanese killed more than 2,000 American soldiers. They destroyed many American ships and airplanes. Americans were very angry. The next day, the United States **declared war** on Japan. A few days later, Italy and Germany said they were at war with the United States. The United States was now at war with all the Axis countries.

The Axis countries were winning the war in 1941. In Chapter 34 we will learn how the United States helped the Allies win the war.

The Japanese destroyed many American ships at Pearl Harbor.

Read and Remember

Choose the Answer   Write the correct answers on your paper.

1. Which of these countries was one of the Allies?
   Japan   Great Britain   Italy

2. Which of these countries was one of the Axis countries?
   Great Britain   Germany   France

3. When did World War II begin?
   1918   1939   1941

4. Which country wanted to conquer and rule much of Europe?
   United States   Poland   Germany

5. Where were millions of Jewish people killed during World War II?
   in battle   in concentration camps   in schools

6. Which country was not captured by Hitler?
   Great Britain   France   Poland

7. Which country attacked the American naval base at Pearl Harbor?
   Italy   Germany   Japan

8. When did the United States begin to fight in World War II?
   1939   1941   1945

Think and Apply

Sequencing Events   Number your paper from 1 to 5. Write the sentences to show the correct order.

The United States went to war against Japan, Germany, and Italy in 1941.

Hitler became the leader of Germany.

World War II began when Germany attacked Poland in 1939.

Japan attacked the American naval base at Pearl Harbor.

Germany conquered France.

Skill Builder

Reading a Chart   This **chart** gives information about some of the countries that fought in World War II. Study the chart.

Nations at War		
Allies	**Axis Countries**	**Neutral Countries**
United States	Germany	Switzerland
China	Italy	Sweden
Great Britain	Japan	Spain
Australia		Portugal
France		Turkey
Soviet Union		Ireland
Canada		
Mexico		

Write on your paper the word or words that finish each sentence.

1. To find a country that was on the same side of the war as the United States, look under _____ .
   Allies   Axis Countries   Neutral Countries

2. The United States and _____ fought against Germany during World War II.
   Japan   Sweden   Great Britain

3. Soldiers from _____ fought against German soldiers.
   Canada   Spain   Sweden

4. Two neutral countries were _____ .
   Switzerland and Sweden   Germany and Italy   Great Britain and France

5. The largest group of nations was the _____ .
   Axis countries   Allies   neutral countries

6. Spain was one of the _____ .
   Axis countries   Allies   neutral countries

THE END OF WORLD WAR II

Think About As You Read

1. How did American life change during World War II?
2. How did General Eisenhower help the Allies win in Europe?
3. Why did the United States drop atomic bombs on Japan?

NEW WORDS

Allied soldiers
rationed
bullets
invaded
atomic bomb

PEOPLE & PLACES

Japanese Americans
General Dwight D. Eisenhower
Italians
General Douglas MacArthur
Harry S. Truman
Hiroshima
Nagasaki

American soldiers helped the Allies win World War II.

The Axis countries were fighting to conquer many countries during World War II. In December 1941 the United States began to fight in the war. Millions of American soldiers would help the Allies win.

Life in America changed in many ways. Millions of people began to work in factories making weapons for the war. Most of the nation's men were fighting in the war. So many women worked in factories to make the ships, airplanes, guns, tanks, and clothing that the soldiers needed. Because there were so many new jobs, the war helped end the Great Depression.

Woman working in a factory during the war

American farmers worked hard to grow extra crops for food. The United States sent food to the American and **Allied soldiers** who were fighting the war. There was not enough food for people at home to have all they wanted. Some foods were **rationed**. Families could buy only small amounts of some foods, such as meat, sugar, and flour.

The United States needed metal during the war. Metal was used to make weapons. Many people collected old metal. Old metal was used to make ships, guns, tanks, and **bullets** for the war.

The United States government was unfair to Japanese Americans during the war. Japanese Americans had always been good citizens. But after Japan bombed Pearl Harbor, many people were angry with the Japanese Americans. The government forced thousands of Japanese Americans to move to special camps. They had to live in small, ugly houses. Guards watched the people in these camps day and night. But some Japanese American men decided they wanted to help the United States win the war. They fought for America even though they were not treated fairly. They were brave soldiers. They helped America win.

General Dwight D. Eisenhower led the American army in Europe. In 1944 he became the leader of all the Allied soldiers. Soldiers from Great Britain, France, Canada, the United States, and other countries were fighting for the

Japanese Americans were forced to leave their homes to move to special camps.

Thousands of Allied soldiers invaded France in June 1944.

Dwight D. Eisenhower

Allies. General Eisenhower helped all these soldiers work together to fight against the Axis countries.

General Eisenhower led the Allied soldiers to Italy. German soldiers went to Italy to help the Italians fight against the Allies. The Allies fought for many months in Italy. At last, in 1944 the Italians surrendered. Italian soldiers would not fight against the Allies again.

Adolf Hitler still ruled France and most of Europe. The Allies wanted France to be free again. In June 1944 General Eisenhower **invaded** France with thousands of Allied soldiers. The Allies fought the Germans in France. After two months the Allies captured Paris. France soon became a free nation again.

The Germans were losing the war. But Adolf Hitler would not surrender. The Allies attacked Germany. American planes dropped bombs on German cities. Much of Germany was destroyed. Finally, on May 7, 1945, the Germans surrendered to the Allies. Europe had peace again.

Thousands of Americans were fighting in Asia at the same time General Eisenhower and his soldiers were fighting in Europe. General Douglas MacArthur led the American soldiers in Asia. Japan had captured the Philippines, Guam, and other islands in the Pacific Ocean. General MacArthur said that he would help Guam and the Philippines become free again.

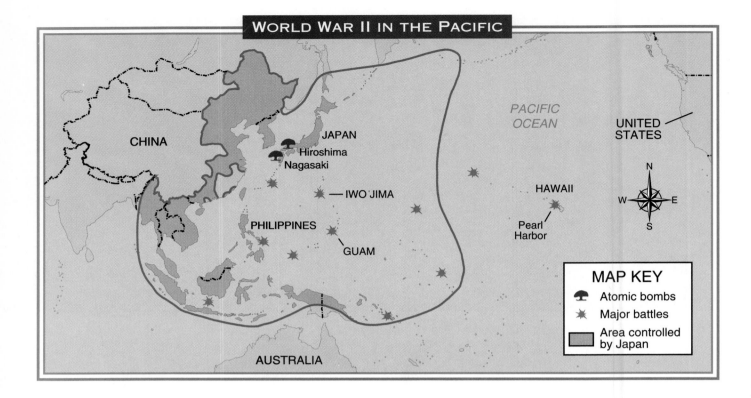

CHINA

JAPAN
Hiroshima
Nagasaki

IWO JIMA

PHILIPPINES

GUAM

AUSTRALIA

PACIFIC
OCEAN

UNITED
STATES

HAWAII

Pearl
Harbor

N
W E
S

MAP KEY
Atomic bombs
Major battles
Area controlled
by Japan

Harry S. Truman

Atomic bomb
destroying Hiroshima

General MacArthur and the American soldiers fought
the Japanese on many islands in the Pacific Ocean. Slowly
the Americans captured many islands from Japan. American
soldiers returned to Guam and the Philippines. In 1944
Guam and the Philippines became free. Then the United
States attacked Japan. The Japanese were losing the war.
But they would not surrender.

The United States had a powerful new weapon. It was
called the **atomic bomb**. Harry S. Truman was now the
President of the United States. He wanted the war to end
quickly. Every day more Americans were killed during the war.
Japan would not stop fighting. President Truman decided
to force Japan to surrender. He decided that an American
plane would drop an atomic bomb on a Japanese city.

On August 6, 1945, the United States dropped the first
atomic bomb. It destroyed most of the city of Hiroshima.
Japan would not surrender. A few days later, Americans
dropped an atomic bomb on the city of Nagasaki. These
powerful bombs killed thousands of Japanese. On August
14, 1945, Japanese leaders surrendered to the Allies. There
was peace in Asia. World War II was over. Americans were
glad that a terrible war had ended.

Read and Remember ★

Finish Up Choose a word or words in blue print to finish each sentence.
Write the correct answers on your paper.

| Truman | World War II | rationed | tanks |
| MacArthur | Eisenhower | surrendered | unfair |

1. Foods such as sugar, flour, and meat were _____ during World War II because there was not enough for everyone in the United States.

2. Women worked in factories to make guns, _____ , ships, and planes.

3. The United States government was _____ to Japanese Americans during the war.

4. In June 1944 General _____ invaded France with thousands of Allied soldiers.

5. The Germans _____ on May 7, 1945.

6. General _____ helped Guam and the Philippines become free from Japan in 1944.

7. Harry _____ was President at the end of World War II.

8. On August 14, 1945, _____ ended.

True or False Write **T** on your paper for each sentence that is true. Write **F** for each sentence that is false.

1. World War II helped end the Great Depression.

2. American farmers grew extra crops during World War II.

3. Americans collected old metal to make guns and tanks.

4. The Allies fought in Italy for one day.

5. Japan was the first nation to surrender.

6. American soldiers fought in Europe and Asia during World War II.

7. Harry S. Truman wanted the war to end quickly.

8. The United States dropped two atomic bombs on Germany.

Think and Apply

Drawing Conclusions   Read each pair of sentences. Then look in the box for the conclusion you can make. Write the letter of the conclusion on your paper.

1. During the war most American men were in the army.
   They could not work in the factories at home.

2. Japanese Americans were forced to move to special camps.
   Guards watched the people in the camps all the time.

3. The Allies attacked Germany.
   Much of Germany was destroyed.

4. The United States dropped the first atomic bomb on a city in Japan.
   Japan still would not surrender.

> a. The United States dropped a second atomic bomb on Japan.
> b. The United States government was unfair to Japanese Americans.
> c. Many women worked in factories in the United States.
> d. The Germans surrendered.

Journal Writing

American soldiers fought against the Axis countries in both Europe and the Pacific Ocean. At home in the United States, many Americans worked hard to help win World War II. Write a paragraph that tells what people did at home in the United States to help win World War II. Name at least three things.

Skill Builder

Reading a Historical Map   The **historical map** on page 216 shows Asia and the Pacific Ocean during World War II. Study the map and the map key. Write a sentence on your paper to answer each question.

1. Name the large country that was partly controlled by Japan during World War II.

2. Name two places in the Pacific Ocean where major battles occurred.

3. Name two Japanese cities that were destroyed by atomic bombs.

Chart Review The chart on this page shows important events from 1914 to 1945. Study the chart. Then use the words in blue print to finish the story. Write the words you choose on your paper.

amendment	1918	Japan
Central Powers	1939	stock market
Depression	vote	

World War I began in 1914 and ended in ___(1)___ . During World War I, the United States, Great Britain, and France were the Allies. The Allies won against the ___(2)___ .

In 1920 an ___(3)___ was added to the Constitution. It gave women in every state the right to ___(4)___ . The ___(5)___ crashed in 1929. Millions of people lost their jobs during the Great ___(6)___ .

World War II began in ___(7)___ . In 1941 Japan attacked Pearl Harbor. Then the United States began to fight in World War II. In 1945 Germany, Italy, and ___(8)___ surrendered.

Important Events from 1914 to 1945		
Event	**Dates**	**What Happened?**
World War I	1914–1918	The Allies and Central Powers fought. The Allies won.
Amendment Added to the Constitution	1920	Women in every state were allowed to vote.
Great Depression	1929–1939	The stock market crashed. Millions of people lost their jobs.
World War II	1939–1945	The United States and the Allies fought against Germany, Italy, and Japan. The Allies won.

UNIT 8

OUR CHANGING NATION

What was it like to be in the United States in August 1963? You could have been one of the 200,000 people who went to march in Washington, D.C. On that day you could hear Martin Luther King, Jr., tell about his dream of a country where everyone was treated fairly. Thousands of people wanted to change laws that were unfair.

The United States did change after World War II. The United States and the Soviet Union became enemies. Martin Luther King, Jr., worked to change laws that were unfair to African Americans. Americans learned to travel in space. The first union to help migrant farm workers was started. Thousands of Americans fought and died in the Vietnam War.

What would you have done if you had lived after World War II? Would you have marched with Martin Luther King, Jr., to change unfair laws? Would you have worked with other people to send rockets into space? As you read Unit 8, think about the many ways the United States changed after World War II.

1945
The United Nations begins.

1950
North Korea invades South Korea.

1961
The Soviet Union builds the Berlin Wall.

1962
The Soviet Union sends missiles to Cuba.

1969
Apollo 11 goes to the moon.

1970
César Chávez wins the first contract for migrant farm workers.

1989
The Berlin Wall is torn down.

1940

1950

1960

1970

1980

1990

1953
The Korean War ends.

1963
Martin Luther King, Jr., leads the March on Washington.

1965
American soldiers start fighting in Vietnam.

1975
South Vietnam surrenders to North Vietnam.

35 THE COLD WAR

The Berlin Wall stopped the people of Communist East Berlin from going to West Berlin.

The United States and the Soviet Union fought against Germany at the end of World War II. After the war the United States and the Soviet Union became enemies. They began to fight against each other in a new kind of war. This new war was called the **Cold War**. The two countries did not fight with guns. Instead each country tried to get other nations to join its side.

The Cold War began because the United States and the Soviet Union had different kinds of governments. The government of the United States is a **democracy**. In a democracy people vote for their leaders. The people have a lot of freedom. The Soviet Union had a **Communist**

Leaders from countries around the world meet in the United Nations building to work for world peace.

The United Nations building

The United Nations flag

government. In a Communist country, the government owns most stores and businesses. The people have little freedom. During the Cold War, a dictator ruled the Soviet Union. The Soviet Union's goal was to start Communist governments in other countries.

The United States had two goals after World War II. America's first goal was to start an **organization** that would work for world peace. The second goal was to stop the **spread of communism** to other countries. How did America meet these goals?

To work for world peace, Americans helped start the **United Nations**. This organization tries to help countries solve problems without fighting. The United Nations building is in New York City.

The United States worked in two ways to stop the spread of communism. First, the United States rebuilt cities and farms in Western Europe and Japan that were destroyed during the war. These countries did not need help from the Soviet Union. So they did not start Communist governments. They became strong democracies. Second, Americans helped start **NATO**. NATO is the North Atlantic Treaty Organization. The United States, Canada, and many nations in Western Europe belong to NATO. The armies of NATO nations will join together to fight an enemy during a war. The Soviet Union did not want to fight against NATO. So it did not spread communism to Western Europe.

The Cold War began in Eastern Europe. The Soviet army fought in Eastern Europe at the end of World War II. When the war ended, the Soviet army forced the nations of Eastern Europe to have Communist governments.

The Cold War was fought in Germany, too. After World War II ended, Germany became two nations. The two nations were called West Germany and East Germany. West Germany became a democracy. East Germany became a Communist country. Soviet leaders told the East German government what to do.

Berlin, the capital city of Germany, was in East Germany. The city of Berlin was also divided after the war. West Berlin became a democracy. East Berlin was a Communist city.

People had a better life in West Germany. They earned more money. They had more freedom, too. So thousands of people escaped from East Germany by going to West Berlin. From West Berlin they could move to West Germany.

The Soviet Union tried different ways to stop people from leaving East Berlin. In 1961 the Soviets built a wall to separate East Berlin and West Berlin. Soldiers in East Berlin stood next to the wall and stopped people who tried to leave. The United States was very angry about the Berlin Wall. But the Soviet Union would not remove the wall. The Berlin Wall was not torn down until 1989.

A divided Berlin

The Soviet army forced nations of Eastern Europe to have Communist governments.

Many American soldiers fought for the United Nations in Korea.

Korea

The Cold War became a real war in Korea. Korea was a nation in eastern Asia. After World War II, Korea was divided into two countries. North Korea became a Communist country. South Korea was not a Communist country. In 1950 North Korean soldiers invaded South Korea. They wanted all of Korea to be one Communist country.

The United Nations sent soldiers to South Korea. Many of the soldiers were Americans. They fought there for three years. The Communists were forced to return to North Korea. The fighting ended in 1953. North Korea and South Korea are two separate countries today.

The Cold War almost became a real war in Cuba, too. Cuba is an island country near Florida. Communists have ruled Cuba since 1959.

In 1962 the Soviet Union gave Cuba dangerous weapons called **missiles**. Cuba could have used those missiles to destroy American cities. John F. Kennedy was President of the United States. He told the Soviet Union to remove the missiles. He said Americans would fight to remove the missiles. After a few days, the Soviets removed the missiles.

The Cold War lasted almost forty years. During that time Americans had real fear that the Cold War might become another world war. In Chapter 42 you will learn how the Cold War ended.

Read and Remember

Match Up   Finish each sentence in Group A with words from Group B. Write the letter of the correct answer on your paper.

Group A

1. In a democracy people _____ .

2. In a Communist country, the government _____ .

3. The armies of NATO will protect _____ .

4. The Soviet Union built the Berlin Wall to _____ .

5. The Soviet Union sent dangerous missiles to _____ .

Group B

a. stop East Germans from escaping to West Berlin

b. Cuba

c. the nations of Western Europe

d. vote for their leaders

e. owns most businesses

Think and Apply

Understanding Different Points of View   During the Cold War, Americans and Soviets had different points of view. Read each sentence below. Write **American** on your paper for each sentence that shows the American point of view. Write **Soviet** for each sentence that shows the Soviet point of view.

1. A dictator should rule the nation.

2. The people should have a lot of freedom.

3. The people should vote for their leaders.

4. The government should own the stores and businesses.

5. Other nations should have Communist governments.

6. NATO is needed to stop the spread of communism.

7. There should not be a wall between East Berlin and West Berlin.

8. People in East Berlin must not move to West Berlin.

Journal Writing

Write a paragraph in your journal that tells how a Communist government is different from a democracy. Write at least four sentences.

Skill Builder

Reading a Historical Map The map below shows Europe in 1960. The map shows Communist nations and NATO nations. It also shows nations that did not have Communist governments and did not belong to NATO. Study the map and the map key. Write a sentence on your paper to answer each question.

1. What is the largest Communist nation?

2. Name four NATO nations.

3. Name four Communist nations.

4. Name three neutral nations.

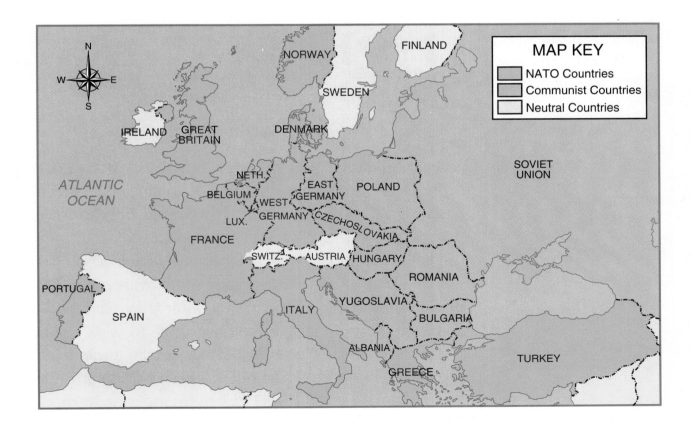

CHAPTER 36

FOUR DOCTORS CHANGE AMERICA

Think About As You Read

1. Why was the work of Dr. Salk and Dr. Sabin important?
2. How did Dr. Charles Drew help many soldiers during World War II?
3. How did Dr. Helen Taussig help sick children?

NEW WORDS

disease
polio
injection
medical school
injured
blood banks
healthy
patients
operation

PEOPLE & PLACES

Jonas Salk
Albert Sabin
Charles Drew
Helen Taussig

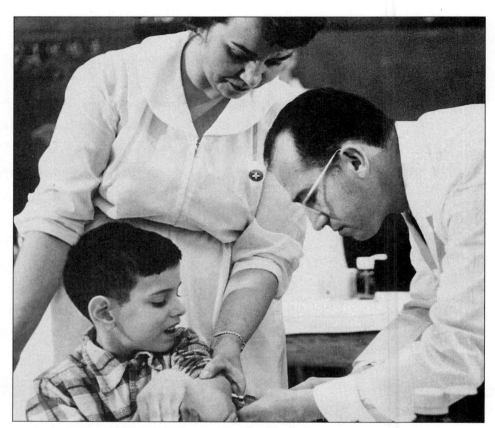

Dr. Jonas Salk made the first medicine for polio.

In this chapter you will learn how four doctors changed America. Two of these doctors are Jonas Salk and Albert Sabin. Dr. Salk and Dr. Sabin discovered how to make wonderful new medicines. People who took their new medicines would not get a terrible **disease**. The disease is called **polio**. Sometimes people die from polio. Often, people's legs become very weak after they have had polio. Sometimes these people are never able to walk again.

Jonas Salk was the first doctor to make a medicine for polio. His parents had been Jewish immigrants. Jonas Salk became a doctor. In 1953 he made a polio medicine. Doctors gave this medicine by **injection**. People who had Dr. Salk's polio injections would not get polio.

Albert Sabin also made a medicine for polio. Albert Sabin was a Jewish immigrant from Poland. In America, Dr. Sabin studied about polio for 30 years. At last, in 1960, he found out how to make a polio medicine. Dr. Sabin put his polio medicine in a sweet liquid. People who swallowed a few drops of this liquid would not get polio. Today, all over the world, doctors give Dr. Sabin's polio medicine to young children. Some doctors still use Dr. Salk's polio medicine.

Charles Drew was a famous African American doctor. He became a doctor in 1933. Dr. Drew taught in a **medical school**. He was also a doctor in a hospital.

Dr. Drew studied all about blood. Sometimes people lose a lot of blood when they are **injured**. People can die if they lose too much blood. Dr. Drew decided that hospitals needed **blood banks**. Doctors could keep **healthy** blood in blood banks. They could give this blood to people who needed it.

Dr. Drew showed doctors how to keep healthy blood in blood banks for many months. Then World War II began. Many soldiers were injured and needed blood. Dr. Drew taught the army how to keep healthy blood in blood banks. Thousands of soldiers were saved because of Dr. Charles Drew's work. Today, hospitals around the world have blood banks.

Dr. Albert Sabin

Dr. Charles Drew taught doctors and hospitals how to keep blood in blood banks.

Dr. Helen Taussig

Helen Taussig was one of the first heart doctors for children in America. Before Dr. Taussig could help sick children, she had to solve two problems of her own. Her first problem was a learning disability. She had to work hard to learn to read. Helen Taussig's second problem was that she lost her hearing soon after she became a doctor. Dr. Taussig could not listen to a child's heart. But she learned to use her hands to feel if a heart was beating the right way.

Dr. Taussig's **patients** were children who were very sick with heart disease. Many of these patients were born with hearts that were not the right shape. Dr. Taussig knew that most of her patients would die if their heart problems were not corrected.

In 1944 Helen Taussig and another doctor did their first heart **operation**. It was the world's first operation to correct a heart problem that a child had been born with. The operation worked! Many more sick children were brought to Helen Taussig. Her heart operation saved thousands of children. Before long, other doctors were learning to do heart operations, too.

American doctors continue to study about diseases. They are still learning to make new medicines. Doctors continue to find new ways to make life better in America.

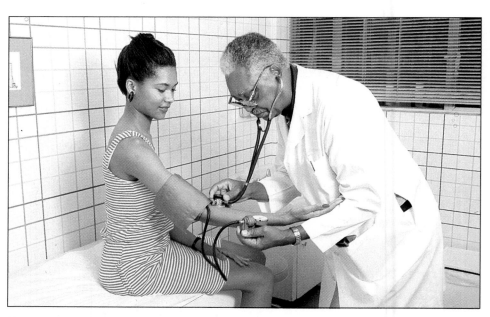

Doctors are working to keep Americans healthy.

Read and Remember

Who Am I? Read each sentence. Then look in the box for the person who might have said it. Write on your paper the name of the person you choose.

Albert Sabin	**Charles Drew**	**Helen Taussig**	**Jonas Salk**

1. "I invented the first polio medicine. I gave it to children with an injection."

2. "I invented a polio medicine that people can swallow."

3. "I taught doctors how to save blood in blood banks."

4. "I invented an operation that corrected heart problems in sick children."

Think and Apply

Fact or Opinion Read each sentence below. Write **F** on your paper for each fact below. Write **O** for each opinion. You should find five sentences that are opinions.

1. Jonas Salk made a medicine so that people would not get polio.

2. Dr. Salk should have made a medicine for a different disease.

3. Albert Sabin studied about polio for many years.

4. Doctors now give Dr. Sabin's polio medicine to young children.

5. The work of Charles Drew was more important than the work of Albert Sabin.

6. Charles Drew showed doctors how to save blood in blood banks.

7. There are too many blood banks in the United States.

8. Since Helen Taussig could not hear well, she should not have worked as a doctor.

9. Dr. Taussig invented an operation to correct heart problems in children.

10. Dr. Taussig was the best children's doctor.

Skill Builder

Reading a Chart   The chart below tells about four American doctors and their important work. Read the chart.

Four American Doctors			
Name of Doctor	**Where Did This Doctor Study?**	**Important Dates**	**Important Work**
Charles Drew	McGill University School of Medicine	1939–1945	Started many blood banks that saved soldiers in World War II
Albert Sabin	New York University School of Medicine	1960	Made polio medicine that is swallowed
Jonas Salk	New York University School of Medicine	1953	Made polio medicine that is given by injection
Helen Taussig	Johns Hopkins University School of Medicine	1944	Invented an operation to correct heart problems in children

Write a sentence on your paper to answer each question.

1. Who studied at the McGill University School of Medicine?

2. What was Charles Drew's important work?

3. Who made a polio medicine that is swallowed?

4. What did Jonas Salk make?

5. Which two doctors studied at New York University School of Medicine?

6. Where did Helen Taussig learn to be a doctor?

7. What happened in 1944?

Journal Writing

Choose one of the four doctors in Chapter 36. Write a paragraph that explains the doctor's work. Tell why you think the work was so important.

37 MARTIN LUTHER KING, JR.

Think About As You Read

1. **What laws were unfair to African Americans?**
2. **How did Martin Luther King, Jr., change the bus law in Montgomery?**
3. **How did the Civil Rights Act of 1964 help Americans?**

NEW WORDS

minister
peaceful
boycott
taxis
march
civil rights
respect
Civil Rights Act
Nobel Peace Prize

PEOPLE & PLACES

Martin Luther King, Jr.
Coretta Scott
Montgomery
Rosa Parks
Christians

Martin Luther King, Jr., worked hard to change laws that were not fair.

After the Civil War, all African Americans were free people. As time passed, laws were written that were not fair to African Americans. In this chapter you will learn how Martin Luther King, Jr., an African American leader, worked to change unfair laws.

Martin Luther King, Jr., was born on January 15, 1929, in Georgia. King's father was a **minister**. King went to college after he finished high school. He worked and studied hard. King became a minister. He met a woman named Coretta Scott. In 1953 King married Scott. They moved to Montgomery, Alabama. King became the minister of a church in Montgomery.

There were laws in the South that Martin Luther King, Jr., did not like. These laws were written after the Civil War. Some laws made it hard for African Americans to vote. Other laws kept African Americans and white people apart. There was a law that said African Americans had to sit in the back seats of buses. Another law said that African American children and white children had to go to separate schools. African Americans and white people could not use the same parks and beaches. They could not drink from the same water fountains. African Americans and white people were not allowed to eat in the same restaurants. Martin Luther King, Jr., said all of these laws were wrong. He said he would find **peaceful** ways to change the laws.

In 1955 Martin Luther King, Jr., began working to change the law that kept African Americans and white people apart on buses. One day an African American woman named Rosa Parks got on a bus in Montgomery. The bus driver told Rosa Parks to get up and let a white person have her seat. Rosa Parks refused to move. A police officer took her to jail.

Martin Luther King, Jr., learned what happened to Rosa Parks. He wanted to change Montgomery's unfair bus law. So he started a **boycott** against the city's buses. During a boycott people stop buying a product or using a service. During this boycott African Americans stopped riding the city's buses. The boycott lasted for a year. Some African

Rosa Parks went to jail because she would not give up her seat on a bus.

Martin Luther King, Jr., led the bus boycott.

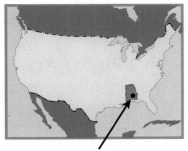

Montgomery, Alabama

Americans went to work in cars and **taxis**. Many African Americans walked to work. They walked to work even in cold, rainy weather.

Newspaper reporters wrote about the Montgomery bus story in newspapers all over America. Martin Luther King, Jr., became a famous leader. The bus boycott worked. The city's buses lost a lot of money. City leaders wanted African Americans to use the buses again. In 1956 the bus law was changed. African Americans could sit anywhere on a bus.

Martin Luther King, Jr., tried to change other laws peacefully. African Americans were not allowed to eat in some restaurants. He told African Americans to sit down and ask for food in these restaurants. King also helped African Americans in the North get better houses and jobs. He helped them go to better schools, too. Many unfair laws were changed because of King's work.

Martin Luther King, Jr., wanted Congress to pass laws that would protect the rights of all people. So he planned a large **march** in Washington, D.C. The march would show all Americans that the nation needed new **civil rights** laws.

In August 1963 Martin Luther King, Jr., led a march called the "March on Washington." More than 200,000 Americans went to the march. African Americans and

Martin Luther King, Jr., made a famous speech during the March on Washington in 1963.

Martin Luther King, Jr., with the Nobel Peace Prize

white Americans marched together. Jews and Christians also marched together.

During the march King made a famous speech. In the speech he said, "I have a dream." He said his dream was that all Americans would be treated fairly. He hoped all Americans would live together in peace. He wanted all people to **respect** each other. People in every state heard King's speech on television and radio.

The next year Congress passed the **Civil Rights Act** of 1964. The law said African Americans and white people could use the same schools, restaurants, parks, and buses. Today we do not have laws that keep African Americans and white people apart.

In 1964 Martin Luther King, Jr., was given the **Nobel Peace Prize**. This prize is given to a man or a woman who has worked hard for peace.

On April 4, 1968, Martin Luther King, Jr., was shot and killed. Martin Luther King, Jr., Day is now an American holiday in January. People in every state remember this great American. Many Americans continue to do the work started by Martin Luther King, Jr. They use peaceful ways to help all Americans live and work together.

★ Read and Remember

Finish Up Choose the word or words in blue print that finish each sentence. Write the correct answers on your paper.

North	boycott	Civil Rights
Nobel	peaceful	Washington

1. Martin Luther King, Jr., told African Americans in Montgomery, Alabama, to _____ the buses.

2. Martin Luther King, Jr., used _____ ways to change unfair laws.

3. Martin Luther King, Jr., helped African Americans in the _____ get better jobs and houses.

4. In 1963 Martin Luther King, Jr., led the March on _____ .

5. In 1964 Congress passed the _____ Act.

6. Martin Luther King, Jr., was given the _____ Peace Prize.

Skill Builder ★

Understanding a Picture Pictures can help you learn about events. The picture on page 236 shows a picture of the March on Washington. Read each pair of sentences. Choose the sentence in each pair that explains the picture. Write the sentence on your paper.

1. Only a few people listened to King's speech.

   Many people listened to King's speech.

2. Men and women went to the march.

   Only men went to the march.

3. There were African Americans and white Americans at the march.

   There were only African Americans at the march.

4. The march was held on a warm day.

   The march was held in winter.

Think and Apply

Drawing Conclusions   Read each pair of sentences. Then look in the box for the conclusion you can make. Write the letter of the conclusion on your paper.

1. Laws in the South said African Americans could not sit with white people in the front of a bus.
   Laws in the South said African American children and white children had to go to separate schools.

2. Rosa Parks was told to let a white person have her seat on the bus.
   When Rosa Parks did not move, a police officer took her to jail.

3. King told African Americans not to ride the buses in Montgomery.
   King told African Americans to ask for food in restaurants where only white people ate.

4. In 1963 more than 200,000 people marched in Washington, D.C., to try to get fairer laws passed.
   African Americans and white Americans went to the March on Washington.

5. The bus law was changed in 1956.
   In 1964 the Civil Rights Act said that African American and white children could go to school together.

---

   a. African Americans were only allowed to sit in certain places on buses.

   b. King used peaceful ways to change unfair laws.

   c. Many Americans wanted Congress to pass new civil rights laws.

   d. Laws were changed so that all Americans would be treated fairly.

   e. Laws in the South kept African Americans and white people apart.

 **Journal Writing**

Write a paragraph in your journal that tells how Martin Luther King, Jr., used peaceful ways to get laws changed.

CHAPTER 38

AMERICANS TRAVEL IN SPACE

Think About As You Read

1. What was America's goal about space before 1970?
2. How are space shuttles different from other spaceships?
3. How do satellites help the United States today?

NEW WORDS

space race
satellite
astronauts
space shuttle
pollution

PEOPLE & PLACES

Cape Kennedy
Neil Armstrong
Edwin Aldrin
Michael Collins
Hispanic American
Sidney Gutierrez

The United States is the only country that has sent people to the moon.

"Which country will be the first to send people to the moon?" Many people asked this question during the 1960s. Americans wanted to be the first to reach the moon.

In 1957 a **space race** began between the United States and the Soviet Union. The race began when the Soviet Union sent the world's first **satellite** into space. The next year Americans sent their first satellite into space.

The space race became part of the Cold War. Americans did not want the Soviets to reach the moon first. President John F. Kennedy promised that the United States would send people to the moon by 1970.

239

Neil Armstrong, Michael Collins, and Edwin Aldrin

An astronaut

The United States sent the first people to the moon in 1969. The trip to the moon started at Cape Kennedy in Florida. The *Apollo 11* spaceship left from Cape Kennedy. Three **astronauts** were inside this spaceship. Neil Armstrong, Edwin Aldrin, and Michael Collins traveled to the moon in *Apollo 11*. After four days in space, *Apollo 11* landed on the moon.

On July 20, 1969, Neil Armstrong and Edwin Aldrin became the first people to walk on the moon. After 22 hours *Apollo 11* left the moon. The three astronauts returned to Earth in *Apollo 11*. They brought back rocks from the moon to Earth.

Five more Apollo spaceships took Americans to the moon. Each trip helped Americans learn more about the moon and space travel.

The Apollo spaceships could be used only once. Each spaceship cost millions of dollars. So Americans worked at inventing a spaceship that could be used many times. They learned to make a new spaceship called the **space shuttle**. The space shuttle lands on Earth almost like an airplane. A space shuttle can be used many times.

In 1981 the first space shuttle took off from Cape Kennedy. After its flight it landed safely on Earth. Since then there have been several space shuttle trips every year.

A space shuttle takes off from Cape Kennedy, Florida.

A teacher, Christa McAuliffe, was one of the seven people who died in the *Challenger* accident.

A space shuttle landing

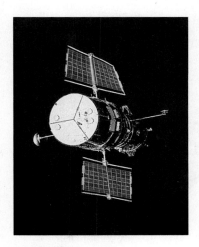

A satellite

Space travel also brought sad times to Americans. In 1986 seven Americans went inside a space shuttle called the *Challenger*. The *Challenger* went up in the sky. Suddenly it blew up into a ball of fire. All seven Americans inside the *Challenger* were killed.

After the *Challenger* accident, Americans worked at building safer space shuttles. In 1988 a new space shuttle traveled safely in space. In 1994 astronauts spent 11 days on one space shuttle flight. The leader of this space trip was a Hispanic American named Sidney Gutierrez. During this trip astronauts studied Earth in order to make better maps. The facts they learned showed where **pollution** was harming our rivers, oceans, and forests. There will be more space shuttle trips in the future.

Today hundreds of satellites are in the sky. Many satellites help the United States. Satellites help us learn about the weather. Television satellites bring us shows from countries around the world. Other satellites send news reports as soon as events happen. Satellites help us make telephone calls to faraway countries.

The United States has explored space more often than any other nation. Space satellites help millions of people have a better life here on Earth.

Read and Remember

Write the Answer   Write a sentence on your paper to answer each question.

1. Which two nations had a space race?

2. Which nation sent the first satellite into space?

3. What was the name of the first spaceship that took Americans to the moon?

4. Who were the first astronauts to walk on the moon?

5. Why did Americans invent the space shuttle?

6. What happened to the *Challenger*?

7. Which Hispanic American led an 11-day space trip in 1994?

8. What did astronauts show was harming our rivers, oceans, and forests?

9. What helps us make telephone calls to faraway countries?

Think and Apply

Categories   Read the words in each group. Decide how they are alike. Choose the best title in blue print for each group. Write the title on your paper.

Space Shuttle
First Americans on the Moon

Space Race
Satellite

1. part of the Cold War
   between the United States and
      the Soviet Union
   send people to the moon first

2. *Apollo 11*
   three astronauts
   brought back moon rocks to Earth

3. first one sent into space in 1957
   helps people make telephone calls
      to other countries
   helps people get weather reports

4. lands like an airplane
   can travel in space many days
   can be used many times

Journal Writing

When Neil Armstrong stepped onto the moon for the first time, he spoke to all the people of Earth. He said, "That's one small step for a man, one giant leap for mankind." What do you think he meant when he said that? Write a paragraph that explains what Armstrong meant.

Skill Builder

Reading a Line Graph   The line graph below compares the amount of time four Apollo spaceships spent on the moon. Study the line graph.

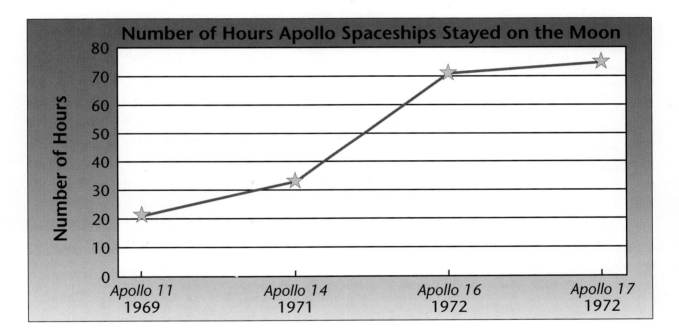

Number of Hours Apollo Spaceships Stayed on the Moon

Write the correct answer that finishes each sentence.

1. *Apollo 11* stayed on the moon for _____ hours.
   22   33   75

2. *Apollo 17* stayed on the moon for _____ hours.
   22   33   75

3. The spaceship that stayed on the moon the most time was _____ .
   Apollo 11   *Apollo 14*   *Apollo 17*

4. Each Apollo spaceship spent _____ time on the moon than the ones before.
   more   less

CHAPTER 39 CÉSAR CHÁVEZ AND THE FARM WORKERS

Think About As You Read

1. What problems do migrant farm workers have?
2. How did the United Farm Workers help the farm workers?
3. Why did César Chávez want farm owners to stop using pesticides?

NEW WORDS

migrant farm workers
United Farm Workers
contracts
grape growers
grape pickers
pesticides
Teamsters

PEOPLE & PLACES

César Chávez

César Chávez was the leader of the United Farm Workers.

César Chávez was a Mexican American leader. He was born in Arizona in 1927. His parents came to the United States from Mexico. When Chávez was ten years old, his family moved to California. There they became **migrant farm workers**. Migrant farm workers work on one farm until there is no more work to do. Then they move to another farm.

Chávez and his family moved many, many times. Every time Chávez's parents moved, Chávez had to go to a different school. César Chávez went to 65 different schools. Most children of migrant farm workers must go to many schools.

Migrant farm workers were paid very little money. Chávez decided to help the migrant farm workers.

Read and Remember

Choose the Answer   Write the correct answers on your paper.

1. What do we call farm workers who move from farm to farm?
   migrant farm workers   union workers   striking workers

2. What do we call a paper that tells workers how much they will be paid?
   a contract   a bill   a salary

3. What did the California grape pickers do to get contracts?
   worked harder   called the President   went on strike

4. César Chávez started a boycott. What did he ask people not to buy?
   cotton   grapes   corn

5. What did most farm owners give the grape pickers in 1970?
   medicine   farms   contracts

6. What did César Chávez want grape growers to stop using?
   migrant workers   pesticides   insects

Think and Apply

Sequencing Events   Number your paper from 1 to 5. Write the sentences to show the correct order.

In 1970 grape growers gave grape pickers their first contracts.

In 1965 César Chávez led a strike and a boycott against the grape growers.

César Chávez died in 1993.

César Chávez started the United Farm Workers in 1962.

As a child, César Chávez went to 65 different schools.

Journal Writing

Imagine you were a migrant farm worker in 1960. What are some things that need to be changed so you can have a better life? Write a paragraph in your journal that tells what needs to be changed.

Riddle Puzzle

Choose a word in blue print to finish each sentence. Write the correct answers on your paper.

California	against	Chávez
Teamsters	strike	respect
thousands	owners	never

1. César _____ used peaceful ways to help the migrant farm workers.

2. Most farm _____ spray pesticides on their grapes.

3. Before 1970 most migrant farm workers _____ had contracts.

4. The _____ is another union that has helped the farm workers.

5. Americans now have more _____ for migrant farm workers.

6. César Chávez started a boycott _____ the grape growers.

7. César Chávez told people not to buy _____ grapes.

8. In 1994 _____ of farm workers marched to honor César Chávez.

9. The _____ against the grape growers lasted five years.

Now look at your answers. Circle the first letter of each answer you wrote on your paper.

The letters you circled should spell a word. The word answers the riddle.

RIDDLE: What papers tell how many hours a day workers will work and what their salaries will be?

Write the answer to the riddle on your paper.

40 WAR IN VIETNAM

Helicopters were often used during the fighting in Vietnam.

Vietnam is a country in Southeast Asia. In 1954 Vietnam was divided into two countries. The northern part was called North Vietnam. The southern part was called South Vietnam. Communists ruled North Vietnam. They wanted to rule South Vietnam. The leaders of South Vietnam did not want their country to be a Communist nation.

Many Communists lived in South Vietnam. They were called the Viet Cong. They wanted to force South Vietnam to become a Communist country. The government of North Vietnam sent soldiers and weapons to help the Viet Cong. Viet Cong soldiers attacked villages. They burned schools and houses. They killed many people in South Vietnam.

During the Cold War, Americans wanted to stop the spread of communism. Americans were worried because China, North Korea, and North Vietnam had become Communist nations. The Soviet Union and China sent many weapons to North Vietnam. The United States did not want the Communists to win in South Vietnam. From South Vietnam the Communists might win control of other countries in southern Asia. The United States did not want this to happen. So the United States decided to help South Vietnam.

The United States sent weapons and planes to South Vietnam. American soldiers went to Vietnam to teach the South Vietnamese how to fight. But the Viet Cong were still winning the war. In 1965 American soldiers began to fight against the Viet Cong. Each year more and more American soldiers were sent to fight in Vietnam. By 1968 there were 550,000 American soldiers in Vietnam. The war lasted many years.

A field in Vietnam

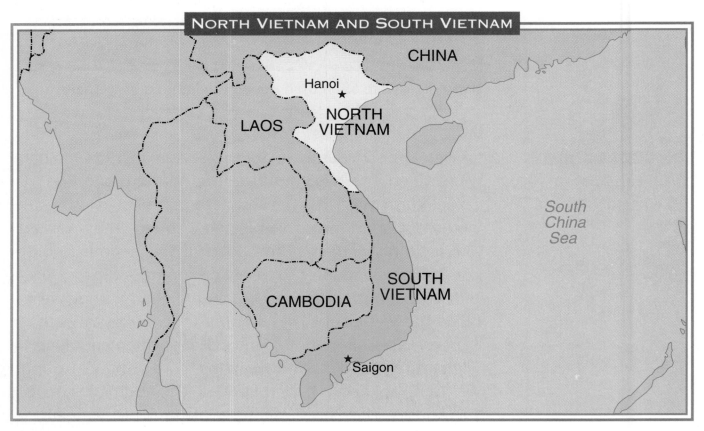

NORTH VIETNAM AND SOUTH VIETNAM

Many protesters wanted the United States to stop fighting in Vietnam.

Every day Americans watched news reports about the Vietnam War on television. They learned how hard it was to fight in Vietnam. The weather was very hot. There were heavy rains. Soldiers often fought in dangerous jungles. Viet Cong soldiers hid in the jungles and attacked American soldiers. Communists from nearby countries helped the Viet Cong fight the Americans. Americans learned from news reports how many soldiers were killed each day.

During the Vietnam War, there were two groups of Americans. One group believed Americans must fight against communism in Vietnam. The other group was against sending Americans to fight in Vietnam. This group grew larger and larger during the war. These people said too many American soldiers were being killed. They wanted the people of Vietnam to fight the war by themselves. It cost millions of dollars for Americans to fight in Vietnam. Many Americans wanted this money to be spent in the United States.

By 1967 many Americans became **protesters** to show they were against the Vietnam War. They marched in large cities against the war. Some protesters burned American flags. Others fought with police. There were fights and **protests** in every part of the country. A few protesters were killed.

Americans honor the people who died in Vietnam at the Vietnam Veterans Memorial in Washington, D.C.

Richard Nixon

Immigrants from South Vietnam

In 1969 President Richard Nixon said that he would bring Americans home from Vietnam. Americans had taught the South Vietnamese to fight the Viet Cong by themselves. The United States gave new weapons to South Vietnam. Thousands of American soldiers returned to the United States.

On January 27, 1973, North Vietnam and South Vietnam promised to stop fighting. This was called a **cease-fire**. Soon most American soldiers were back home in the United States.

The Viet Cong and the South Vietnamese had promised to stop fighting. But they started fighting again after the American soldiers left Vietnam. By 1975 North Vietnam had captured most of South Vietnam. On April 30, 1975, South Vietnam surrendered. Vietnam became one nation again. It is now a Communist country. Many people from South Vietnam left their country. Thousands of them became immigrants to the United States.

About 2,000 American soldiers never returned home. They are missing in Vietnam. Americans are still trying to learn what happened to these missing soldiers.

A **memorial** was built in Washington, D.C., to honor the Americans who died in Vietnam. Almost 58,000 Americans died in Vietnam. Their names are on the black walls of this memorial. Millions of people visit the Vietnam Veterans Memorial each year.

Read and Remember

Finish the Sentence   Write on your paper the word or words that finish each sentence.

1. Vietnam is in _____ Asia.
Northeast   Southeast   Northwest

2. In 1954 _____ was divided into two countries.
Vietnam   Russia   the United States

3. The United States did not want _____ Vietnam to become a Communist nation.
North   South   West

4. The _____ in South Vietnam were Communists.
protesters   Viet Cong   employers

5. Almost 58 _____ Americans died in Vietnam.
hundred   thousand   million

Think and Apply

Cause and Effect   Write sentences on your paper by matching each cause on the left with an effect on the right.

Cause

1. North Vietnam wanted South Vietnam to be a Communist country, so _____

2. The United States did not want South Vietnam to be a Communist country, so _____

3. Many Americans wanted the United States to stop fighting in Vietnam, so _____

4. In 1975 North Vietnam won control of South Vietnam, so _____

Effect

a. American soldiers went to fight in South Vietnam.

b. all of Vietnam became one Communist nation.

c. they marched in protests against the war.

d. North Vietnam helped the Viet Cong fight in South Vietnam.

Journal Writing

Many protesters marched to show they were against the war in Vietnam. Why did they want soldiers from the United States to stop fighting in this war? Write a paragraph in your journal that tells what the protesters believed about the war.

Skill Builder

Reading a Bar Graph   The bar graph below shows the number of United States soldiers in Vietnam during the Vietnam War. Study the graph.

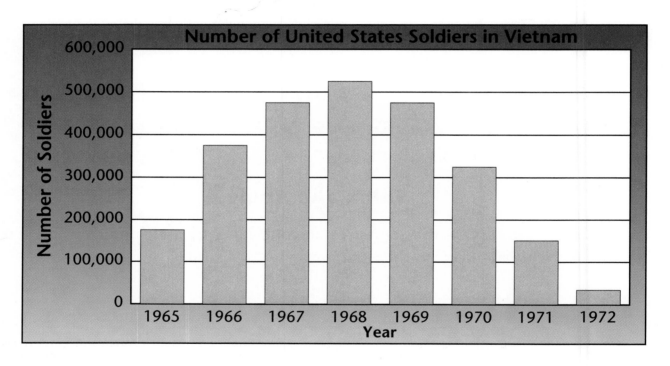

Write a sentence on your paper to answer each question.

1. When did United States soldiers first go to Vietnam?

2. In which year was the greatest number of United States soldiers in Vietnam?

3. In which years did the United States have more than 400,000 soldiers in Vietnam?

4. Did the United States have more soldiers in Vietnam during 1969 or during 1970?

5. In what year did the United States have the smallest number of soldiers in Vietnam?

Study the time line on this page. Then use the words in blue print to finish the story. Write the words you choose on your paper.

Cuba	North Korea	shuttle
polio	Berlin Wall	boycott
moon	South Vietnam	Communist

After World War II, the Cold War began between the United States and the Soviet Union. The United States was very angry when the Soviet Union built the __(1)__ in 1961. In 1962 the Soviet Union sent missiles to __(2)__ . In 1950 __(3)__ attacked South Korea. In 1965 Americans began to fight in __(4)__ . In 1975 Vietnam became one __(5)__ country.

The United States changed in other ways. In 1953 Dr. Salk made the first __(6)__ medicine. Martin Luther King, Jr., led a bus __(7)__ to change bus laws that were unfair to African Americans. In 1969 Americans were the first people to reach the __(8)__ . Seven Americans died when the *Challenger* space __(9)__ blew up. In 1994 a space shuttle trip helped Americans learn more about Earth's pollution.

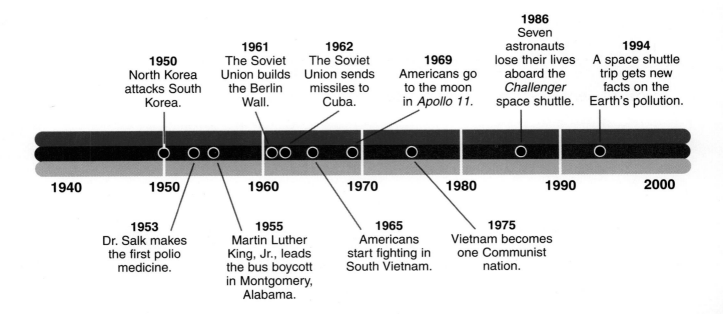

1950 North Korea attacks South Korea.

1961 The Soviet Union builds the Berlin Wall.

1962 The Soviet Union sends missiles to Cuba.

1969 Americans go to the moon in *Apollo 11.*

1986 Seven astronauts lose their lives aboard the *Challenger* space shuttle.

1994 A space shuttle trip gets new facts on the Earth's pollution.

1940   1950   1960   1970   1980   1990   2000

1953 Dr. Salk makes the first polio medicine.

1955 Martin Luther King, Jr., leads the bus boycott in Montgomery, Alabama.

1965 Americans start fighting in South Vietnam.

1975 Vietnam becomes one Communist nation.

255

UNIT 9

CHALLENGES IN TODAY'S WORLD

The United States is a changing nation. As it changes, Americans must find new ways to solve problems. We need better ways to get along with other nations around the world. Pollution is a problem. We need clean air and clean water. As we get closer to the year 2000, we must find new ways to solve our problems.

Think about how our country has changed since it first became a nation. Then think about the problems we have to solve. How can we have better trade with our neighbors? How can the United States work towards world peace? As you read Unit 9, think about what you can do to build a better America for tomorrow.

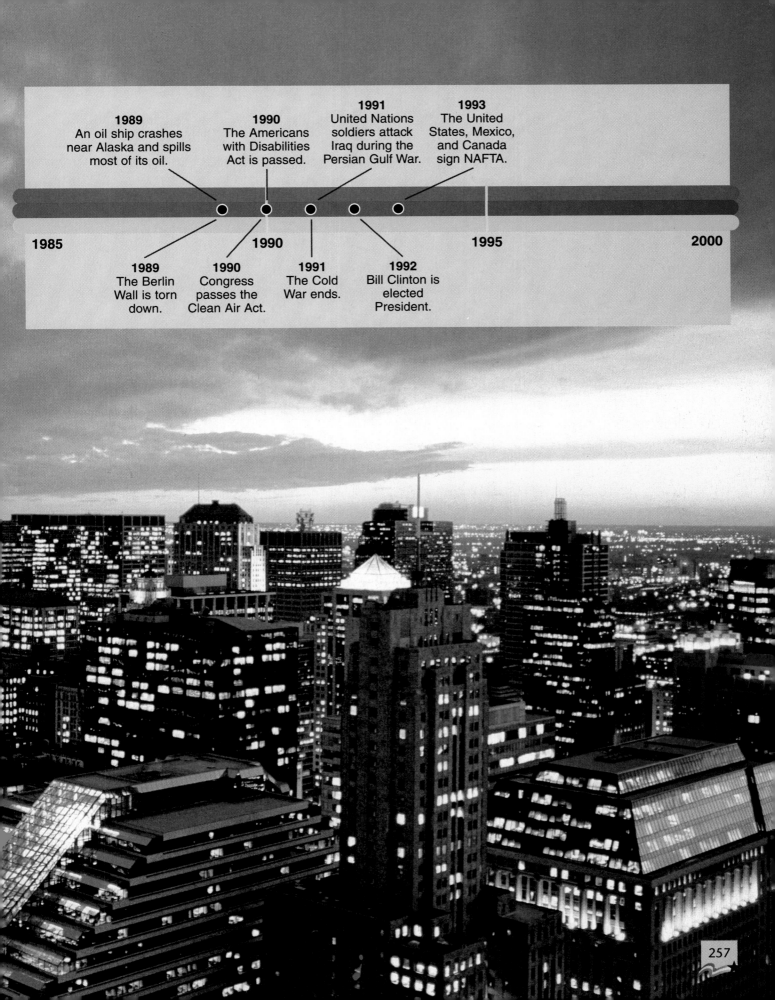

1989
An oil ship crashes near Alaska and spills most of its oil.

1990
The Americans with Disabilities Act is passed.

1991
United Nations soldiers attack Iraq during the Persian Gulf War.

1993
The United States, Mexico, and Canada sign NAFTA.

1989
The Berlin Wall is torn down.

1990
Congress passes the Clean Air Act.

1991
The Cold War ends.

1992
Bill Clinton is elected President.

1985

1990

1995

2000

CHAPTER 41 · THE UNITED STATES AND ITS NEIGHBORS

Think About As You Read

1. How have Canada and the United States worked together?
2. How does selling oil help Mexico?
3. How will NAFTA help Canada, Mexico, and the United States?

NEW WORDS

unguarded border
water power
acid rain
chemicals
debt
permission
illegal aliens
agreement
North American Free Trade Agreement (NAFTA)

PEOPLE & PLACES

Quebec
St. Lawrence Seaway
Great Lakes
Latin America
Brazil
Chile

Leaders from Canada, the United States, and Mexico signed the North American Free Trade Agreement.

Canada and Mexico are the closest neighbors of the United States. Each year millions of people from the United States visit Canada and Mexico. The map on page 259 shows the United States, Canada, and Mexico.

Canada is our northern neighbor. There is a strong friendship between the United States and Canada. The longest **unguarded border** in the world separates the two countries. The government of Canada is a democracy. Canada, like the United States, was settled by the English. Canada was also settled by the French. Today most French people in Canada live in the area of Quebec. Some leaders in Quebec have wanted Quebec to be a separate nation. So far all of Canada has remained one nation.

The United States and Canada work together. In 1954 they began building the St. Lawrence Seaway together. The seaway allows large ships to travel from the Atlantic Ocean all the way through the Great Lakes. Electricity is made by **water power** at the seaway. Both countries use this electricity.

Acid rain is a problem that both nations are trying to solve together. Factories and cars send smoke, dirt, and **chemicals** into the air. The smoke, dirt, and chemicals cause pollution. Pollution in the air causes acid rain.

American pollution often causes acid rain in Canada. Canada is angry because acid rain destroys forests and farm soil. It also kills fish and plants in lakes and rivers. In 1990 the United States Congress passed the Clean Air Act. This law said that Americans must cause less air pollution. New cars and factories now send less pollution into the air.

The United States also has a strong friendship with Mexico. Mexico is our southern neighbor. The language of Mexico

Factory Pollution

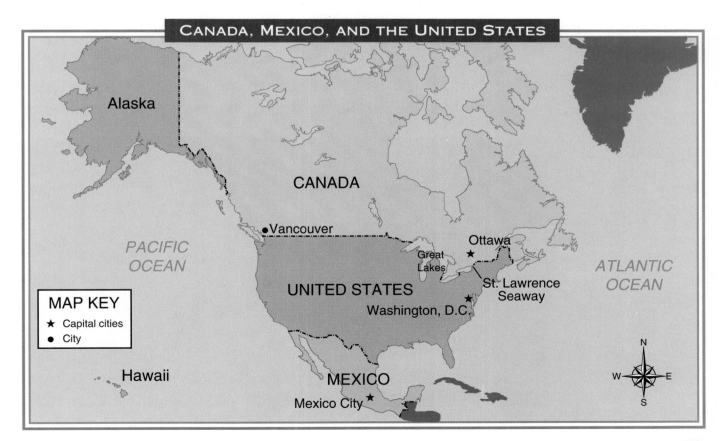

CANADA, MEXICO, AND THE UNITED STATES

Alaska

CANADA

Vancouver

PACIFIC OCEAN

Ottawa
★
Great Lakes

St. Lawrence Seaway

ATLANTIC OCEAN

UNITED STATES

Washington, D.C.
★

MAP KEY
★ Capital cities
● City

Hawaii

MEXICO

Mexico City ★

N
W E
S

is Spanish. Today Mexico is a democracy. Mexico City is the capital of Mexico. It is the largest city in North America. Air pollution is a problem in this city. Mexico has passed new laws to control the city's pollution.

Mexico has huge amounts of oil. It earns most of its money by selling oil to the United States and other countries. Mexico is using some of the money earned from selling oil to pay its **debt**. Mexico has borrowed millions of dollars from other countries. The problem is that Mexico does not earn enough money to pay back all of the debt.

Mexico has another problem. Millions of people in Mexico are very poor. The Mexican government is using some of the money earned from selling oil to solve this problem. The government is building schools, roads, houses, and hospitals with the money. These projects give jobs to many people.

Many Mexicans are poor because they do not have jobs. They want to come to the United States to find jobs. Some Mexicans have **permission** to move to the United States. But thousands of Mexicans come to the United States each year without permission. They are called **illegal aliens**. The United States and Mexico work together to stop illegal aliens from coming into the United States.

Trade is important between the United States, Canada, and Mexico. In 1993 the three nations signed an **agreement**

Border between Mexico and the United States

Mexico City is one of the largest cities in the world.

Vancouver is a large port city in Canada near the border of the United States.

President Clinton signing NAFTA

Latin America

to make trade easier with one another. This important agreement is called the **North American Free Trade Agreement**. It is often called NAFTA.

NAFTA is supposed to help trade because there will be fewer tariffs. A tariff is a special tax. Tariffs make products more expensive. NAFTA says that by the year 2009, most products from the three countries will be bought and sold without tariffs.

NAFTA may help trade in other ways. NAFTA says it will be easier for people in each country to own businesses and factories in the other two countries. It will also be easier for people in one country to work in the other countries.

Some people believe that NAFTA may hurt workers in the United States. They say that businesses will move from the United States to Mexico. Businesses may move to Mexico because many workers in Mexico will work for less money. We will not know for a few years if NAFTA is helping or hurting workers in the United States.

The United States has other neighbors. These neighbors are the countries of Latin America. The United States trades with its neighbors in Latin America. Americans buy shoes from Brazil. They buy fruit from Chile. There is friendship between the United States and its neighbors.

Read and Remember

Finish Up Choose the word or words in blue print that finish each sentence. Write the correct answers on your paper.

illegal aliens   tariffs   acid rain
Clean Air Act   NAFTA   Seaway

1. Canada and the United States built the St. Lawrence _____ together.

2. Fish and plants are killed by _____ .

3. Congress passed the _____ to control air pollution.

4. _____ is supposed to help trade between the United States, Canada, and Mexico.

5. By the year 2009, there will be few _____ on products traded between the United States, Mexico, and Canada.

6. Many _____ come to the United States from Mexico.

Think and Apply

Finding the Main Idea Read each group of sentences below. One of the three sentences is a main idea. The other two sentences support the main idea. Write on your paper the sentence that is the main idea.

1. There is a long unguarded border between the United States and Canada.

   The United States and Canada share electricity made from the St. Lawrence Seaway.

   There is friendship between the United States and Canada.

2. Mexico has to pay back a very large debt.

   Mexico has two big problems.

   Many Mexicans are very poor.

3. The United States buys shoes from Brazil.

   The United States trades with its neighbors in Latin America.

   The United States buys fruit from Chile.

Skill Builder

Reading a Double Bar Graph   A **double bar graph** compares facts by using two different colored bars. The double bar graph below shows how much the United States traded with its neighbors. The green bars show how much money the United States earned by selling products to four neighbors. The white bars show how much the United States spent buying products from its neighbors.

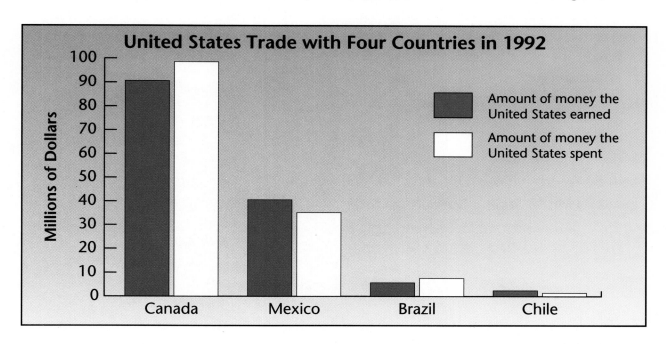

United States Trade with Four Countries in 1992

Millions of Dollars

Amount of money the United States earned

Amount of money the United States spent

Canada   Mexico   Brazil   Chile

Write on your paper the word or words that finish each sentence.

1. The United States had the most trade with _____ .
   Chile   Canada   Brazil

2. The United States spent more than it earned from _____ .
   Canada   Mexico   Chile

3. The United States earned about _____ in trade with Mexico.
   $2 million $41 million $91 million

4. The United States spent about _____ on products from Brazil.
   $8 million $40 million $98 million

5. The United States earned _____ than it spent in trade with Canada.
   more   less

CHAPTER 42 THE UNITED STATES AS A WORLD LEADER

Think About As You Read

1. How did the Cold War end?
2. How is the United States a world leader?
3. How does the United States work with the United Nations?

NEW WORDS

Middle East
Persian Gulf War

PEOPLE & PLACES

Kuwait
Iraq
Colin Powell
H. Norman Schwarzkopf
Palestinians
Israel
Somalia

Germans celebrated as the Berlin Wall was torn down.

You read about the Cold War in Chapter 35. The Cold War between the United States and the Soviet Union ended in 1991. Since then the United States has been the strongest world leader.

The Cold War ended when the Soviet Union and the nations of Eastern Europe started new governments. These countries were no longer ruled by Communists. In 1989 the Berlin Wall was torn down in East Germany. A year later East Germany and West Germany became one nation again.

The Soviet Union also changed. The Soviet Union was one country that was made up of 15 smaller countries. A Communist government ruled the 15 countries of the

Soviet Union. In 1991 the 15 countries of the Soviet Union became independent. Each of these 15 independent countries started its own government. These countries were not ruled by Communists. This was the end of the Soviet Union.

Russia had been the largest country in the Soviet Union. Russia is now a poor country with many problems. The United States is lending money to Russia and some of the other countries that had been in the Soviet Union. Many American businesses are starting to sell their products in Russia.

Since the Cold War ended, the main goal of the United States has been world peace. The United States works with the United Nations to keep peace. Sometimes the United Nations sends soldiers to countries where there is fighting. Many of the United Nations soldiers are Americans.

The United States worked with the United Nations to help Kuwait. Kuwait is a small nation in the **Middle East**. Kuwait is very rich in oil. One of Kuwait's neighbors is a country called Iraq. Iraq wanted Kuwait's oil. So in 1990 Iraq's army took control of Kuwait.

The United States asked 28 nations to join together to help Kuwait. These nations said they would fight with the United Nations against Iraq. The United Nations said Iraq had to leave Kuwait by January 15, 1991.

Iraq and Kuwait

The Persian Gulf War was fought in the deserts of Kuwait and Iraq.

Colin Powell

Somalia

Iraq refused to leave Kuwait. So on January 17, 1991, the United Nations soldiers attacked Iraq's army in both Kuwait and Iraq. This war was called the **Persian Gulf War**. The soldiers from the United States and many other countries won the war. General Colin Powell and General H. Norman Schwarzkopf were the leaders of the American soldiers. Kuwait became a free nation again.

The United States has also worked for peace in the Middle East between the Palestinians and the people of Israel. They have been enemies for more than forty years. In 1993 Israeli and Palestinian leaders met in Washington, D.C. They signed a plan that would help bring peace to their people. American leaders helped them sign another agreement in 1994.

In 1993 the United States worked in Africa with the United Nations to help the people of Somalia. The people of Somalia fought a long civil war. In 1992 there was very little food in Somalia. More than a million people were starving. United Nations soldiers went to Somalia. About two thirds of the soldiers were Americans. They gave food to thousands of starving people. The United States saved the lives of many people in Somalia.

The United States as a world leader is working to bring peace to many parts of the world.

American soldiers worked with the United Nations to help the people of Somalia.

Read and Remember ★

True or False   Write **T** on your paper for each sentence that is true. Write **F** for each sentence that is false.

1. Today East Germany and West Germany are two separate nations.

2. The Berlin Wall has been torn down.

3. Today the Soviet Union is the strongest world leader.

4. The 15 countries of the Soviet Union became independent countries in 1991.

5. Russia is still part of the Soviet Union.

6. Businesses from the United States are selling their products in Russia.

7. The United States and 28 other nations fought together against Iraq.

8. Kuwait is rich in gold and silver.

9. Kuwait became free again after the Persian Gulf War.

10. There was a civil war in Somalia.

Choose the Answer   Write the correct answers on your paper.

1. What did Iraq try to get when it took control of Kuwait in 1990?
    gold   oil   silver

2. What has been the main goal of the United States since the Cold War?
    communism   independence   world peace

3. Who was one of the leaders of American soldiers in the Persian Gulf War?
    Neil Armstrong   Colin Powell   Douglas MacArthur

4. In what area of the world are Kuwait and Israel?
    Western Europe   Southeast Asia   the Middle East

5. What did United Nations soldiers give to people in Somalia?
    food   freedom   jewels

Think and Apply

Cause and Effect   Write sentences on your paper by matching each cause on the left with an effect on the right.

Cause

1. The Soviet Union and the nations of Eastern Europe no longer had Communist governments, so _____

2. The 15 countries of the Soviet Union became independent, so _____

3. Iraq's army took control of Kuwait, so _____

4. Israelis and Palestinians had been enemies, so _____

5. The United States wanted to help the starving people of Somalia, so _____

Effect

a. the United Nations told Iraq to leave Kuwait.

b. the United States helped Israelis and Palestinians sign a peace plan.

c. the United States sent food and soldiers to Somalia.

d. the Cold War ended.

e. that was the end of the Soviet Union.

Sequencing Events   Number your paper from 1 to 5. Write the sentences to show the correct order.

In 1989 the Berlin Wall was torn down.

The Cold War started after World War II.

East Germany and West Germany became one nation again.

Americans worked with the United Nations to help the people of Somalia.

Americans fought in the Persian Gulf War in 1991.

43 WORKING FOR TOMORROW

Ten thousand people became citizens during this ceremony. Many of them were immigrants from Latin America.

The United States continues to change every year. Before 1965 most immigrants came to the United States from Europe. A 1965 law has helped people from other parts of the world come to America. Millions of Asians and Latin Americans have become immigrants.

Two hundred years ago, all government leaders in the United States were white men. Now many other Americans are government leaders. Many women are now government leaders. African Americans, Asian Americans, and Hispanic Americans are members of Congress. In 1992 Ben Nighthorse Campbell became the first Native American senator.

New laws protect the rights of people with disabilities.

Computers in a school

Bill Clinton

American laws have changed so that all people will be treated fairly. In Chapter 37 you read about the Civil Rights Act of 1964. This law changed America. It said all people have equal rights. In 1990 Congress passed the **Americans with Disabilities Act**. This new law said that Americans with disabilities have the same rights as other Americans. This law makes it easier for people with disabilities to get jobs.

Technology is changing America. Technology means the inventions that change the way we live. The way we **communicate** has changed. Many people have telephones in their cars. **Fax machines** have changed the way we send letters. A letter can be sent across the ocean in only minutes with a fax machine. Technology has helped doctors to do many kinds of operations. New machines have been invented to study the inside of the human body.

In one important way, America has not changed. It has always been a democracy. In 1992 Americans proved that their democracy was still working. They elected a new President. Bill Clinton became the forty-first President.

There have been many good changes in the United States. There have also been problems. One problem is that more than 30 million Americans are very poor. Many people do not have jobs. Many people are **homeless**.

More people became homeless in the summer of 1993. During that summer there were terrible floods on the Mississippi River. Farms, homes, and towns were destroyed in nine states. The government gave those states money to rebuild what the floods destroyed.

Our country also has an **energy** problem. Three kinds of energy are light, heat, and electricity. We need energy for our cars, homes, and factories. We use coal, oil, and **natural gas** to make energy. Coal, oil, and natural gas are **natural resources**. Many people are afraid that one day our natural resources will be used up.

Many Americans are trying to save energy. They use less electricity. People use less heat in their homes in the winter. They save energy by washing clothes in cold water. People drive smaller cars that use less gasoline. Many people ride buses, trains, and bicycles instead of driving cars.

A bus that uses natural gas

Many people lost their homes when the Mississippi River flooded in 1993.

Everyone can help save our natural resources by recycling.

Ship that spilled oil near Alaska

Water, fish, animals, and trees are other natural resources. An accident in 1989 destroyed many of Alaska's natural resources. A large ship was carrying oil from Alaska to other parts of the nation. The ship crashed near Alaska. Most of the oil spilled into the sea. The oil killed thousands of birds, fish, and other sea animals.

Recycling is a good way to save natural resources. Many people do not throw away plastic bottles, metal cans, newspapers, and glass bottles. These things are sent to be recycled. New plastic, metal, paper, and glass are made from old plastic, metal, paper, and glass. Recycling saves our natural resources for tomorrow.

America's story is not yet finished. In the years ahead, we must find new ways to make energy. We must save our natural resources. Many people will be working for America. You can work with them. You can save energy for our country. You can recycle. You can write letters to government leaders. Tell them how you think they should solve our problems. As an adult you can vote for the best leaders for our nation. You will be building a better America for tomorrow.

Read and Remember

Match Up   Finish each sentence in Group A with words from Group B. Write the letter of the correct answer on your paper.

Group A

1. Millions of immigrants now come from _____ .

2. A 1990 law helped _____ .

3. To save gasoline, people should _____ .

4. To save energy, people should _____ .

5. To save natural resources, people should _____ .

Group B

a. people with disabilities get jobs

b. recycle glass bottles, metal cans, newspapers, and plastic bottles

c. use buses, trains, and bicycles instead of cars

d. Asia and Latin America

e. use less heat and electricity

Think and Apply

Sequencing Events   Number your paper from 1 to 5. Write the sentences to show the correct order.

In 1990 Congress passed the Americans with Disabilities Act.

An oil ship crashed near Alaska in 1989.

Congress passed the Civil Rights Act.

Floods on the Mississippi River destroyed homes in nine states in 1993.

Bill Clinton was elected President.

Journal Writing

What problem in our nation do you think needs to be solved? Write a letter to your United States senator. Tell your senator about the problem. Tell the senator how you think the problem should be solved. Mail it to your senator in Washington, D.C.

Skill Builder

Reading a Double Line Graph A **double line graph** compares facts by using two different lines. The lines on the graph below show how much glass and paper was recycled from 1960 to 1990. Glass and paper are measured in **tons**. A ton is 2,000 pounds. Study the graph.

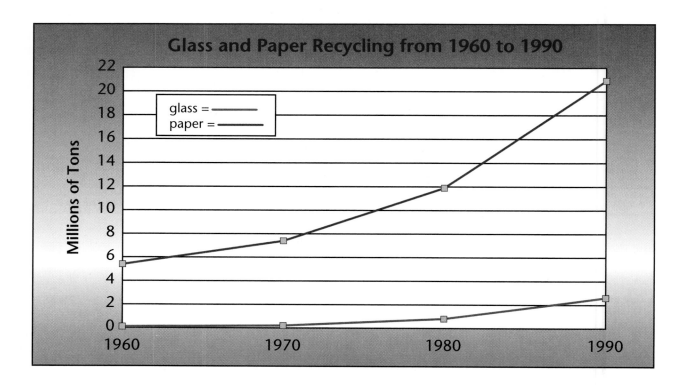

Use the graph to answer the questions below. Write the correct answers on your paper.

1. What color is the line that shows the amount of recycled glass?
red   blue

2. In 1960 about how many tons of paper were recycled?
5 million   7 million   12 million

3. In what year were the most glass and paper recycled?
1960   1980   1990

4. In 1990 about how many tons of glass were recycled?
3 million   5 million   21 million

5. Are people recycling more glass or more paper?
more glass   more paper

Chart Review   The chart on this page shows important events from 1989 to 1993. Study the chart. Then use the words in blue print to finish the story. Write the words you choose on your paper.

natural	Iraq	food
Persian Gulf	Cold War	NAFTA
Disabilities	Somalia	Alaska

In 1989 a large oil ship crashed near ___(1)___ . Oil from the ship destroyed many ___(2)___ resources. Congress helped many Americans by passing the Americans with ___(3)___ Act. The United States sent soldiers to Kuwait during the ___(4)___ War. The United Nations forced ___(5)___ to leave Kuwait.

The ___(6)___ ended in 1991. More than a million people were starving in ___(7)___ . American soldiers helped the United Nations bring ___(8)___ to Somalia. In 1993 the United States, Canada, and Mexico signed a trade agreement called ___(9)___ .

Important Events from 1989 to 1993		
Date	**Event**	**Results**
1989	An oil ship crashes near Alaska.	The oil that spilled from the ship destroyed natural resources.
1990	Congress passes the Americans with Disabilities Act.	Americans with disabilities have the same rights as other Americans.
1991	The Persian Gulf War begins.	The United Nations forced Iraq to leave Kuwait.
1991	The Cold War ends.	The United States is the stongest world leader.
1992	The United States sends soldiers to Somalia.	The American army gave food to thousands of starving people in Somalia.
1993	NAFTA is signed by the United States, Canada, and Mexico.	There will be fewer tariffs between the three nations.

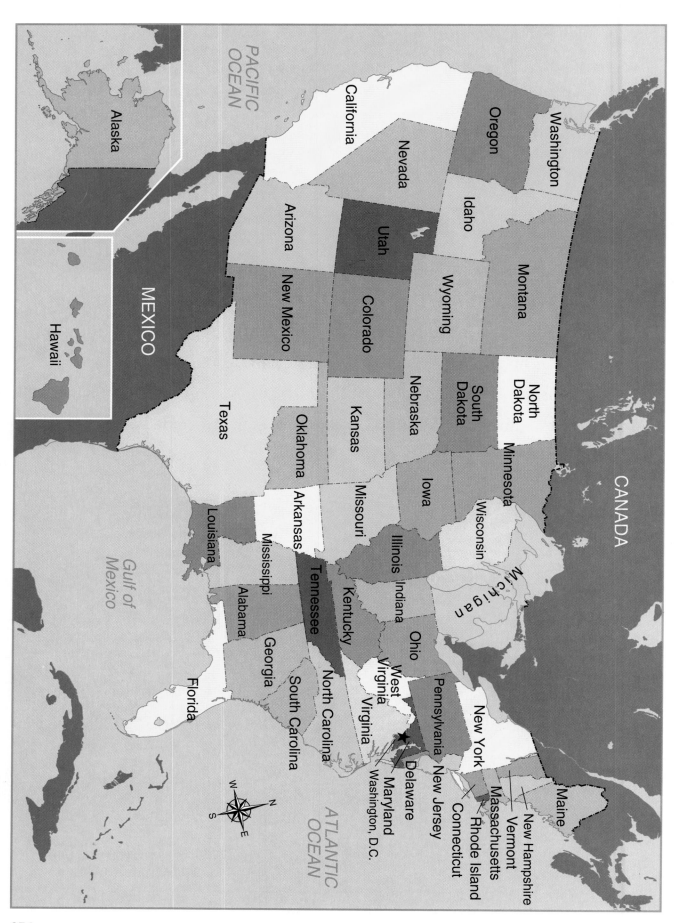

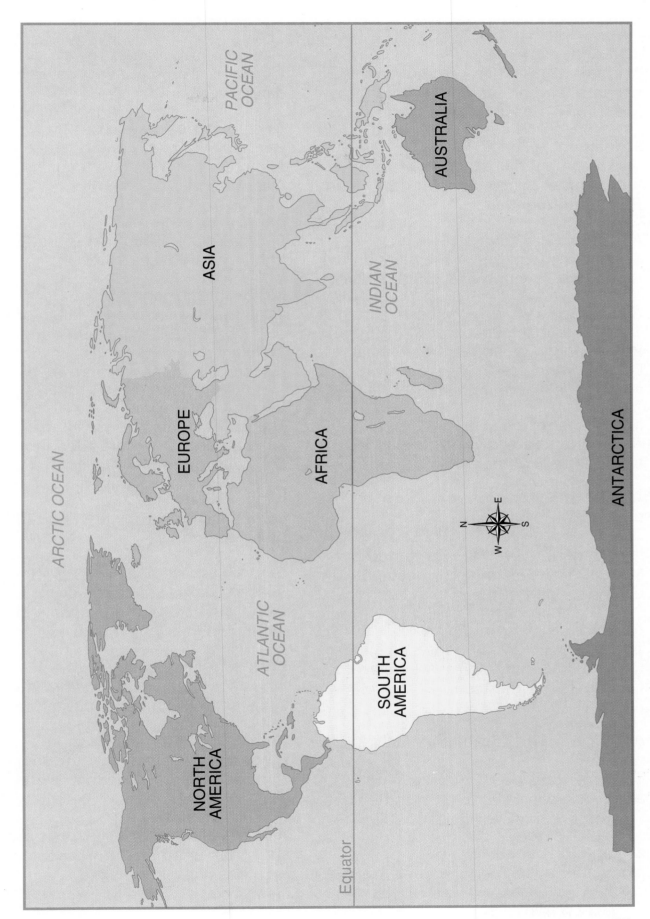

acid rain page 259
Acid rain forms when pollution in the air becomes part of the rain. It can destroy forests and can kill fish and plants.

agreement page 261
An agreement is a paper that tells how two or more people or countries will do something together.

Allied soldiers page 214
Soldiers who fought for the Allies during World War II were called Allied soldiers.

Allies page 190
The nations that fought against the Central Powers during World War I were the Allies. During World War II, the Allies fought against the Axis countries.

amendments page 55
Amendments are laws that are added to the Constitution.

American Federation of Labor (AFL) page 173
The American Federation of Labor is a large organization that was started by Samuel Gompers to help workers. Many unions are part of the AFL.

American Revolution page 43
The American Revolution was the war that the American colonies fought against Great Britain. It started in 1775 and ended in 1781.

Americans with Disabilities Act page 270
The Americans with Disabilities Act was a law passed in 1990 to protect the rights of people with disabilities.

astronauts page 240
Astronauts are people who travel in space.

atomic bomb page 216
An atomic bomb is a very powerful, dangerous bomb.

Axis countries page 208
Germany, Italy, and Japan were the main Axis countries that fought against the Allies during World War II.

battleship page 147
A battleship is a ship that is used for fighting wars at sea.

big business page 166
Big business means one person or one business controls many other businesses. An example of big business is that one person owned most American railroads.

Bill of Rights page 55
The Bill of Rights is the first ten amendments that were added to the Constitution.

blew up page 147
Something blew up if it was destroyed by exploding.

blood bank page 229
A blood bank is a place to store blood. This blood can be given to people who lose a lot of blood because they are sick or hurt.

body of water page 32
A body of water is a large area of water. Lakes and oceans are bodies of water.

bomb page 208
A bomb is a weapon that destroys things when it is made to explode.

border page 85
A border is a line that separates one state from another. A border can also separate cities, towns, and countries.

Boston Tea Party page 42
During the Boston Tea Party, Americans went on three British tea ships. They threw all the tea into the ocean because they did not want to pay for the tea.

boundaries page 66
Boundaries are the lines around a city, state, or country. Rivers, oceans, and mountains can be boundaries. Boundaries are often shown as lines drawn on maps.

boycott page 234
During a boycott, people stop buying or using a product or a service.

buffalo page 5
A buffalo is an ox. It is a large animal with horns and fur.

building armies page 190
Nations that are building armies are making many weapons and are teaching many people to be soldiers.

bullet page 214
A bullet is a small piece of metal that is shot out of a gun.

capital page 54
The capital of a country is the city where the government meets.

capture page 79
To capture means to take and hold a person, place, or thing by using force.

Catholics page 17
Catholics are people who believe in the Christian religion. The pope is the leader of the Catholic religion.

cease-fire page 252
A cease-fire happens when enemy countries agree to stop fighting during a war.

Central Powers page 191
The Central Powers were the nations that fought against the Allies during World War I.

chemicals page 259
Chemicals are dry or liquid materials that can make things change.

Church of England page 20
Church of England means all the churches in England that accept the king of England as the head of the church.

citizens page 108
Citizens are members of a country.

civil rights page 235
Civil rights are the rights that the Constitution gives all American citizens. These rights cannot be taken away because of race, religion, sex, or age.

Civil Rights Act page 236
A Civil Rights Act is a law passed by Congress that protects the rights of citizens. The Civil Rights Act of 1964 said that all people should be treated equally.

Civil War page 126
The Civil War was the war fought between the North and the South. The war was fought between 1861 and 1865.

claimed page 12
When a country claimed land, it meant it would own and rule that land.

coast page 114
The coast is land along the ocean.

Cold War page 222
The Cold War was a struggle between the United States and the Soviet Union over the spread of communism.

colony page 25
A colony is land that is ruled by another nation.

commander in chief page 64
The commander in chief is the most important leader of the army.

communicate page 270
To communicate means to give information to others by writing or speaking. Newspapers and TV news reports communicate news to people.

Communist page 222
In a Communist nation, the government owns most businesses, and people have little freedom.

concentration camp page 209
A concentration camp was a place where captured people were forced to stay during World War II. Millions of Jews and other people were killed in concentration camps.

Confederates page 125
The people of the Confederate States of America were called Confederates.

Confederate States of America
page 122
Eleven southern states left the United States and started their own country. The new country was called the Confederate States of America.

Congress page 53
Congress is all the people in the United States Senate and House of Representatives who write laws for the nation.

conquer page 208
To conquer means to win control of a country during a war.

constitution page 52
A constitution is a set of laws. The United States Constitution is a set of laws for the United States.

contract page 245
A contract is a paper that tells employers and workers the amount of money workers will be paid and how long a job will last.

conveyor belt page 153
A conveyor belt is a long, moving belt that carries materials past workers in a factory.

cotton page 5
Cotton is a plant that is used to make cloth. You can wear clothes made of cotton.

covered wagons page 113
Covered wagons are wagons that are covered with heavy cloth and pulled by horses or other animals. People traveled west in covered wagons.

crashed page 202
When the stock market crashed, the price of stocks became very, very low.

crops page 73
Crops are plants grown by farmers. Corn and cotton are two kinds of crops.

debt page 260
A debt is borrowed money that must be paid back.

Declaration of Independence page 46
The Declaration of Independence was an important paper that said the American colonies were a free nation.

declared war page 210
If a country says that it is going to fight in a war against another country, it has declared war on that country.

democracy page 222
A democracy is a government that allows people to choose their own leaders and help write their own laws.

depression page 201
A depression is a time when most businesses lose money. Many people might lose their jobs and their money during a depression.

destroy page 127
To destroy means to break and to ruin. A war can destroy homes, farms, and cities.

dictator page 207
A dictator is a ruler who has full control over the government of a country. A dictator can take away the rights and freedoms of the people.

disabilities page 92
People with disabilities are less able to do certain things. Not being able to see is a disability.

disease page 228
A disease is a sickness.

doubled page 74
When the United States doubled in size, it became twice as large as it had been in 1776.

drill page 167
When people drill for oil, they use a machine that makes a hole that goes deep into the earth.

education page 92
Education means the things you learn from school and from different people and places.

elect page 203
Americans elect a President by giving that person enough votes to win.

electric sparks page 59
Electric sparks are tiny bits of electricity that give off small amounts of light for a few seconds.

employers page 172
Employers are people who hire other people to work for them.

energy page 271
Energy gives things power. Heat, light, and electricity are three forms of energy.

equal page 46
People who are equal have the same importance.

equal rights page 136
Equal rights means all people have the same rights.

escape page 121
To escape means to become free by leaving a person, place, or thing.

fax machine page 270
A fax machine is a machine that can send a copy of a written paper to another fax machine anywhere in the world.

First Lady page 65
The wife of the President of the United States is called the First Lady.

flight page 183
A flight is a trip in an airplane.

flour page 140
Flour is a powder made from wheat. It is used for making breads, cakes, cookies, and macaroni.

fort page 102
A fort is a building from which an army can fight its enemies.

freedom of religion page 20
Freedom of religion means you can pray the way you want to pray.

freedom of the press page 54
Freedom of the press means you can write what you want to write in newspapers and books.

freedom of the seas page 79
Freedom of the seas means that ships can go wherever they want to go.

Gadsden Purchase page 108
The United States bought land from Mexico called the Gadsden Purchase.

gasoline engine page 182
A gasoline engine is a machine that uses gasoline to power things. It can make cars, trucks, and airplanes move. Gasoline is a liquid made from oil.

general page 47
A general is an important army leader.

goal page 127
A goal is something a person wants and tries to get.

gold rush page 116
A gold rush is a time when many people move into an area in order to find gold.

governor page 21
A governor is a government leader for a state, town, or area.

grape growers page 245
Grape growers are farm owners who grow grapes.

grape pickers page 245
Grape pickers are farm workers who pick grapes.

Great Depression page 201
The Great Depression was the depression in the 1930s when many people lost their jobs and had little money.

healthy page 229
To be healthy means to be well.

Holocaust page 209
The killing of about six million Jews and many other people during World War II was called the Holocaust.

homeless page 271
A homeless person does not have a home to live in.

Homestead Act page 139
The Homestead Act was a law that gave settlers land for a low price. Settlers had to build a house and a farm on their land.

House of Representatives page 53
The House of Representatives is one of the two houses, or parts, of Congress. It has 435 members.

icebox page 146
An icebox is a box filled with ice that was used to keep food cold. In the 1800s people used iceboxes because they did not have refrigerators.

illegal aliens page 260
Illegal aliens are people who come to America from other countries without getting papers from the American government that say they are allowed to live in America.

immigrants page 142
Immigrants are people who come from other countries to live.

imperialism page 145
Imperialism is the idea that one country should rule other countries or colonies.

in debt page 27
A person who is in debt owes money to other people.

independent page 46
An independent country rules itself. It is not ruled by another country.

injection page 228
An injection is a way to send medicine through a needle so it goes into a person's body.

injured page 229
An injured person is a person who has been hurt.

invade page 215
To invade means to enter a country by using force.

invent page 152
To invent means to make something that is new and different. Garrett Morgan invented the traffic light.

invention page 151
An invention is a new machine that makes life better for people. The car was an important invention.

judges page 54
Judges are people who rule on cases in court.

kindergarten page 178
A kindergarten is a class for children who are four to six years old.

labor union page 172
A labor union is an organization of workers who work together to get paid more money and to improve their jobs.

lead page 179
Lead is a very soft gray metal that is found in the earth. It is used in factories to make many different products, such as pipes.

lead poisoning page 179
Lead poisoning happens when people have too much lead in their bodies. People get this sickness by breathing in lead or swallowing products that have lead in them.

Liberty Bonds page 192
Americans bought Liberty Bonds to help the government pay for World War I. Years later all Americans got back the money they paid for the bonds.

Louisiana Purchase page 74
The Louisiana Purchase was the sale of a large piece of land west of the Mississippi River. The United States bought it from France in 1803.

Loyalists page 47
Loyalists were Americans who did not want the colonies to become independent. They helped Great Britain during the American Revolution.

manage page 63
To manage means to control and take care of something.

Manifest Destiny page 106
Manifest Destiny was the idea that the United States should rule all land from the Atlantic Ocean to the Pacific Ocean.

march page 235
A march is a group of people walking together for something they believe in. They walk in a march to win support from government leaders and other people.

Mayflower Compact page 21
The Mayflower Compact was the Pilgrims' plan for ruling themselves in America.

medical school page 229
A medical school is a school where people study to become doctors.

memorial page 252
A memorial is a building or object that is made to help people honor and remember others who have died.

Mexican Cession page 108
The land that the United States won during the Mexican War was called the Mexican Cession.

Middle East page 265
The Middle East is an area in Asia that is northeast of Africa. Israel, Kuwait, and Iraq are Middle East nations.

migrant farm workers page 244
Migrant farm workers are workers who move from one farm to another in order to have work.

millionaire page 167
A person who has more than a million dollars is a millionaire.

minister page 233
A minister is a leader in a church.

missile page 225
A missile is a rocket with a bomb in it. The bomb explodes when the missile lands. A country can send missiles to attack enemy nations.

missions page 17
Missions are places where people teach others how to become Christians.

motorized page 182
A motorized machine has a motor or engine that makes it work.

nation page 40
A nation is a large group of people living together in one country.

NATO page 223
NATO is the North Atlantic Treaty Organization. The armies of NATO nations will fight for each other during a war.

natural gas page 271
Natural gas is a gas that is found in the earth. It can be burned to make heat and electricity.

natural resources page 271
Natural resources are things we get from the earth. Water, metals, trees, animals, and oil are natural resources.

naval base page 210
A naval base is a place near the sea where the navy keeps many ships, weapons, airplanes, and sailors.

navy page 80
The navy is a nation's warships and all the people who work on the warships.

neutral page 191
A neutral nation does not fight or help other nations during a war.

New Deal page 203
Franklin D. Roosevelt's plan for ending the Great Depression was called the New Deal.

New World page 12
People in Europe called North America and South America the New World because they had not known about these continents.

Nobel Peace Prize page 236
The Nobel Peace Prize is a prize that is given to a person whose work helps people live together in peace.

North American Free Trade Agreement (NAFTA) page 261
NAFTA is a plan for making trade easier between the United States, Canada, and Mexico.

oil page 146
Oil is a dark liquid that is found in the earth. It is used for making gas for cars. Oil from the earth is also called petroleum.

oil refineries page 167
Oil refineries are factories that clean oil after it is taken out of the earth. After oil is cleaned, it can be used in cars, trucks, and buses.

operation page 230
An operation is work that is done to a person's body by a doctor in order to improve the person's health.

ore page 167
Ore is rock with metal in it that is found in the earth. We find iron in ore from the earth.

Oregon Trail page 114
The trail that wagons followed through the West to Oregon was called the Oregon Trail.

organization page 223
An organization is a group of people or a group of nations that work together.

oxen page 113
An ox is an animal like a cow. Oxen is the word used for more than one ox.

Parliament page 41
All the people who are chosen to write the laws for Great Britain and the building they work in are called Parliament.

pass page 116
A pass is a trail through the mountains.

patient page 230
A patient is a person who is cared for by a doctor, nurse, dentist, or hospital.

peaceful page 234
People who are peaceful like peace and do not cause fighting or trouble.

peace treaty page 22
A peace treaty is an agreement not to fight.

permission page 260
Permission means being allowed to do something. Many immigrants have permission to move to the United States.

Persian Gulf War page 266
The Persian Gulf War was the war when the United Nations fought against Iraq in 1991.

pesticides page 246
Pesticides are chemicals that are sprayed on crops so insects will not eat the crops. Pesticides help farmers grow more food.

photographer page 174
A person who takes pictures with a camera is a photographer.

photographs page 163
Photographs are pictures taken with a camera.

pilot page 183
A pilot is a person who flies airplanes.

plantations page 120
Plantations are very large farms where crops like cotton and tobacco are grown.

polio page 228
Polio is a sickness that can cause leg muscles to become so weak that a person cannot walk. People can die from polio.

pollution page 241
Pollution is dirt in the air or water. Water pollution can be found in lakes, rivers, and oceans.

popular page 203
To be popular means to be liked by many people.

port page 42
A port is a place on an ocean or river where ships are loaded and unloaded.

priests page 17
Priests are people who lead religious services and teach about the Catholic religion.

printer page 58
A printer is a person who prints books and newspapers.

printing shop page 58
A printing shop is a place with machines for printing books and newspapers.

products page 121
Products are things that are made by people or by nature. Shoes are a factory product. Apples are a natural product.

property page 109
All the land and other things you own are your property.

protesters page 251
Protesters are people who march, give speeches, or do other things to show they are against something. Many people became protesters against the Vietnam War.

protests page 251
Protests are the things people do to show they are against something. During the Vietnam War, marches against the war were one kind of protest.

public schools page 92
Public schools are schools that are paid for with tax money. You do not pay to study in a public school.

publish page 58
To publish means to prepare a book or newspaper so it can be sold.

quarrel page 119
To quarrel means to argue or not agree about something.

rationed page 214
When foods and other products are rationed, people are allowed to buy only certain amounts.

rebuild page 128
To rebuild means to build something again.

Reconstruction page 134
The years after the Civil War were called Reconstruction. During Reconstruction the southern states rejoined the Union, and cities were rebuilt.

recycling page 272
Recycling is a way to turn old metal, plastic, paper, and glass into new metal, plastic, paper, and glass.

rejoin page 134
To rejoin means to join again. The South rejoined, or became part of, the United States after the Civil War.

religion page 4
Religion is the way people believe in and pray to God or to many gods.

religious page 26
Religious means having to do with religion.

reporter page 163
A reporter learns about important news and then writes about it in the newspaper.

representatives page 53
People who make laws in the House of Representatives are called representatives.

republic page 103
A republic is a country where people vote for their leaders. These leaders make laws for the people and lead the government.

reservations page 141
Reservations are lands that Native Americans were given to live on.

respect page 236
To show respect for others means to honor and care about them.

salary page 172
A salary is the money earned at a job.

satellite page 239
A satellite is a machine that is sent into space by a rocket. In space the satellite moves around and around Earth.

Senate page 53
The Senate is one of the two houses, or parts, of Congress. It has 100 members.

senators page 53
People who make laws in the Senate are senators.

settlers page 25
Settlers are people who come to live in a new place.

share of stock page 201
A person who owns a share of stock owns a small part of a business.

short cut page 31
A short cut is a shorter way to go to a place.

slavery page 15
Slavery means people being owned by other people. Slaves were forced to work without pay.

snowshoes page 33
Snowshoes are wooden frames that you attach to your shoes. They help you walk on deep snow.

space race page 239
The space race was a race between the United States and the Soviet Union to see which nation could send people to the moon first.

space shuttle page 240
A space shuttle is a spaceship that can be used many times.

Spanish-American War page 148
The war that the United States fought against Spain in 1898 was the Spanish-American War.

spend her life page 197
If a woman has a goal that will take many years to reach, she may spend her life working for that goal.

spices page 10
Spices are added to food to improve the way it tastes and smells.

spike page 142
A spike is very large nail that is used to join railroad tracks.

spread of communism page 223
The spread of communism happens when Communist countries force other nations to have Communist governments.

Stamp Act page 41
The Stamp Act said that Americans in the British colonies had to pay a tax on things like newspapers.

starving page 161
People are starving when they do not get enough food to eat.

steel mills page 167
Steel mills are large factories that use iron to make steel.

stock page 202
A person who buys stock becomes part owner of a business. A stock can be bought or sold.

stock market page 202
The stock market is the place where stocks are bought and sold.

strike page 172
A strike is when workers stop working in order to force their employers to give them more money and to improve their jobs.

subjects page 94
The courses that you study in school, such as math and science, are subjects.

sugar cane page 120
We get most of our sugar from the tall plant called sugar cane.

sunk page 192
A ship that has been attacked and goes underwater has sunk.

supervisor page 198
A supervisor is a person who is in charge of a group of workers.

Supreme Court page 54
The Supreme Court is the highest court. It decides if laws agree with the Constitution.

surrender page 64
To surrender in a war means to give up, stop fighting, and agree that your side has lost.

tank page 196
A tank is a large, heavy machine that has a big gun on top and is used for war. A tank moves over rough ground on two long strips of metal around its wheels.

tariffs page 88
Tariffs are taxes on goods from other countries.

tax page 41
Tax is money that you must pay to the government.

taxis page 235
Taxis are cars that people pay to ride in.

Teamsters page 246
The Teamsters is a labor union that helps migrant farm workers.

technology page 270
Technology is the inventions that are improving the way we live and work.

Texas Revolution page 103
The war that Texans fought to win their independence from Mexico was the Texas Revolution.

tobacco page 26
Tobacco is a plant. The leaves of this plant are smoked in pipes, cigars, and cigarettes.

Trail of Tears page 88
The trip that Native Americans were forced to make to the West was called the Trail of Tears.

unguarded border page 258
A nation has an unguarded border when there are no soldiers guarding a line or fence that separates two countries.

Union page 125
The Union is the United States.

United Farm Workers page 245
The union that César Chávez started for migrant farm workers is called the United Farm Workers.

United Nations page 223
The United Nations is an organization that tries to help nations solve their problems without fighting.

wagon train page 113
Covered wagons that traveled together on a trail formed a wagon train.

water power page 259
Water power is energy that comes from the moving water of a river, waterfall, or stream. Water power can be used to make electricity.

weapons page 140
Weapons are objects used to attack or protect something. Guns and knives are two kinds of weapons that are used in fighting.

wheat page 140
Wheat is a plant from which we make flour.

women's rights page 197
Women's rights are rights that all women should have. Being able to vote and earning the same salaries as men are two kinds of women's rights.

Polio, 228–229
Polk, James, 107, 114, 115
Pollution, 241, 259, 260
Powell, Colin, 266
President, 54
   of Mexico, 102
   of the Republic of Texas, 103
   of the United States, 54, 65, 66, 72, 73,
      74, 80, 81, 85, 86, 87, 88, 107, 114,
      115, 122, 125, 126, 127, 128, 161,
      192, 193, 198, 203, 204, 210, 216,
      225, 239, 252, 270
Protest(s), 251
Providence, Rhode Island, 26
Puerto Rico, 147, 148
Puritans, 26

Quakers, 27
Quebec, 258
Queen Isabella, 11

Railroad(s), 108, 109, 126, 134, 141–142,
   161, 163, 166, 167, 168
Reconstruction, 134–136
Recycling, 272
Representatives, 53, 136, 139, 197, 198
Republic of Texas, 103
Reservations, 141
Rhode Island, 26
Richmond, Virginia, 127–128
Riis, Jacob, 163
Rio Grande, 107, 108
Rockefeller, John D., 167–168
Rocky Mountains, 75, 113, 139, 142
Roosevelt, Franklin D., 203–204, 210
Russia, 145, 146, 162, 190, 265

Sabin, Albert, 228–229
Sacajawea, 75
St. Lawrence River, 31, 32
St. Lawrence Seaway, 259
St. Louis, Missouri, 32, 34

Salk, Jonas, 228–229
Salomon, Haym, 49
Sampson, Deborah, 48
San Jacinto River, 103
Santa Anna, 102, 103, 106
Santa Fe, New Mexico, 17
Santa Maria, 11
Schwarzkopf, H. Norman, 266
Scotland, 152, 167
Scott, Coretta, 233
Seminoles, 88
Senate, 53
Senators, 53, 136, 139, 197, 198, 269
Sequoya, 86–87
Serbia, 190, 191
Slave(s), 15, 26, 33, 74, 82, 101, 119–121,
   127, 134, 135, 136, 161
Slavery, 15, 66, 119–122, 126, 127, 136
Somalia, 266
South, 119, 120, 121, 122, 125, 126,
   127, 128, 134, 136, 161, 234
South America, 15, 184
South Carolina, 85, 88, 125
Southeast Asia, 249
South Korea, 225
South Vietnam, 249–252
South Vietnamese, 250, 252
Soviet Union, 222–225, 239, 250, 264–265
Space race, 239
Space shuttle, 240–241
Spain, 11, 12, 15, 16, 17, 34, 73, 86, 100,
   147, 148
Spanish, 15–17, 31, 33, 147, 148
   language, 101, 259–260
Spanish-American War, 147–148
Squanto, 22
Stamp Act, 41
Stanton, Elizabeth Cady, 197–198
Steel, 167, 168
Steuben, Friedrich von, 48
Stock market, 202

CREDITS

Photo Credits continued: pp. 132–133, 134, 135, 136, 139 The Granger Collection; p. 140b © Mickey Gibson/Animals Animals; p. 140c The Granger Collection; p. 142 The Bettmann Archive; p. 145 © Johnny Johnson/Earth Scenes; pp. 146, 147a The Granger Collection; p. 147b © Ric Ergenbright; p. 148a The Granger Collection; p. 148b The Bettmann Archive; p. 151 The Granger Collection; p. 152a & b Courtesy AT&T; p. 152c National Park Service Edison Historic Site; p. 153a & b The Granger Collection; p. 154a UPI/Bettmann; p. 154b Culver Pictures; pp. 158–59, 160 The Granger Collection; p. 161a National Portrait Gallery, Smithsonian Institution; pp. 161b, 163a, b & c The Granger Collection; p. 166 The Bettmann Archive; p. 167a The Granger Collection; p. 167b Culver Pictures; p. 168a Pach/Bettmann; p. 168b Culver Pictures; p. 171 The Bettmann Archive; pp. 172, 173a The Granger Collection; p. 173b UPI/Bettmann; p. 174a The Bettmann Archive; p. 174b The Granger Collection; p. 177 University of Illinois at Chicago, the University Library Jane Addams Memorial Collection; p. 178a The Granger Collection; p. 178b Culver Pictures; p. 178c © Doris De Witt/Tony Stone Worldwide; p. 179a Museum of the City of New York; p. 179b University of Illinois at Chicago, the University Library Jane Addams Memorial Collection; p. 182 The Granger Collection; p. 183a The Bettmann Archive; p. 183b National Air and Space Museum, Smithsonian Institute; p. 183c The Granger Collection; p. 184a UPI/Bettmann; p. 184b The Bettmann Archive; pp. 188–89, 190, 192a & b The Granger Collection; p. 192c The Bettmann Archive; p. 193a & b The Granger Collection; p. 196 The Bettmann Archive; p. 197a & b The Granger Collection; p. 197c UPI/Bettmann; p. 198a AP/Wide World; p. 198b The Granger Collection; p. 201 The Granger Collection; p. 202a UPI/Bettmann; p. 202b The Granger Collection; p. 203a & b The Granger Collection; p. 204a Culver Pictures; p. 204b National Portrait Gallery, Smithsonian Institution; p. 207 Culver Pictures; p. 208 The Granger Collection; p. 209a Art Resource; p. 209b The Bettmann Archive; p. 210a National Portrait Gallery/Art Resource; pp. 210b, 213 UPI/Bettmann; p. 214a & b The Bettmann Archive; p. 215a Culver Pictures; p. 215b The Granger Collection; p. 216a & b The Granger Collection; pp. 220–221 © Charles Moore/Black Star; p. 222 UPI/Bettmann; p. 223a Reuters/Bettmann; p. 223b Courtesy The United Nations; p. 223c © Quinn Stewart; p. 224 © Gamma-Liaison; pp. 225, 228 AP/Wide World; p. 229a UPI/Bettmann; p. 229b National Portrait Gallery/Art Resource; p. 230a National Library of Medicine; p. 230b © Merritt Vincent/PhotoEdit; p. 233 © Dennis Brack/Black Star; pp. 234, 235 AP/Wide World; p. 236a © Leonard Freed/Magnum; p. 236b AP/Wide World; pp. 239, 240a, b & c, 241a, b & c NASA; p. 244 © Bob Fitch/Black Star; p. 245a The Library of Congress; p. 245b © Paul Fusco/Magnum; p. 246a © Richard Balsam; p. 246b © Ron Sanford/Black Star; p. 249 © James Pickerell/Black Star; p. 250 © Jean Kugler/FPG; p. 251 © Magnum; p. 252a UPI/Bettmann; p. 252b National Portrait Gallery, Smithsonian Institution; p. 252c Reuters/Bettmann; pp. 256––257 © Alan Klehr/Tony Stone Worldwide; p. 258 © Bob Dammrich/Sygma; p. 259 © Mark Lewis/ Gamma-Liaison; p. 260a © Rolf Adlercreutz/Gamma Liaison; p. 260b © Bryon Augustin/D. Donne Bryant; p. 261a © H Richard Johnston/Tony Stone Worldwide; p. 261b © Dirck Halstead/Gamma-Liaison; p. 264 © Eric Bouvet/ Gamma-Liaison; p. 265 AP/Wide World; p. 266a © Dirck Halstead/Gamma-Liaison; p. 266b Reuters/Bettmann; p. 269 UPI/Bettmann; p. 270a © Michael Newman/ PhotoEdit; p. 270b © Billy E Barnes/PhotoEdit; p. 270c AP/Wide World; p. 271a © Richard Balsam; p. 271b Reuters/Bettmann; p. 272a © Tony Freeman/PhotoEdit; p. 272b AP/Wide World.